The Status of the Education Sector in Sudan

AFRICA HUMAN
DEVELOPMENT SERIES

The Status of the Education Sector in Sudan

AFRICA HUMAN
DEVELOPMENT SERIES

THE WORLD BANK
Washington, D.C.

© 2012 International Bank for Reconstruction and Development / International Development Association or
The World Bank
1818 H Street NW
Washington DC 20433
Telephone: 202-473-1000
Internet: www.worldbank.org

1 2 3 4 15 14 13 12

This volume is a product of the staff of The World Bank with external contributions. The findings, interpretations, and conclusions expressed in this volume do not necessarily reflect the views of The World Bank, its Board of Executive Directors, or the governments they represent.

The World Bank does not guarantee the accuracy of the data included in this work. The boundaries, colors, denominations, and other information shown on any map in this work do not imply any judgment on the part of The World Bank concerning the legal status of any territory or the endorsement or acceptance of such boundaries.

Rights and Permissions
The material in this work is subject to copyright. Because The World Bank encourages dissemination of its knowledge, this work may be reproduced, in whole or in part, for noncommercial purposes as long as full attribution to the work is given.

For permission to reproduce any part of this work for commercial purposes, please send a request with complete information to the Copyright Clearance Center Inc., 222 Rosewood Drive, Danvers, MA 01923, USA; telephone: 978-750-8400; fax: 978-750-4470; Internet: www.copyright.com.

All other queries on rights and licenses, including subsidiary rights, should be addressed to the Office of the Publisher, The World Bank, 1818 H Street NW, Washington, DC 20433, USA; fax: 202-522-2422; e-mail: pubrights@worldbank.org.

ISBN (paper): 978-0-8213-8857-0
ISBN (electronic): 978-0-8213-8867-9
DOI: 10.1596/978-0-8213-8857-0

Library of Congress Cataloging-in-Publication Data
The status of the education sector in Sudan.
    p. cm.
 "This report was prepared by the World Bank and the Government of National Unity (GoNU) of the Republic of Sudan"—T.p. verso.
  Includes bibliographical references.
  ISBN 978-0-8213-8857-0 — ISBN 978-0-8213-8867-9
  1. Education—Sudan—Evaluation. I. World Bank. II. Sudan.
  LA1651.S83 2011
  370.9624—dc23

2011029392

Cover photo: Amir Abdallah, Blue Nile State © Hassan Zakaria / Sudanese Organization for Education Development (SOED).

Table of Contents

Foreword xiii
Acknowledgments xvii
Abbreviations xix
Map: States Featured in This Study, Sudan, 2010 xxi

OVERVIEW   1
   The Main Findings   2
   Equity-Oriented Education Spending   14
   Conclusion   15
   Notes   16
   References   16

CHAPTER 1. SETTING THE SCENE   19
   Scope of This Education Sector Status Report   19
   Administrative Structure of General Education in Northern Sudan   26
   Annex 1A: Population by Age in 2008   28
   Annex 1B: Administrative Structure of the Education System   30
   Notes   33
   References   34

CHAPTER 2. OVERALL ENROLLMENT PATTERNS   37
   Structure of the Education System and Enrollments   37
   Schools for Nomadic and Internally Displaced Populations   47
   The Gross Enrollment Rate   49
   Measuring Education Coverage More Precisely   53
   Summary   55
   Annex: Number of Basic Schools   56
   Notes   57
   References   58

CHAPTER 3. PATTERNS OF STUDENT FLOW 59
Schooling Profile and Distance from Universal Primary Completion   59
Other Aspects of Student Flow Efficiency and Projections   68
Projection of Access and Completion Rates for Basic Education   75
Summary   77
Annex: Basic and Secondary Education Enrollments   78
Notes   79
References   79

CHAPTER 4. DISPARITIES 81
Regional Disparities   81
Social Disparities   85
Out-of-School Children in Urban and Rural Areas   92
Structural Disparities   93
Summary   97
Annex 4A: Enrollment of Girls in Education in
    Northern Sudan   99
Annex 4B: Probability of Children Ever Enrolling in Basic School   99
Notes   100
References   101

CHAPTER 5. SERVICE DELIVERY AND LEARNING OUTCOMES IN BASIC SCHOOLS IN THREE STATES 103
Sample Description   105
Characteristics of Government Basic Schools in the Sample   107
Student Learning Outcomes   119
Secondary Education Examination Results   125
Summary   129
Annex: Probability of Still Being in School by Grade 8   130
Notes   131
References   131

CHAPTER 6. TEACHERS 133
Profile of Teachers in Northern Sudan   133
Teacher Recruitment, Deployment, and Transfer   140
Teacher Utilization   144
School Record Keeping: Teacher Leave and Time/Attendance   147
Teacher Supervision   150
Teacher Salaries and Motivation   153
Summary   155

Notes 156
References 156

CHAPTER 7. EDUCATION FINANCE 159
Background 159
Analysis of Public Education Spending 161
Public Per-Student Spending 168
Analysis of State-Level Education Spending 174
Summary 182
Annex: Spending on Education 183
Notes 187
References 188

APPENDIX: STATE-LEVEL DATA SHEETS 191

GLOSSARY 237

BOXES

1.1	Education Sector Status Report Data Sources	20
7.1	State Visits to Collect Information on Education Spending	160

FIGURES

O.1	Average Annual Growth Rates for Basic School Enrollment, by State, 2004–05 to 2008–09	3
O.2	Educational Access: Probability of Ever Enrolling in Basic School, by Location, Income, and Gender, circa 2005	8
O.3	Share of Girls in Enrollments, by Type of Basic School, 2008–09	10
O.4	International Comparisons: Degree of Randomness in Teacher Allocations in Basic Education, by Country	12
O.5	Public Education Spending, by Administrative Level, 2000–09	14
1.1	Growth of GDP per Capita in Sudan, 1975–2008	22
1A.1	Raw Population Data in Sudan, Ages 0–24 Years, 2008	28
1A.2	Raw and Smoothed Population Data in Sudan, Ages 2–24 Years, 2008	29
1B.1	Organizational Structure of the FMoGE	31
1B.2	Ministries Providing Technical and Vocational Training	32
2.1	Trends in Student Enrollments in Northern Sudan, 2000–01 to 2008–09	40
2.2	Evolution in Basic School Enrollments in Selected States, 2000–01 to 2008–09	41
2.3	Average Growth Rates for Basic School Enrollments, by State, 2004–05 to 2008–09	41

2.4	Share of Students Enrolled in Nongovernment Schools, 2008–09 or Latest Available Year	44
2.5	Trends in Gross Enrollment Rates for General Education in Northern Sudan, 2000–01 to 2008–09	51
2.6	Comparing the Gross Enrollment Rate Calculated from Different Sources, 2005–06 to 2008–09	55
3.1	Schooling Profile for the Primary and Secondary Levels, 2008–09	60
3.2	Educational Pyramid for Northern Sudan, 2008–09	61
3.3	Access to Grade 1: Share of Population between Ages 5 and 29 Who Had Ever Accessed Basic School, 2005–06	63
3.4	Ages of Girls and Boys Attending Grade 1, 2005–06	64
3.5	Enrollment Status of Girls and Boys by Age, 2005–06	66
3.6	Schooling Status and Level of Education of Girls and Boys by Age, 2005–06	67
3.7	School Life Expectancy in Sudan and Comparator Countries, Latest Available Year	68
3.8	International Comparison of the Share of Repeaters in Primary and Secondary Schools, Latest Available Year	71
3.9	Projection of the Rate of Access and Completion of Basic Education to 2015	76
4.1	Access: Regional Disparities in the Share of Children between Ages 5 and 17 Who Had Ever Accessed Basic School, 2005–06	84
4.2	Ratio of Boys to Girls in the Basic School-Age Population, by State, 2008	87
4.3	Access: Probability of Ever Enrolling in Basic School (Grade 1) according to Location, Income, and Gender, circa 2005	89
4.4	Retention: Probability of Still Being in School by Grade 8, by Location, Income, and Gender, circa 2005	91
4.5	Schooling Status of Urban and Rural Children by Age, 2005–06	93
4.6	Lorenz Curve for the Distribution of Public Education Spending, 2008–09	96
5.1	Grade 5 Student Learning Assessment Scores in Mathematics and Reading in Kassala, North Kordofan, and River Nile, 2009	120
5.2	International Comparison of Student Performance in Mathematics between Morocco, Northern Sudan, Singapore, and Tunisia, 2008–09	122
5.3	International Comparison of Student Performance in Reading between Benin, Northern Sudan, and Singapore, 2008–09	123
5.4	Average Student Performance in Mathematics and Reading, by Household Wealth, 2009	126
5.5	Average Student Performance in Mathematics and Reading, by Father's Education Level, 2009	127
6.1	Types of Staff in Northern Sudan, by Education Level, 2009	135
6.2	Percentage of Female and Male Teachers in Basic Education in Northern Sudan, by State, 2009	136
6.3	Percentage of Female and Male Teachers in Secondary Education in Northern Sudan, by State, 2009	136

6.4	Percentage of Trained and Untrained Teachers in Northern Sudan, by State, 2009	139
6.5	Full-Time Government Teachers' Academic Qualifications and Preservice Training in Kassala, North Kordofan, and River Nile States, 2009	139
6.6	Number of Teachers in Relation to Student Enrollment in Basic Education Schools in Northern Sudan, 2008–09	141
6.7	Number of Teachers in Relation to Student Enrollment in Basic Education Schools, Red Sea State, 2008–09	142
6.8	International Comparisons: Randomness in Teacher Allocations in Basic Education, by Country	143
6.9	Average Number of Leave Days by Purpose over Six Months in Kassala, North Kordofan, and River Nile States, 2009	149
6.10	Local Supervision: Visits to the Teachers in Kassala, North Kordofan, and River Nile States, 2009	152
6.11	Payment of Teacher Salaries in Kassala, North Kordofan, and River Nile States, by Teacher Type, 2009	153
7.1	Recurrent Public Education Spending per School-Age Child, 2000–09	162
7.2	Comparison of Public Education Spending, by Country, 2005–08	163
7.3	Development and Recurrent Public Education Spending Shares, 2000–09	164
7.4	Public Education Spending, by Administrative Level, 2000–09	165
7.5	Composition of Recurrent Public Education Spending, by Education Level, 2009	168
7.6	State Education Spending as a Share of State Total Public Spending, 2009	176
7.7	Average Public Per-Student Spending, by GER Group, 2009	177
7.8	Public Per-Student Spending, by Education Level and State, 2009	178
7.9	Federal Transfers and State Own Revenues as a Share of Total Revenues, 2008	180
7.10	Federal Transfers per Capita and Average GER, by State, 2008–09	181

TABLES

O.1	Anthropometric Measures of Sudan's Children	11
1.1	Trends in GoNU Revenues and Expenditures, 2000–09	23
1.2	Anthropometric Measures of Sudan's Children	25
1A.1	Population of Sudan by Census Year and Average Growth in Intervening Years, 1956–2008	28
1B.1	Availability of Job Descriptions in the FMoGE	31
2.1	Trends in Student Enrollments by Level of Education in Northern Sudan, 2000–01 to 2008–09	38
2.2	Increase in the Number of Schools, Teachers, and Students from 2004–05 to 2008–09	43
2.3	School Size and Student-Teacher Ratios in Government and Nongovernment Schools, 2008–09	46

2.4	Number of Schools and Enrollments in Government Nomadic, IDP, and Village Schools, 2007–08 and 2008–09	48
2.5	Primary Education GERs in Northern Sudan and Comparator Countries, 2008 or Latest Available Year	52
2.6	Upper Secondary Education GERs in Northern Sudan and Comparator Countries, 2008 or Latest Available Year	53
2.7	Higher Education Enrollments in Northern Sudan and Comparator Countries, 2008 or Latest Available Year	54
2A.1	Number of Basic Schools by State and Type of School, 2008–09	56
3.1	Gross Intake Rate and Primary Completion Rate, 2008–09	62
3.2	Basic School Intake and Completion Rates Based on Two Data Sources, 2005–06	63
3.3	Share of Repeaters in Basic Schools from Different Sources, 2005–06 to 2008–09	69
3.4	Estimation of Repetition in Government and Nongovernment Academic Secondary Schools, 2008–09	70
3.5	Retention and Other Indicators for Basic and Secondary Education, 2000–01 to 2008–09	72
3.6	Internal Efficiency Coefficients in Basic and Secondary Education, 2005–06 to 2008–09	74
3.7	International Comparison of Internal Efficiency Coefficients in Basic Education	75
3.8	Gross Intake and Primary Completion Rates for Basic Education, 2000–01 to 2008–09	76
3A.1	Enrollments by Grade in Basic and Secondary Education, Northern Sudan, 2008–09	78
4.1	Comparison of GERs in Preschool, Basic, and Secondary Schools across States, 2008–09	82
4.2	Share of Girls in Enrollments by Level of Education, 2000–01 and 2008–09	85
4.3	Share of Girls in Enrollments by Type of Basic School, 2008–09	86
4.4	Gender Disparities at All Levels of Education, 2008–09	87
4.5	International Comparison of Gender Parity Index by Level of Education, Latest Available Year	88
4.6	Access: Interaction of Gender with Poverty and Rurality	90
4.7	Retention: Interaction of Gender with Poverty and Rurality	92
4.8	Estimated Number of 10- to 17-Year-Olds in Northern Sudan Who Have Never Been in School, by Gender, 2008	94
4.9	Distribution of Public Education Spending among Members of the Same Cohort, 2008–09	95
4.10	Distribution of Public Spending on Education within a Cohort of Children, Northern Sudan Compared to Sub-Saharan Africa, 2008–09	97
4A.1	Share of Girls in Total Enrollments, by State and Level of Education, 2008–09	99

4B.1	Logistic Regression Results: Probability of Ever Enrolling in Basic School (Grade 1), by Location, Income, and Gender, circa 2005	99
5.1	Basic Education Indicators for the Three Surveyed States and the Northern Sudan Average, 2008–09	104
5.2	Sample Information for the Three Northern Sudan States Chosen, 2009	106
5.3	Rural/Peri-urban and Urban Composition of the School Sample, 2009	107
5.4	Availability of Chalkboards and Desks in Observed Classrooms, 2009	108
5.5	Availability of Textbooks in Observed Classrooms	110
5.6	Syllabus Coverage in Observed Classrooms, 2009	111
5.7	Class Size in Observed Classrooms, 2009	113
5.8	Average Student Attendance in Observed Classrooms, 2009	114
5.9	Official and Actual Number of School Days in the Academic Year, State Averages, 2009	115
5.10	School Record Keeping on Student Enrollment and Performance, State Averages, 2009	116
5.11	Characteristics of Education Councils, State Averages, 2009	117
5.12	School Support Provided by Educational Councils, State Averages, 2009	118
5.13	Grade 5 Student Learning Assessment Scores in Mathematics and Reading, 2009	121
5.14	Average Student Learning Assessment Scores, by Gender, 2009	124
5.15	Pass Rates for Secondary School Examinations in Northern Sudan, by School Type and State, 2008	128
5A.1	Logistic Regression Results: Probability of Still Being in School by Grade 8, by Location, Income, and Gender, circa 2005	130
6.1	Numbers of Education Staff in Northern Sudan, by Education Level, 2009	134
6.2	Sudan Open University Bachelor of Education Degree Output, 2008–12	138
6.3	Student-Teacher Ratios in Northern Sudan, by State, 2009	145
6.4	Average Class Size in Northern Sudan, by School Type and Grade, 2008–09	146
6.5	Number of Hours Taught by Teachers in Different Salary Scales	147
6.6	School Record Keeping in Kassala, North Kordofan, and River Nile States State Averages, 2009	150
6.7	Number of Teachers, Inspectors, Volunteers, and National Service Staff in Basic and Secondary Education, by State, 2009	151
6.8	Outside Jobs and Private Tutoring in Kassala, North Kordofan, and River Nile States, by Teacher Type, 2009	154
6.9	Teacher Incentives to Perform, or Not	155
7.1	Estimated Total Public Education Spending, 2000–09	161
7.2	Recurrent Public Education Spending, by Education Level, 2009	166

7.3	Comparison of Public Education Spending, by Region/Country and Education Level, 2005–08	167
7.4	Composition of Recurrent Public Education Spending, by Education Level, 2009	167
7.5	Composition of Per-Student Spending, by Education Level, 2009	169
7.6	Comparison of Public Per-Student Spending, by Region and Education Level, 2002–08	170
7.7	Composition of Education Staff, by Education Level, 2009	171
7.8	Average Salaries of School-Based Staff in Northern Sudan, by Education Level, 2009	172
7.9	Comparison of Average Primary Teacher Salaries, by Region/Country, 2002–08	173
7.10	Average Annual Household Out-of-Pocket Spending per Student, Selected States, 2008–09	174
7A.1	Comparison of Public Education Spending, by Region/Country, 2005–08	183
7A.2	Total, Recurrent, and Development Education Spending, by Administrative Level, 2000–09	183
7A.3	Preschool: Overview of State Education Spending and STRs, by Group and State, 2009	184
7A.4	Basic Education: Overview of State Education Spending and STRs, by Group and State, 2009	185
7A.5	Academic Secondary Education: Overview of State Education Spending and STRs, by Group and State, 2009	185
7A.6	Technical Secondary Education: Overview of State Education Spending and STRs, by Group and State, 2009	186

Foreword

As the Republic of Sudan embarks upon a new phase in its history, its government has reaffirmed its commitment to achieve the Education for All (EFA) targets and the Millennium Development Goals (MDGs)—if not by 2015, then soon thereafter. This year, the Government of National Unity is preparing a new education sector strategic plan, for 2012–16, that will set the direction for reform and investment in basic, secondary, and higher education over the coming five years. The aim of the current report is to contribute to the knowledge base that informs the preparation of this plan by providing a diagnostic of the country's education system. With detailed data on enrollments, teachers, learning outcomes, and education financing, the report contextualizes valuable information about the challenges and emerging priorities for Sudan's education sector.

The positive impact of peace on education following the Comprehensive Peace Agreement (CPA) signed in 2005 is evidenced in the substantial increase in basic school enrollments among those previously affected by conflict. In absolute terms, enrollments in basic education grew by almost 1.6 million in the eight years since the 2000–01 academic year. However, regional disparities in education access exist. Also, children in rural areas, children from poorer households, and girls are at a disadvantage in terms of access to schooling. The strongest predictor of access to schooling is whether a child lives in an urban or rural area, with urban children being 17 percentage points more likely than rural children to access school. Preliminary estimates also suggest low basic education coverage of internally displaced persons and nomadic populations. There are also indications of inadequate literacy and numeracy among students based on a learning assessment administered as part of this analysis in 195 government schools across three states. These weak learning outcomes could be linked to many factors, including widespread malnutrition among young children (which has consequences for learning ability), too few instructional hours, and a lack of textbooks. Finally, primary school completion rates are low: whereas roughly 80 percent of children were enrolled in grade 1 in 2008, only about 50 percent of students completed basic education, indicating that a large number of students are dropping out of school.

Secondary education also has a high number of students who drop out, and it has a large number of students who are repeaters. As many as 36 percent of students in the final year of secondary school are estimated to be repeaters, giving a repetition rate of 15 percent across the secondary level. Nevertheless, the estimated transition rates between basic and secondary education and between secondary and higher education of 74 percent and about 87 percent, respectively, are fairly high, and they indicate that most pupils drop out of the education system within the basic or secondary levels rather than between the levels. With such high transition rates, the current expansion in basic school enrollments (and assuming that the dropout rate improves) is likely to result in considerable pressure on secondary education, technical and vocational training, and higher education systems, which will need to accommodate a rapidly increasing number of basic school graduates seeking to continue their studies. Whether the system is able to respond to this increased pressure will determine whether the transition rates can remain at these high levels in the years ahead.

From a regional perspective, enrollment in higher education is higher in Sudan than in other Sub-Saharan African countries and is similar to that in Middle Eastern and North African countries. The gender parity index for higher education in Sudan is also similar to that for countries in the Middle East and North Africa, and accounted for 56 percent of enrollment in higher education in 2009. Given the relatively high enrollment rate in higher education, it is important that while in the education system, students acquire the skills that match those needed by the labor market to contribute to economic growth and development in the country. Further research, including a labor market survey, is required to understand and strengthen the links between the skills imparted to higher education students and the skills required to support the expansion and diversification of the economy.

The independence of South Sudan and the expiration of the CPA are likely to lead to a significant decline in government financing. All sectors—including education—will be affected by this contraction, placing at risk the significant gains of the last decade. Maintaining the momentum and expanding the existing education system will require a commitment to promote a strong, efficient, equity-oriented approach to service delivery. Sudan's upcoming education sector plan will highlight priorities and can be used to mobilize both internal and external financing. The analytic foundation that this report provides and its identification of the key bottlenecks to progress are thus both timely and relevant.

This report was prepared in collaboration with a national team from the Ministry of General Education (MoGE) and partners active in the education sector in Sudan. The MoGE's national team, led by the undersecretary of the federal MoGE, comprised representatives from both the federal and state levels. Over a period of 18 months, this collaboration facilitated considerable capacity building in data collection and analysis, as well as regular dissemination of the analysis to a wider audience.

This publication is the first comprehensive overview of the education sector in Sudan. The challenge that remains is to design policy responses to the issues identified within the forthcoming education sector strategic plan. More important, these policies—already being discussed with the MoGE—must be effectively implemented so that Sudan can make faster progress toward achieving the EFA targets and MDGs. It is my hope that this report will serve as the basis for an evidence-based and equity-oriented approach to education planning and investment. This approach will have positive repercussions for overall economic growth, poverty alleviation, and human development in 21st-century Sudan.

Ritva Reinikka
Director, Human Development
Africa Region
The World Bank

Acknowledgments

This report was prepared by the World Bank and the Government of National Unity (GoNU) of Sudan. The GoNU team worked under the overall guidance of a management committee headed by Dr. El Mustassim El Hassan, undersecretary of the Ministry of General Education (MoGE).[1] The GoNU team comprised Dr. El Tahir Hassan El Tahir, director general for the Planning Unit of the federal MoGE; Dr. Ibtissam M. Hassan, director general for the Teacher-Training Unit of the federal MoGE, and the director generals of all the state ministries of education. Other team members within the GoNU included Dr. Khaled El Amin El Mosharaf, Omar Alebied Ahmed, and Najla Basheer. The team wishes to express gratitude to Mrs. Souad Abelrazig, State Minister of the MoGE for her leadership in finalizing this book.

The World Bank team consisted of Elizabeth Ninan, task team leader; Yasser El-Gammal, task team leader for the concept note stage; Ramahatra Mam Rakotomalala; Kirsten Majgaard; Moctar Ould Djay; Gunilla Pettersson; Prema Clarke; Koffi Segniagbeto; Deepa Sankar; and Aymen Ali Musmar. Michel Welmond, lead education specialist, provided overall technical guidance on the report. The peer reviewers for the concept note, also from the Bank, were Soren Nelleman, Linda English, and Peter Buckland. The peer reviewers for the final report were Alberto Begue, Education for All Fast-Track Initiative secretariat; Peter Buckland, consultant; Yasser El-Gammal, lead social protection specialist and sector leader for Sudan, World Bank; Safaa El-Kogali, regional director, West Asia and North Africa, Population Council; and Cem Mete, senior economist, World Bank. The team would also like to thank the World Bank's William Battaile, senior economist, and Michael Geiger, economist, for their inputs throughout the development of the report.

The report benefited substantially from the support provided by other ministries and development partners in northern Sudan. Staff participation from the Ministry of Finance and National Economy (MoFNE) included Mirghani Golood and Sadia Alkhidir Ahmed. Donor partners in Khartoum contributed to the development of the report and included Cecilia Baldeh and Parvez Akhtar, United Nations Children's Fund; Mauro Ghirotti, Italian Cooperation; Mustafa Yassin, European Commission; and David Dean, Education Management Information System, European Commission.

The report also benefited from the support of World Bank staff in Khartoum, especially Alassane Sow, country manager for northern Sudan, and Isabel Soares, senior operations officer. Christopher Thomas, former sector manager for the Africa Region's education team, and Peter Nicolas Materu, acting sector manager, provided support to the team throughout the process.

The team is grateful for the excellent administrative support received from World Bank staff members Rosario Aristorenas in Washington, DC, and Enas Suleiman Mohammed in Sudan.

The team acknowledges with great appreciation the financial support received from the Education Program Development Fund of the Fast-Track Initiative and the GoNU Multi-donor Trust Fund.

NOTE

1. Established under Administrative Order 22 in 2009, the management committee provided overall strategic guidance in the preparation of the education sector report for northern Sudan.

Abbreviations

CPA	Comprehensive Peace Agreement
EFA-FTI	Education for All Fast-Track Initiative
ESPA	Eastern Sudan Peace Agreement
ESR	education sector report
ESSP	Education Sector Strategic Plan
EU	European Union
FMoGE	Federal Ministry of General Education
GDP	gross domestic product
GER	gross enrollment rate
GIR	gross intake rate
GoNU	Government of National Unity
GoSS	Government of Southern Sudan
GPI	gender parity index
IDP	internally displaced person
IEC	internal efficiency coefficient
ISETI	in-service education training institute
MDG	Millennium Development Goal
MoFNE	Ministry of Finance and National Economy
MoGE	Ministry of General Education
MoHESR	Ministry of Higher Education and Scientific Research
MoLPSHR	Ministry of Labor, Public Service and Human Resource Development
NCTTE	National Council for Technical and Technological Education
PCR	primary completion rate
PIRLS	Progress in International Reading Literacy Study
SDG	Sudanese pound

SDS	service delivery survey ("Quality of Service Delivery in Basic Education Study")
SHHS	Sudan Household Health Survey
SLE	school life expectancy
SOU	Sudan Open University
STR	student-teacher ratio
TIMSS	Trends in International Mathematics and Science Study
UNHCR	United Nations High Commissioner for Refugees
UNICEF	United Nations Children's Fund

Map: States Featured in This Study, Sudan, 2010

Overview

The Sudan Government of National Unity (GoNU) has committed itself to achieving the Education for All (EFA) targets and the education-related Millennium Development Goals (MDGs) by 2015, which signals its readiness to continue to invest in education and expand educational opportunities. The current five-year (2007–11) Education Sector Strategic Plan (ESSP) expresses the country's commitment to the EFA goals and outlines activities to meet the MDG education targets. In developing its ESSP for 2012–16, the GoNU seeks to assess the status of the education system in order to identify priority areas for development in the sector.

This report is a diagnostic of the education system and provides a knowledge base to inform the GoNU's preparation of the ESSP. It also contributes to the dialogue among relevant stakeholders on the challenges and emerging strategic priorities for the education sector in northern Sudan.

The report begins by setting the scene in historical and economic terms. It then provides an outline of the administrative setup, which is particularly important in northern Sudan's decentralized education system. It also examines trends in enrollments, followed by the schooling profile and an assessment of the efficiency of the education sector. Next, the report describes existing disparities in the education system along several dimensions: rural-urban location, income, gender, nomadic population, internally displaced persons (IDPs), and state. An analysis of education service delivery presents indicative findings on student learning outcomes and on resource availability and management in basic schools in three states; it also presents a brief overview of examination performance in secondary education.[1] The report then addresses teacher-related issues, including recruitment, deployment, utilization, and supervision. Finally, education spending is discussed, both at the national and state levels, and the composition of education spending is explored for each subsector.

THE MAIN FINDINGS

There are 11 main findings of this diagnostic of the education system in northern Sudan. They range from the peace dividend's effect on enrollments and the high dropout rates in basic and secondary education to disparities in resources at the local level and low spending on education relative to similar countries in the region.

ACCESS TO EDUCATION

The peace dividend is especially apparent in the growth in student enrollments in basic education in states previously affected by conflict. The number of students enrolled across subsectors has grown annually over the past decade, with the fastest relative growth in enrollments since 2000–01 occurring in preschool (10 percent), followed by higher education (7 percent), secondary education (6 percent), and basic education (5 percent). Basic education is by far the largest subsector of education in terms of student enrollments and, in absolute terms, grew by almost 1.6 million in eight years. The growth in enrollments for basic education is evidence of both strong demand for education and commitment by the GoNU to achieving the EFA goals and the MDGs.

At the state level, evidence (figure O.1) points to a positive impact of peace on basic school enrollment for the populations that were affected by conflict prior to 2005: Northern, Southern, and Western Darfur states in the western part; North Kordofan, South Kordofan, and Blue Nile states in the southern part (the Nuba Mountains area); and Kassala and Red Sea states in the eastern part (the third eastern state, Al Qadarif, has registered a negative growth rate since 2005). In most of the other states, basic enrollment growth has slowed down since 2005 because these states were already close to full capacity in basic education.

The education sector in northern Sudan has characteristics of both low-income Sub-Saharan Africa and the Middle East education sectors. The coverage of higher education in northern Sudan, at 1,500 students per 100,000 inhabitants, is higher than that for most of its neighboring countries (except the Arab Republic of Egypt) and also higher than that for the lower-middle-income countries of Sub-Saharan Africa. It is lower, however, than the coverage in almost all of the lower-middle-income countries in the Middle East and North Africa region (except Morocco).

Figure O.1 Average Annual Growth Rates for Basic School Enrollment, by State, 2004–05 to 2008–09

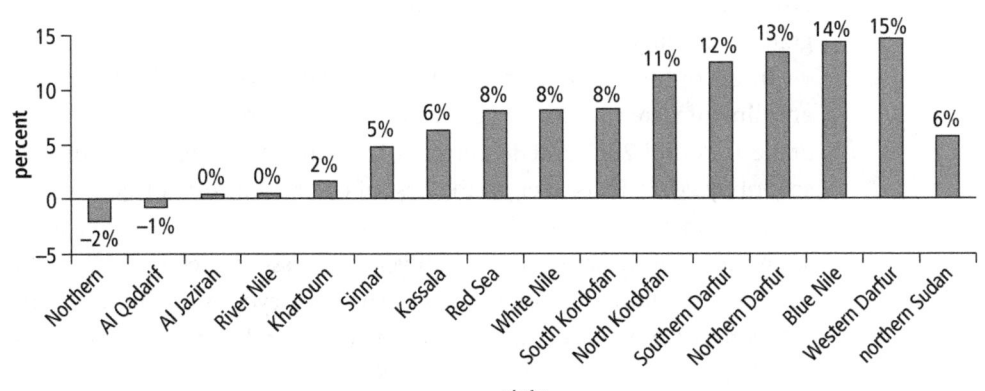

Source: Federal Ministry of General Education (FMoGE) statistical yearbooks for the years indicated; World Bank estimates.

Northern Sudan also has a higher secondary school gross enrollment rate (GER), 34 percent, than most of its neighbors (except Kenya), which is comparable to other lower-middle-income countries in Sub-Saharan Africa. However, its relatively high GER for secondary school is partly the result of a large number of repeaters. Northern Sudan's GER for secondary schools is also similar to that for countries such as Morocco and the Syrian Arab Republic, but it is lower than the average for countries in the Middle East and North Africa region.

However, basic education gross enrollment rate in northern Sudan (76 percent) does not compare favorably to the average GER for basic education in lower-middle-income Sub-Saharan African countries (105 percent) and lower-middle-income Middle East and North African countries (106 percent). The GER for northern Sudan is higher only than that for Eritrea and comparable to that for countries such as the Central African Republic, Chad, and Côte d'Ivoire.

DROPOUT RATES

Northern Sudan experiences a high number of dropouts in basic and secondary education. While there was a fairly high rate of intake (80 percent) of new students to grade 1 of basic school in 2008, the primary completion rate (PCR) was low (54 percent), indicating that many students drop out of school before completing basic education. A study following a group of students that enrolled in grade 1 in 2000 until they reached grade 8 in 2007 revealed that only 57 of every 100 students were still in school by grade 8.

This means that the probability of a student's dropping out before grade 8 is 43 percent, indicating an average dropout rate of 6 percent per grade from grades 1 through 7.

In an optimistic scenario, if the observed increase in basic education enrollment were to continue, then almost all children could be enrolling in grade 1 around 2012 and 80 percent of children could be completing basic school by 2015. Thus, even in the best of circumstances, northern Sudan is not likely to reach universal primary completion by 2015. However, it could soon attain universal or almost universal access—a precondition for universal completion. Because the basic schooling cycle is eight years, universal primary completion can be achieved no earlier than eight years after universal access to grade 1, that is, by 2020 or later. However, these outcomes are within reach only if efforts to ensure intake does not decline and only if targeted interventions to enroll vulnerable populations and retain all students in school for the full cycle are put in place and sustained.[2]

The number of dropouts in secondary education is higher than that in basic education when adjusted for the length of the cycles. A study following a group of students that enrolled in secondary 1 in 2005 until they reached secondary 3 in 2007 revealed that only 74 of every 100 students were still in school by secondary 3. This finding corresponds to a dropout rate of 13 percent per year in the first two years of the secondary cycle.

The high rates of dropout in both basic education and secondary education are of serious concern in northern Sudan, yet there is insufficient information to ascertain the main causes. However, international evidence suggests that students are at risk of dropping out of school when parents do not perceive that additional schooling is worth the investment in terms of time and money—when the cost of schooling exceeds the expected benefits. High dropout rates could therefore indicate that the quality of the schooling is too low to justify the student's time and the direct costs in terms of parental financial contributions or the opportunity costs of a child who would otherwise be contributing to the household income or helping with chores. Other factors also put children at risk of dropping out. For example, when schools do not offer all the grades of the basic cycle (as is the case for village and nomadic schools in northern Sudan) and children have to change schools to access the higher grades, the students' travel time to school increases, which may lead to their dropping out. Also, late entry to school by overage children is strongly associated with dropout, which seems to be the case in northern Sudan, where 40 percent of children entering grade 1 in 2005 were overage (that is, 8 years or older).

Going forward, as the GoNU moves to design appropriate policies to improve student retention, more research will be required to determine the main causes of the high dropout rates.

LEARNING OUTCOMES

The education sector shows weak learning outcomes. A student learning assessment administered in 195 schools across three states (Kassala, North Kordofan, and River Nile) in 2009 found that student learning outcomes were generally weak: the average male student in the sample answered only 35 percent of the mathematics questions correctly and 38 percent of the reading questions compared to 37 percent and 41 percent, respectively, for the average female student. Within the sample, girls on average performed significantly better than boys, which is consistent with findings from both developing and developed countries. Students among the richest 20 percent performed better on average than students in the middle 60 percent, who in turn performed better than students in the poorest 20 percent. From a regional perspective, students in the three states performed similarly to their counterparts in Morocco and Tunisia and somewhat better than students in Benin. However, it should be noted that the students in northern Sudan were assessed in grade 5 rather than grade 4, as was the case in Morocco and Tunisia, meaning that Sudanese students had the advantage of roughly one additional year of schooling.

Northern Sudan does not currently have a system to continuously assess student learning in order to determine whether public investments in basic education translate into the provision of quality education and learning for all students. The GoNU should consider instituting a national student learning assessment system, which can be combined with data on school resources from the new Education Management Information System, in order to identify factors that promote or hinder learning. Such systems already exist or are being introduced in many developed and developing countries.

INSTRUCTIONAL TIME

The weak learning outcomes may also be partly related to inadequate instructional time. Unlike many other countries in the region, teachers in northern Sudan specialize by subject area from grade 4 onward. This means that even though the average student-teacher ratio for basic education is 34 to 1, the average class size is 48 students. The official instructional time for basic schooling is 25 hours per week, but based on the number of teachers in the system, students receive an average of only 17 hours. Put another way, students fail to receive about 30 percent of instructional time. Compounding the problem is the fact that senior teachers, who are more experienced, teach fewer hours than junior teachers. There are several additional reasons for the loss in instructional time, such as teacher absenteeism, in-service teacher training, strikes, conflict, the use of schools as polling stations, and closures due to weather conditions.

The 2009 basic education service delivery study in Kassala, North Kordofan, and River Nile states also showed students receiving fewer instructional hours than the official policy; it showed incomplete syllabus coverage as well. The official school year in northern Sudan is 210 days, but in the sample schools in the three states, the average number of actual school days was 189. This result implies that students are missing about one month of teaching each year, which has negative implications for student learning outcomes. As for syllabus coverage, of the 195 sample schools, the average coverage was 72 percent in mathematics and 75 percent in reading when 80 percent of the syllabus should have been covered. Going beyond averages, however, reveals notable differences in syllabus coverage across schools. For example, 4 percent of urban schools and 11 percent of rural and peri-urban schools in Kassala had covered only 40–59 percent of the syllabus. These schools are of particular concern because a complete catch-up in terms of syllabus coverage would be nearly impossible.

These findings strongly suggest the need to put standards into place that clearly communicate official policy on the length of the school year, make up for lost days, and enable schools (for example, by constructing durable school buildings) to be open as intended.

SCHOOL RESOURCES

Studies indicate that resources are inadequate at the school level in northern Sudan. According to the United Nations Children's Fund (UNICEF) baseline survey conducted in 2008, 42 percent of classrooms in basic schools in northern Sudan were in need of repairs, and 9 percent required replacement. The UNICEF survey also found wide variation in the quality of school infrastructure by state: 29 percent of classrooms in Khartoum state needed to be renovated or replaced, whereas the figure rose to 66 percent for classrooms in South Kordofan. In addition, many schools are built with local materials and are either unsuitable for learning (no light, insufficient space, no roof) or inaccessible during the rainy season. Despite the lack of adequate infrastructure, development spending remains low in northern

Sudan at 9 percent of total public education spending in 2009. Although this is an increase from 2000, when its share was 1 percent of total public education spending, the lack of school infrastructure remains a significant challenge.

Aside from problems with infrastructure, the findings of the 2009 basic education service delivery study and a 2008 European Union (EU 2008) study point to the lack of textbooks within the classroom. The average student-textbook ratio for mathematics and reading in the three states surveyed through the service delivery study was 3 to 1, compared to the official policy of 2 to 1. At the extreme, rural sample schools in North Kordofan had a 9 to 1 student-textbook ratio. Considering that education councils provided textbooks for students in several of the survey schools, the higher-than-recommended average student-textbook ratio points to a serious failure of the public education system, with negative consequences for student learning. The EU study, based on visits to 71 government basic schools in seven states, also documents the lack of textbooks with an average student-textbook ratio of 4 to 1.

Spending on goods and services by the government is generally low, and particularly so for basic education. This situation means that households have to contribute to a school's running costs, such as maintenance, water and electricity, and supplementary teacher payments. The average estimated out-of-pocket spending by households each year on operating costs was 15 Sudanese pounds (SDG) per student in 2008–09, higher than the SDG 12 public spending per student on such costs.[3] Whereas the official policy of the GoNU is free basic education, the available data suggest that households pay a large share of school running costs in addition to other costs, such as uniforms, textbooks, and meals.

DISPARITIES

Substantial disparities exist in the education system, by region, rural-urban location, gender, and income. At all three levels of education, the GER varies enormously from one state to another, ranging from 13 percent to 65 percent for preschool, about 65 percent to 94 percent for basic school, and 15 percent to 61 percent for secondary school. As noted earlier, the states with the highest GERs were the central states, which were largely unaffected by the conflict, whereas the states with the lowest GERs were those previously affected by conflict, such as Northern and Southern Darfur; Kassala and Red Sea, which were part of the Eastern states conflict; and Blue Nile, at the border of south Sudan.

Aside from regional disparities in access to education, children in rural areas, those from poorer households, and girls are at a disadvantage (see figure O.2). Of the three dimensions—rural-urban location, income, and gender—the strongest predictor of access to schooling is whether a child lives in an urban or rural area, with urban children being 17 percentage points more likely than rural children to have access to education. Overall, boys are 8 percentage points more likely than girls to have access, and rich children are 2 percentage points more likely than poor children to have access to school. A poor rural girl is the most disadvantaged of all and is about 25 percentage points less likely to ever access basic school than a rich urban boy. In village schools, which are rural by nature, only 41 percent of students enrolled are girls.

When northern Sudan is compared with its neighbors, the gender parity indexes (GPIs) for academic secondary and higher education are 0.97 and 1.27, respectively, and are more similar to the average GPIs seen in Egypt, the Islamic Republic of Iran, Jordan, and Tunisia (1.02 and 1.25, respectively) than to the averages for Cameroon, Kenya, Nigeria, and Uganda (0.84 and 0.74, respectively). However, the average GPI of 0.90 for basic education is lower than the average for Egypt, the Islamic Republic of Iran, Jordan, and Tunisia, which is 1.09, and also lower than the average for Cameroon, Kenya, Nigeria, and Uganda, which is 0.93.

Out of the population of 6 million 10–17-year-olds in northern Sudan, it is estimated that one in six, that is, close to 1 million, never had access to school in 2010. Among this group of children, 62 percent were girls and 84 percent were from rural areas. A UNICEF study conducted in

Figure O.2 Educational Access: Probability of Ever Enrolling in Basic School, by Location, Income, and Gender, circa 2005

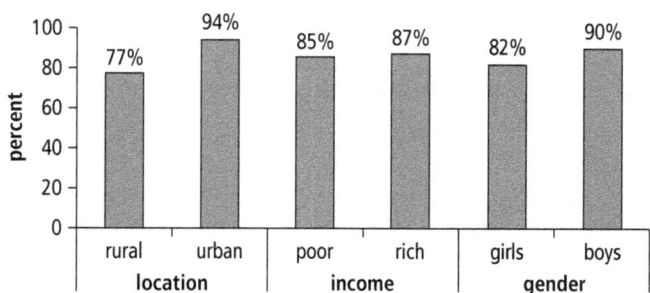

Source: Authors' analysis of the 2006 Sudan Household Health Survey (GoNU and GoSS 2006). The figure is based on responses of children ages 11–15.
Note: The figure gives the probability of ever enrolling in grade 1 of basic school. For this chart, *poor* means belonging to the lowest income quintile and *rich* means belonging to the two richest quintiles of the population.

southern Sudan may provide some insights into why some girls are being held back in rural areas of Sudan (UNICEF/GoSS 2008). One of the main conclusions of the study is that parents generally do want to educate their daughters, but many are not sending them to school out of concern for their safety as they walk to school or even in the schools themselves. The study concludes that safer and more child-friendly school environments—for girls as well as for boys—can be achieved by making fairly modest changes. Such actions as increasing parent involvement in school management or providing tuition waivers for girls are likely to be enough to convince parents to send their daughters to school. The study also emphasizes the need for teaching life skills both in schools and in the community.

POPULATIONS IN TRANSIT

Education access for vulnerable populations (nomads, internally displaced persons [IDPs]) needs to be expanded. Providing education services for IDPs and nomads in northern Sudan remains a significant challenge because they are perpetually on the move. Data on the size of these population groups are scarce, and there is great variation in available estimates. For example, according to the United Nations High Commissioner for Refugees (UNHCR), there were 4.9 million IDPs in Sudan (including South Sudan), with 2.6 million located in the Darfur region alone and 1.7 million in Khartoum state. However, according to the 2008 population census, there are approximately 780,000 IDPs, and the difference in numbers is probably a result of the definitions used. Nomads also make up a large share of the population in northern Sudan. According to the existing estimates, nomads account for 8.5–8.7 percent of the total population (GoS and others 2005; UNHCR 2010).

In 2008–09, 8.7 percent of basic schools in northern Sudan were nomadic and 1.6 percent were IDP (Education Yearbook 2009). IDP schools are large. Their average enrollment was 815 students in 2008–09, with an average of 92 students per class, which potentially results in lower learning levels. Nomadic schools, on the other hand, are smaller, multigrade schools, though teachers follow the general curriculum.

Among these vulnerable groups, the share of girls in basic education is smaller than that in regular schools (figure O.3). The share of girls in nomadic schools is 38 percent and in IDP schools, 44 percent compared with 47 percent in regular government schools. These figures suggest that girls are at a greater disadvantage within the vulnerable population groups, particularly nomads.

Figure O.3 Share of Girls in Enrollments, by Type of Basic School, 2008–09

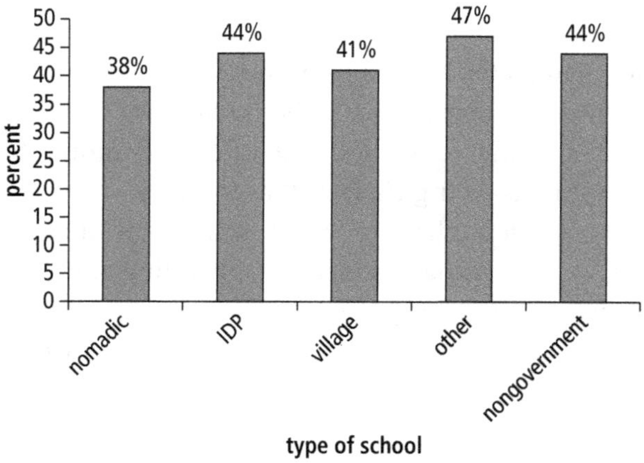

[Bar chart showing percent by type of school: nomadic 38%, IDP 44%, village 41%, other 47%, nongovernment 44%]

Source: FMoGE 2008–09 statistical yearbook.

Moving forward, to effectively target the nomadic and IDP population groups (which is a necessary step if universal primary completion is to be achieved), data need to be disaggregated to reflect the participation of nomads and IDPs within regular schools. These data could be captured through the new Education Management Information System.

MALNOURISHED STUDENTS

Malnourished children are an underlying problem (table O.1). A large proportion of children ages 0–59 months in northern Sudan are malnourished, with negative consequences for learning at preschool and beyond. The percentage of children who are underweight and stunted in northern Sudan is high compared with that of other countries with variation between the states. In Northern Darfur, 55 percent of children are underweight, whereas in Kassala, 69 percent are stunted. These figures are higher than the averages in Sub-Saharan Africa (28 percent underweight and 9 percent wasting), and much higher than the averages for the Middle East and North Africa region (17 percent underweight and 8 percent wasting) (SHHS 2007; UNICEF 2009). International literature shows that malnourished children tend not to reach their potential either physically or mentally, are less likely to go to school, and once in school, register lower levels of learning achievement (EFA 2011).

Table O.1 Anthropometric Measures of Sudan's Children
percent

State	Underweight	Stunted	Wasted
Northern	41.6	38.7	26.3
River Nile	34.5	40.0	15.2
Red Sea	43.3	45.2	19.8
Kassala	53.9	68.5	23.7
Al Qadarif	42.5	55.2	11.4
Khartoum	24.5	37.2	13.1
Al Jazirah	28.5	41.3	9.7
Sinnar	38.0	50.4	14.0
Blue Nile	46.5	59.8	14.5
White Nile	40.2	48.7	15.3
North Kordofan	42.9	51.0	15.5
South Kordofan	35.3	43.0	14.9
Northern Darfur	55.0	48.6	28.5
Western Darfur	51.3	44.8	23.2
Southern Darfur	41.6	47.3	11.4
Sub-Saharan Africa (2000–07)	28	38	9
Middle East and North Africa (2000–07)	17	26	8

Source: For northern Sudan, the data are from the World Bank staff calculations (World Bank forthcoming) using data from the SHHS 2006 (GoNU and GoSS 2006). For Sub-Saharan Africa and the Middle East and North Africa, the data are from the National Center for Health Statistics of the U.S. Centers for Disease Control and Prevention and from the World Health Organization.

STAFFING NEEDS

Attracting teachers to hardship areas and remote schools remains a challenge. In northern Sudan, basic education teachers are not effectively deployed based on school needs. Specifically, the number of teachers allocated to a school frequently does not increase with the number of students enrolled in that school, and teachers tend to be concentrated in urban areas. The degree of randomness in the allocation of teachers in northern Sudan is only about 49 percent (see figure O.4), which is worse than all Sub-Saharan African countries shown except Liberia. Two of the main constraints to effective deployment of teachers appear to be (a) the policy that deploys female teachers close to their spouses

Figure O.4 International Comparisons: Degree of Randomness in Teacher Allocations in Basic Education, by Country

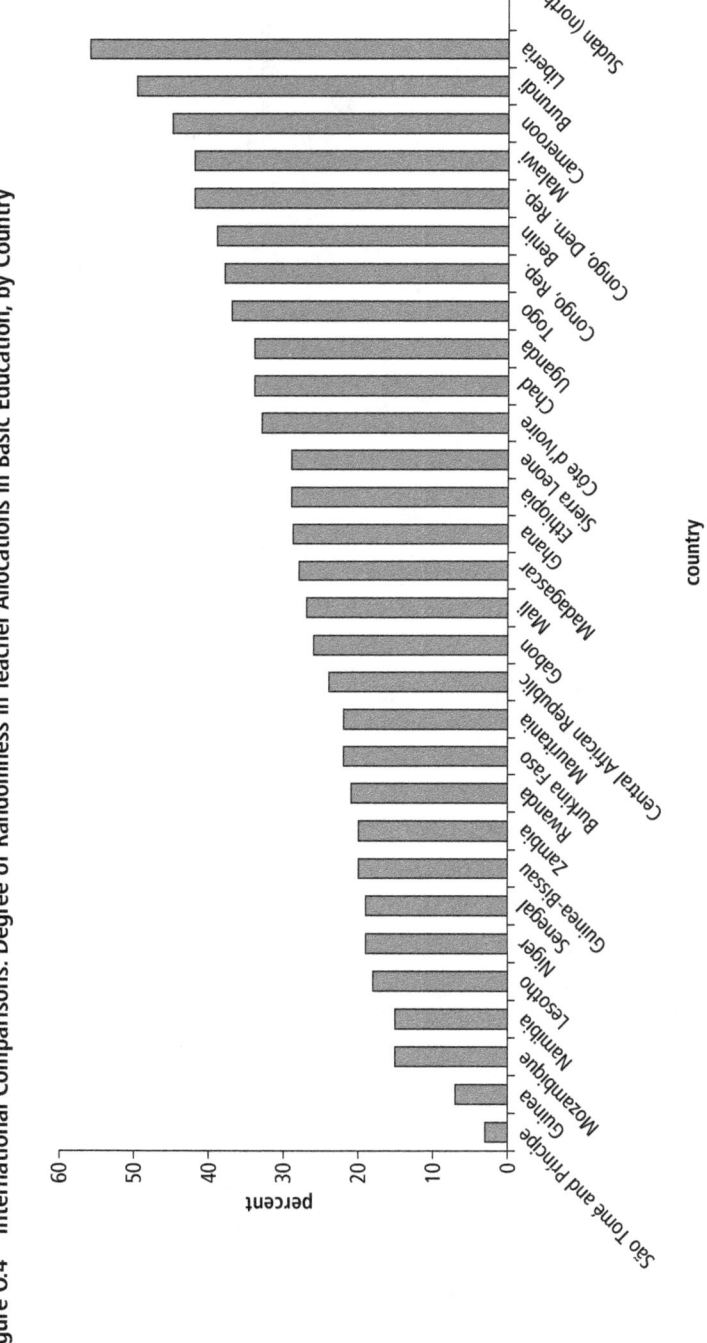

Source: Authors' estimates from the various country status reports.

(67 percent of teachers are female) and (b) the fact that there are no incentives (financial or otherwise) provided by the government to work in rural or remote schools.

One of the critical areas to be addressed moving forward is how to attract teachers to hardship or remote areas. Some of the solutions could include recruiting teachers from those areas and providing financial incentives such as bonuses, faster promotions, or housing for teachers in remote schools.

FEDERAL EDUCATION SPENDING

Although government spending on education has increased, it remains low compared with other countries, particularly for basic education. Between 2000 and 2009, there was a substantial increase in education spending—from SDG 660 million in real terms to SDG 2.4 billion—which indicated the government's commitment to expand and improve education. The share of gross domestic product (GDP) allocated to education doubled to 2.7 percent over this period, but northern Sudan still spends less on education compared with similar lower-middle-income countries in Africa and the Middle East. Furthermore, average spending on basic education as a share of total education spending, that is, 37 percent, is lower than that in Egypt, Kenya, and Morocco, which allocate 40 percent, 55 percent, and 46 percent, respectively. It is evident therefore that more resources are needed in the sector.[4] This need will become an increasing challenge if economic growth slows down or government revenues decline, making the shift to efficiency in the use of resources all the more urgent.

Following the government's decentralization policy, the responsibilities of the states have increased significantly since the 2005 Comprehensive Peace Agreement. Education spending at the state level has followed this pattern: in 2009, states covered 83 percent of total public education spending (see figure O.5). In practice, however, the fiscal autonomy of some states has been limited because they rely heavily on federal transfers driven by federal policies that influence areas such as salary determination (World Bank 2007).

Government spending on goods and services in the education sector has been low, particularly for basic education, where goods and services account for only 5 percent of total recurrent spending. This relatively small share of public spending is offset by household spending on school running costs (EU 2008), which in 2009 were estimated to be an annual average of SDG 84 per person among urban households and SDG 24 per person among rural households World Bank 2010).

Figure O.5 Public Education Spending, by Administrative Level, 2000–09

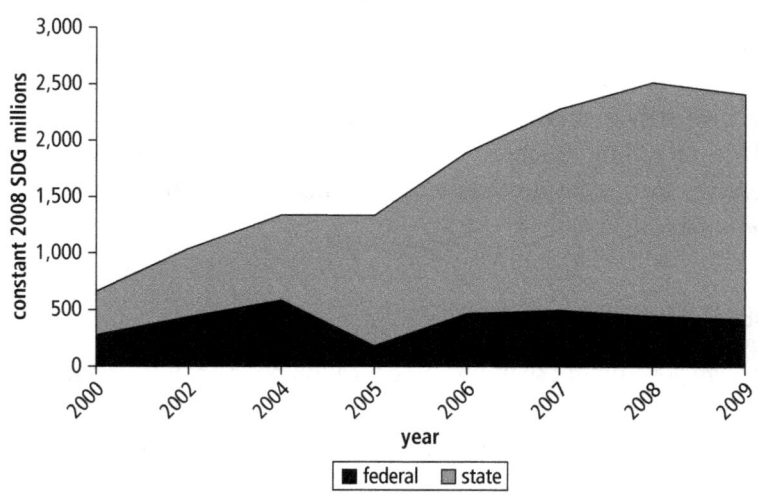

Source: Authors' estimates based on state ministry of education data collected in 2010.

EQUITY-ORIENTED EDUCATION SPENDING

Education needs, which vary within and across states, should drive overall spending. Federal transfers are intended to redistribute resources so that all states are given equal opportunity to provide public services, including education, to their citizens.[5] The rationale behind this decentralized service delivery system supports an environment conducive to addressing regional and social disparities by bringing the decision-making process and resources closer to the citizens. However, decentralization poses a challenge in terms of the varying capacities at the local level to raise revenues through taxes. In addition, decentralization presents a challenge in terms of reporting to and coordinating with the Federal Ministry of General Education, particularly when the roles and responsibilities of each level of government are not clearly defined.

Federal resources are supposed to be allocated based on states' financial performance, population size, natural resources, human resources, infrastructure, education status, security status, and per capita income where each component is assigned a weight (EU 2008). However, a lack of data does not allow confirmation that this formula is followed in all cases. Rather, discussions with the states indicate that transfers for education are primarily based on states' existing payroll and obligations (last year's budget plus a negotiated increment) (see EU 2008). Although this formula helps states honor their payroll obligations and keep existing education services running, it tends to perpetuate existing inequalities and reduce states' spending autonomy.

Further, the analysis of education spending in northern Sudan is hampered by several challenges. A consolidated budget for the three levels of government (federal, state, and local) is lacking; spending is not classified by function and purpose; data exist typically for budget allocations rather than executed amounts; and financial management capacity is weak at the state and local levels, which results in the incomplete reporting of spending at these levels (World Bank 2007).

Although the GoNU supports a strong equity-orientated approach to education service delivery in the ESSP, there is an urgent need to link the planning and budgeting processes with the education resource needs of different regions and vulnerable populations. A prerequisite for an equity-orientated approach to education service delivery is the regular collection and analysis of data on (a) key educational outcomes by region and population groups, (b) past trends in investments and outcomes, and (c) gaps that need to be bridged in terms of key education outcomes (Jhingran and Sankar 2009). Moving forward, the Education Management Information System, currently being instituted by the Ministry of General Education in collaboration with the EU, will be critical in capturing such disaggregated educational input and output data. However, the collection of state-level education spending data remains an issue that needs to be dealt with more broadly to improve the public financial management system within the Ministry of Finance and National Economy.

CONCLUSION

The GoNU has made great efforts to increase access to education for children in northern Sudan across education subsectors over the past decade. In particular, educational access for children in areas previously affected by conflict has improved substantially since the signing of the peace agreements of 2005 and 2006. Estimates suggest that, on average, 90 percent of all children in northern Sudan had access to a formal school in 2010. However, inequities in access to schooling by gender and location persist. There continue to be regional disparities in access by children in rural areas, with girls facing the greatest disadvantage.

The challenges ahead relate not only to reducing these inequities in access but also to improving the efficiency of the education system to produce young adults equipped with the skills and knowledge to secure their livelihoods and contribute to society. If northern Sudan is to achieve its target of Education for All, it needs to focus on three things: enrolling all children, keeping them in school, and creating an environment that facilitates learning. The critical constraints facing the efficiency of the system in northern Sudan include the large number of dropouts at both basic and secondary levels, the ineffective deployment of teachers across schools (and the inability to attract teachers to remote schools), insufficient resources (particularly textbooks) for students, and inadequate instructional time.

Finally, two critical risks face the education sector. One is a contraction in public spending—because of the heavy reliance of the country on oil revenues—resulting in reduced transfers to the states. The other is the lack of alignment between the educational needs of a state and the resources provided.

NOTES

1. A similar learning assessment and service delivery study for secondary education was being conducted by the United Nations Educational, Scientific, and Cultural Organization/United Nations Children's Fund (UNESCO/UNICEF) at the time this report was being compiled, as well as an early childhood development (ECD) assessment by UNICEF. A separate higher education learning paper was also being prepared by the World Bank at the time.

2. In 2007–08, there was a government campaign encouraging parents to send their children to school, and as a result, grade 1 enrollments increased. In 2008–09, there was no such campaign, and grade 1 enrollments dropped.

3. For the purpose of this comparison, *public spending per student on school operating costs* is defined as spending on goods and services.

4. Calculations were made after adjusting for the fact that basic education in northern Sudan is eight years rather than six.

5. The rules governing fiscal transfers are scattered in many documents, including the Comprehensive Peace Agreement of 2005, the Darfur Peace Agreement of 2006, and the Eastern Sudan Peace Agreement of 2006.

REFERENCES

EFA (Education for All). 2011. *EFA Global Monitoring Report 2011. The Hidden Crisis: Armed Conflict and Education.* Paris: United Nations Educational, Scientific, and Cultural Organization. Available at http://unesdoc.unesco.org/images/0019/001907/190743e.pdf.

EU (European Union). 2008. Cost and Financing Study.

FMoGE (Federal Ministry of General Education). Various years. "Statistical Yearbooks." Khartoum.

———. 2008. "Baseline Survey on Basic Education in the Northern States of Sudan: Final Report June 2008." Online document available at http://planipolis.iiep.unesco.org/epiweb/E029336e.pdf.

GoNU (Government of National Unity). 2010. "Poverty in Northern Sudan: Estimates from the National Baseline Household Survey of 2009." Khartoum.

GoNU (Government of National Unity) and GoSS (Government of Southern Sudan). 2006. *Sudan Household Health Survey (SHHS) 2006*. Khartoum/Juba: Central Bureau of Statistics and Southern Sudan Center for Census, Statistics and Evaluation.

GoS (Government of Sudan), SPLM (Sudan Peoples Liberation Movement), World Bank, and UNDP (United Nations Development Programme). 2005. *Joint Assessment Mission: Framework for Sustained Peace, Development, and Poverty Eradication*. Vols. I–III. Available at http://www.unsudanig.org/docs/Joint%20Assessment%20Mission%20(JAM)%20Volume%20I.pdf.

Interim Constitution of the Republic of Sudan. 2005. Available at http://www.sudan-embassy.de/c_Sudan.pdf.

Jhingran, Dhir, and Deepa Sankar. 2009. "Addressing Educational Disparity: Using District Level Education Development Indices for Equitable Resource Allocations in India." Policy Research Working Paper 4955, South Asia Region, Human Development Network, World Bank, Washington, DC.

UNHCR (United Nations High Commissioner for Refugees). 2010. Available at http://www.unhcr.org/cgi-bin/texis/vtx/home/opendocPDFViewer.html?docid=4dfdbf480&query=IDPs%20Sudan%202010.

UNICEF (United Nations Children's Fund). 2009. *The State of the World's Children 2009: Maternal and Newborn Health*. New York: UNICEF. Available at http://www.unicef.org/sowc09/report/report.php.

UNICEF/GoSS (United Nations Children's Fund/Government of Southern Sudan). 2008. *Socio-Economic and Cultural Barriers to Schooling in South Sudan*. Juba.

World Bank. 2007. "Sudan. Public Expenditure Review. Synthesis Report." Report 41840-SD. World Bank, Washington, DC.

———. Forthcoming. "Public Expenditure Tracking Survey (PETS) for Northern Sudan: From Spending More to Spending Smart–Case Study of the Health Sector." Poverty Reduction and Ecomonic Management Network, World Bank, Washington, DC.

CHAPTER 1

Setting the Scene

This chapter provides the context for education in Sudan. It begins with an overview of the demographic, macroeconomic, and socioeconomic environment and is followed by a brief description of the administrative structure of education. The six subsequent chapters focus on details related to (a) overall enrollment trends, (b) patterns in student flow, (c) disparities in education provision, (d) status of educational service delivery in three states, (e) management of teachers, and (f) financing of the education system.

SCOPE OF THIS EDUCATION SECTOR STATUS REPORT

Sudan is committed to the Education for All (EFA) Initiative and the education Millennium Development Goals (MDGs) and to providing universal access to quality education in both primary and secondary education. The five-year (2007–11) Education Sector Strategic Plan (ESSP) based on the 2001 Education Act of the Government of National Unity (GoNU) directs activities in the education sector. In developing its new ESSP, for 2012–16, the GoNU sought to assess the status of the education system in order to identify priority areas for development in the sector. This Education Sector Status Report is a diagnostic of the system for that purpose. It provides the knowledge base (box 1.1) that will inform the preparation of the 2012–16 ESSP and contribute to dialogue among relevant stakeholders on the continuing challenges and emerging strategic priorities for the education sector. The focus of this report is northern Sudan, which encompasses 15 states.[1]

The period since 2005 has been characterized by relative peace between northern and southern Sudan. Following decades of civil war, the Comprehensive Peace Agreement (CPA) was signed on January 9, 2005.

> **BOX 1.1 EDUCATION SECTOR STATUS REPORT DATA SOURCES**
>
> **This status report draws on existing data sources as well as primary data collected by targeted studies. They are as follows:**
>
> - School data from the federal Ministry of General Education statistical yearbooks (FMoGE various years)
> - Demographic data from the 2006 Sudan Household Health Survey (GoNU and GoSS 2006) and the short form of the 2008 population census (data from the Sudan Household Health Survey 2009 and the long form of the 2008 population census [GoNU and GoSS 2009] were not available at the time this report was being prepared)
> - Financing data from the national accounts of the Ministry of Finance and National Economy
> - School characteristics data from the 2008 baseline survey (FMoGE 2008) and the 2008 European Union Cost and Financing Study (EU 2008)
> - Primary data on state-level education expenditure collected by the team for 13 of the 15 northern states
> - Primary data collected in 3 of the 15 northern states for the service delivery chapter
> - Interviews with education stakeholders for individual chapters

Through the institutionalization of autonomy for southern Sudan and the sharing of resources, the agreement offered an environment for both sides to concentrate their efforts on reconstruction and development. The Eastern Sudan Peace Agreement in 2006 brought peace to that region, though conflict has continued in the Darfur region after the Darfur Peace Agreement in 2006.

DEMOGRAPHIC CONTEXT

Sudan is a multicultural society and is undergoing rapid change. Located at the crossroads between North and East Africa and the Middle East, it was Africa's largest country by area prior to the secession of South Sudan on July 9, 2011. Sudan is characterized by cultural, ethnic, and religious diversity and is home to numerous tribes, languages, and dialects. The official languages of Sudan are Arabic and English, though Arabic is the dominant language in northern Sudan. As in most African countries,

Sudan is undergoing rapid urbanization, with 43 percent of the population living in urban areas in 2008, which is up from 36 percent in 2000 and 27 percent in 1990.[2] The strong rural-urban migration is in part driven by drought and desertification, as well as insecurity in rural areas (World Bank 2009).

The accuracy of demographic data has always been an issue in Sudan. The combination of a vast territory, a large nomadic population, civil conflict, and security concerns makes it difficult to count the population. Much effort was therefore invested in the 2008 population census (GoNU and GoSS 2009), the first postwar census in Sudan.[3] The census estimated the total population of Sudan at 39.2 million. The population of just the 15 northern states was 30.9 million, corresponding to 79 percent of the total population of Sudan.

The 15 northern states vary widely in population size. Khartoum State and neighboring Al Jazirah State are the main centers of economic activity in Sudan (World Bank 2009). They are also among the largest states in terms of population: Khartoum State is home to 5.3 million inhabitants and Al Jazirah State to 3.6 million. Other large states include Southern Darfur (4.1 million), North Kordofan (2.9 million), and Northern Darfur (2.1 million), whereas the remaining 10 states have fewer than 2 million inhabitants each.

The demographic context for providing universal basic education in northern Sudan is more advantageous than that for Sub-Saharan Africa generally. The share of 5–16-year-olds in the total population of northern Sudan in 2008 was 31.9 percent compared with the average across Sub-Saharan Africa of 34.4 percent. The share of 5–16-year-olds in the populations of some of Sudan's neighbors was larger, notably Ethiopia, with 36 percent, and Chad, with 37 percent. Thus, northern Sudan will be in a better position to shoulder the cost of providing basic education to all children than will several of its African neighbors.

The pace of population growth has declined. This fact suggests that Sudan is nearing a demographic transition, where the size of the generations will stabilize, which has positive implications for the affordability of the education system. The pattern of slowing population growth is most pronounced in Kassala, Northern, and Red Sea states; however, it is not present in all states.

MACROECONOMIC CONTEXT

The past 15 years have been a period of unprecedented economic growth in Sudan. Between 1975 and 1995, GDP per capita—a measure of average income per person—remained within a narrow band of

US$600–US$800 (in real terms). During this period, Sudan was a low-income country with an average income similar to that of Chad or Kenya in 2010. Since 1995, and especially since 1999 when Sudan started exporting oil in significant amounts, the country has experienced strong economic growth. Between 1995 and 2008, GDP per capita almost doubled in real terms, from US$780 to more than US$1,400 (figure 1.1).

The economic expansion has brought with it increased investment and improved macroeconomic management. A 2009 World Bank report argues that Sudan's oil wealth has led to considerable investment in infrastructure and utilities. For example, the length of the Sudanese road network grew by 80 percent between 2000 and 2008, and electricity generation doubled over the same period. There are also improvements in macroeconomic management since the discovery of oil; for example, inflation was reduced from an average of 33 percent per year during the 1970s and 1980s to 8 percent per year since 1999.

In spite of the benefits, Sudan's overdependence on oil revenues threatens the stability of the economy. In the short term, the volatility of oil prices and uncertainties about oil production present challenges for fiscal management. In the long term, Sudan's oil reserves are not unlimited, so future economic growth will depend on the development of nonoil sectors.

GOVERNMENT REVENUE AND EXPENDITURE

The strong economic growth in Sudan has been accompanied by an even stronger expansion of the public sector. Total GoNU spending grew from 11 percent of GDP in 2000 to 17 percent in 2009 (table 1.1). However, the

Figure 1.1 Growth of GDP per Capita in Sudan, 1975–2008

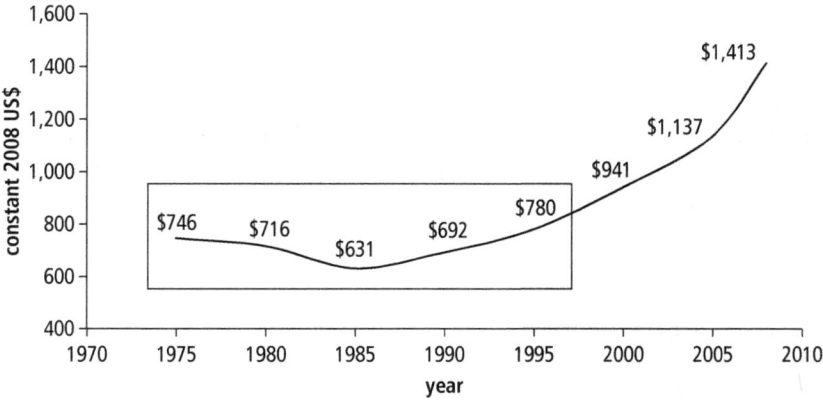

Source: Adapted from World Bank 2009.

Table 1.1 Trends in GoNU Revenues and Expenditures, 2000–09

Indicator	2000	2002	2004	Actual 2005	2006	2007	2008	Budgeted 2009
Total GoNU revenue[a]	6,901	8,800	15,152	16,071	18,569	20,768	24,274	16,591
As percentage of GDP	11	12	18	18	19	19	21	15
Percentage from oil	43	42	49	50	51	56	66	43
Total GoNU expenditure[a]	7,277	9,657	16,333	18,906	22,597	24,275	25,985	19,442
As percentage of GDP	11	13	20	21	23	23	22	17
Federal government expenditure[a]	6,665	9,044	15,087	13,564	14,481	15,318	14,413	11,028
Transfer to northern states[a]	612	613	1,246	2,832	4,453	5,078	5,411	5,555
Transfer to GoSS[a]	0	0	0	2,510	3,664	3,880	6,161	2,858
Memo item: GDP[a]	65,696	73,484	82,761	87,999	97,933	107,886	116,887	112,209

Source: Data for 2007–10 are from the Ministry of Finance and National Economy revenue and expenditure accounts. Data for earlier years are from World Bank (2007). Estimated figures for GDP for 2009 and 2010 are from EIU (2010).
Note: Current prices are shown in annex 1A to this chapter. GDP = gross domestic product; GoNU = Government of National Unity; GoSS = Government of Southern Sudan.
a. Figures are in 2008 constant million Sudanese pounds (SDG).

GoNU expenditure figures do not include all public spending. They exclude spending by other levels of government, notably states and localities, which draw from their own locally generated sources of revenue. In absolute terms, GoNU revenues and expenditures were at their highest in 2008 as a result of that year's spike in oil prices. Similarly, the decline in overall GoNU revenues and expenditures in 2009 can be attributed to the precipitous drop in oil export revenues (World Bank 2010a).

Public spending in Sudan is still relatively modest relative to the size of its economy. In Sub-Saharan Africa, public spending of middle-income countries averages 35 percent of GDP, whereas public spending of low-income countries averages 25 percent of GDP, compared to 17 percent in Sudan.

Since the 2005 CPA, the structure of the GoNU budget reflects the increasing level of decentralization in northern Sudan. Both the Government of Southern Sudan (GoSS) and the 15 northern states now receive very significant transfers from the GoNU. Transfers to the northern states have grown from 8 percent of total GoNU spending in 2004 to as much as 29 percent in 2009.

Economic development has been unbalanced between the center and the periphery. Sudan's growth process has historically been unbalanced because the majority of its manufacturing firms and irrigated land were concentrated in Khartoum and Al Jazirah states. The capital city consumes nearly one-third of the total electricity produced in the country, whereas less than 7 percent of households in the country have access to the national grid (CEM 2010). Within northern Sudan, poverty is significantly higher in rural areas: one out of four urban dwellers is poor, as defined by the national poverty line, but three out of five are poor in rural areas. Poverty levels also vary by state, with the incidence of poverty ranging from one-fourth of the population in Khartoum State to more than two-thirds of the population in Northern Darfur (GoNU 2010).

SOCIOECONOMIC BACKGROUND

Despite the economic gains and increased government spending in recent years, socioeconomic indicators for northern Sudan remain weak. Poverty is widespread, with almost half the population (46.5 percent) in northern Sudan living below the national poverty line (GoNU 2010).[4] Table 1.2 shows that anthropometric measures for children are worse in several states in Sudan compared to the regional average. In 12 of the 15 northern Sudan states, more than 34 percent of children are considered

Table 1.2 Anthropometric Measures of Sudan's Children
percent

State	Underweight	Stunted	Wasted
Northern	41.6	38.7	26.3
River Nile	34.5	40.0	15.2
Red Sea	43.3	45.2	19.8
Kassala	53.9	68.5	23.7
Al Qadarif	42.5	55.2	11.4
Khartoum	24.5	37.2	13.1
Al Jazirah	28.5	41.3	9.7
Sinnar	38.0	50.4	14.0
Blue Nile	46.5	59.8	14.5
White Nile	40.2	48.7	15.3
North Kordofan	42.9	51.0	15.5
South Kordofan	35.3	43.0	14.9
Northern Darfur	55.0	48.6	28.5
Western Darfur	51.3	44.8	23.2
Southern Darfur	41.6	47.3	11.4
Sub-Saharan Africa (2000–07)	28	38	9
Middle East and North Africa (2000–07)	17	26	8

Source: For northern Sudan, the data are from the World Bank staff calculations (World Bank forthcoming) using data from the SHHS 2006 (GoNU and GoSS 2006). For Sub-Saharan Africa and the Middle East and North Africa, the data are from the National Center for Health Statistics of the U.S. Centers for Disease Control and Prevention and from the World Health Organization.

underweight compared with the Sub-Saharan African average of 28 percent. Similarly, table 1.2 shows that except for Khartoum and Al Jazirah states, the average percentages of stunted and wasted children in northern Sudan are consistently higher than the 26 percent and 8 percent, respectively, in Sub-Saharan Africa. The prevalence of HIV/AIDS among 15–49-year-olds in all of Sudan is estimated to be 1.4 percent, which is below the 5 percent average in Sub-Saharan Africa and above the 0.3 percent average in the Middle East and North Africa region. However, the Joint United Nations Programme on HIV/AIDS (UNAIDS 2009) estimates that the HIV prevalence rate for adults in northern Sudan is 0.67 percent, which is lower than the average for all of Sudan.

Sudan's population includes the largest number of internally displaced persons (IDPs) in Africa.[5] Out of the total 11.6 million IDPs in 19 countries on the continent, there are an estimated 4.1 million IDPs in

Sudan, including South Sudan, (UNHCR 2010) as a result of conflict and instability. Of these, the United Nations High Commissioner for Refugees (UNHCR) estimates that 2.6 million are located in the Darfur region alone, with another 1.7 million in Khartoum State. About 400,000 of the IDPs in Khartoum State reside in four sites recognized by the authorities, while the rest live in informal squatter areas in and around the city. Children who have been displaced often do not have access to education because it is not considered a priority humanitarian or early reconstruction response.

Sudan also has a large nomadic population. The total number of nomads in Sudan is not clear, but the Joint Assessment Mission (GoS and others 2005) estimated that 8.5 percent of both northern and South Sudan's population were nomads at the time. Providing education services for nomads remains a significant challenge because they are perpetually on the move, they often attach little value to education, and old traditions require girls to marry young (UNICEF 2009).

ADMINISTRATIVE STRUCTURE OF GENERAL EDUCATION IN NORTHERN SUDAN

General education in northern Sudan is 13 years, including 2 years of preschool, 8 years of basic school, and 3 years of secondary school.[6] The official length of the academic year at all levels of general education is 210 working days, and the year is divided into two semesters. The length of the academic year and the timing of the secondary school certificate examination are determined by the federal Ministry of General Education (FMoGE), while the states decide on a suitable school calendar (see annex 1B for details).

Basic education in northern Sudan is intended to be free and compulsory.[7] According to the Interim Constitution of the Republic of Sudan (2005), basic education is compulsory and should be provided by the state free of charge. Similar clauses are documented within the Eastern Front Peace Agreement and the Darfur Peace Agreement.

The CPA has necessitated the development of a national curriculum framework that addresses the multicultural, multiethnic, and multireligious context of Sudan. The National Center for Curriculum and Education Research (NCCER), which is responsible for all aspects of developing and supporting the national curriculum framework for basic and secondary education, is currently undertaking an assessment of the curriculum across Sudan in order to propose a framework for developing a new curriculum in line with the requirements of the CPA. Curriculum development for preschools and IDP schools is the responsibility of the state ministries of education. Nomadic schools operate with the same curriculum as that used in regular schools.

There are five core areas in the basic education curriculum and nine in the secondary school curriculum. The five areas in basic education are religion, language, mathematics, man and the universe, and applied arts. Rather than a subject-oriented approach, the basic education curriculum focuses on thematic areas; for example, the area of man and the universe includes instruction in science, history, geography, and religion. With the assistance of the United Nations Children's Fund (UNICEF), a comprehensive life skills curriculum was also introduced in 2008 and is being rapidly implemented across schools. The life skills curriculum includes developing self-confidence and dealing with conflict, HIV/AIDS, and gender issues. In secondary education, there are nine core subjects including Arabic, Islamic studies, English, mathematics, physics, chemistry, biology, geography, and history. Optional subjects include computers, agricultural and animal protection, commercial science, family studies, military studies, and engineering studies.

As a result of the CPA and the Interim Constitution of the Republic of Sudan (2005), northern Sudan has a decentralized system of education service delivery. Within the education sector, the federal government, through the FMoGE in Khartoum, is in charge of planning, coordinating, and monitoring across the three general education levels. In addition, the FMoGE directs policy development in three key areas: secondary school certification, the qualification framework for teachers, and development of the basic and secondary education curricula. Policies related to human resource management and certification for basic education fall under the purview of the state government. Further, the states and *mahalyas* (localities) are responsible for the delivery of preschool, basic, and secondary education. In contrast, higher education is managed (both policies and service delivery) by the federal Ministry of Higher Education and Scientific Research (MoHESR).

On the one hand, a decentralized service delivery system supports the creation of an environment conducive to addressing regional and social disparities by bringing the decision-making process and the resources closer to the people of a region. On the other hand, decentralization poses a challenge in terms of the varying capacities that exist at the local level to raise revenue through taxes and design and to implement policies. In addition, decentralization presents a challenge for subnational governments in terms of reporting to and coordinating with the FMoGE, particularly because the roles and responsibilities of each level of government are not clearly defined.

Education service delivery in Sudan is severely hampered by the uncertainties that surround the disbursal of funds to subnational governments (World Bank 2010a). The Country Integrated Fiduciary Assessment for 2005–2007 found that the northern states are highly dependent on interfiscal transfers from the federal government, yet budget allocations are rarely realized outside of Chapter I (that is, salary and staff costs). This situation makes both the planning and delivery of education services difficult.

ANNEX 1A: POPULATION BY AGE IN 2008

Table 1A.1 provides the total population in each of the five census years starting with 1956, and calculates the rate of population growth in the intervals between censuses. There is no clear trend in the population growth rate per year, first increasing from 2.2 percent to 3.7 percent, then declining from 3.7 percent to 1.9 percent, and increasing again to 2.9 percent. This uneven trend suggests that some censuses attained a better coverage of the population than did others.

The 2008 population data are not smooth. Figure 1A.1 zooms in on the population ages 24 years and younger and shows the distribution of this group by age. The chart shows a very uneven population curve, with

Table 1A.1 Population of Sudan by Census Year and Average Growth in Intervening Years, 1956–2008

Item	1956 (million)	Growth (percent)	1973 (million)	Growth (percent)	1983 (million)	Growth (percent)	1993 (million)	Growth (percent)	2008 (percent)
Total population	10.3	2.2	14.8	3.7	21.3	1.9	25.6	2.9	39.2

Source: Authors' construction based on data from the Population Census Council/Technical Working Group 2009.

Figure 1A.1 Raw Population Data in Sudan, Ages 0–24 Years, 2008

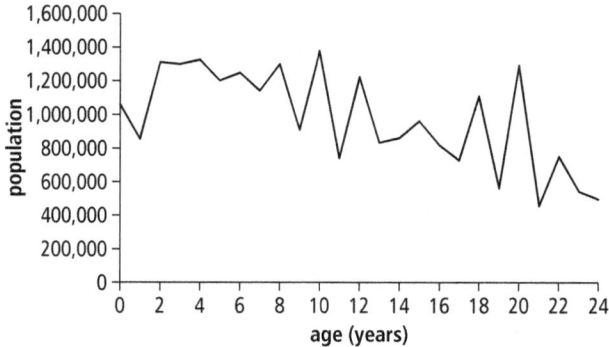

Source: 2008 population census (GoNU and GoSS 2009).

the numbers for most of the even ages (6, 8, 12, and so on) being higher than those for the uneven ages (7, 9, 11, and so on), as well as very high numbers of 10- and 20-year-olds. These peaks reflect errors, or biases, in the data that arise because parents may not know the exact ages of their children and find it easier to report the approximate ages (which tends to be easier, rounded numbers, such as 10, 20, and the like). If the raw census data are used to calculate age-specific indicators—such as the gross intake rate or the primary completion rate—the errors in the population data will translate into errors in the analysis of, in this example, education coverage. For these errors in the data to be corrected, the population data by single ages therefore need to be smoothed.

There appears to be an underreporting of infants in the census data.[8] Figure 1A.1 also shows that the number of infants, that is, children ages 0 and 1 year, in the population data is very low. This finding could have two explanations: (a) a sudden drop in fertility in Sudan or (b) an underreporting of infants in the census. According to Ahmed (2008), it is commonly known that some tribes in Sudan "report lesser number of their children believing that the evil eyes of the enumerators will kill their children if they report many." Therefore (and because there are no other sources to suggest a sudden drop in fertility), we may conclude that there are errors in the data on the number of infants.

For the purposes of this study, population data for the 2–24 age group were smoothed. That choice was made because of the two data issues mentioned. Here, smoothing simply means redistributing population across single ages while holding the total population constant. The smoothing was done at the level of each state and then aggregated to national-level smoothed population data. In the following, figure 1A.2 shows the smoothed population data for all of Sudan.

Figure 1A.2 Raw and Smoothed Population Data in Sudan, Ages 2–24 Years, 2008

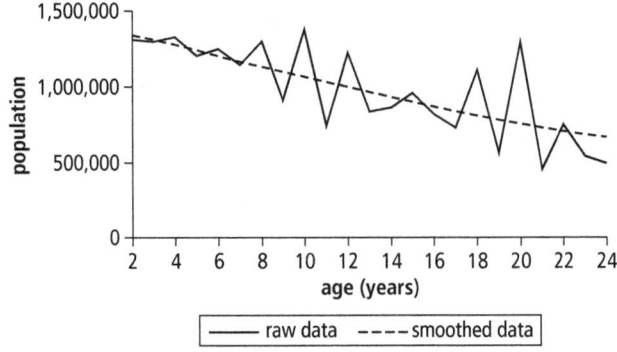

Source: Authors' construction based on the 2008 population census (GoNU and GoSS 2009).

Although it is hard to see this trend in figure 1A.2, the shape of the smoothed curve indicates a deceleration in the pace of growth in the size of each generation born in Sudan. This finding suggests that Sudan is nearing a demographic transition, where the size of the generations will stabilize (with obvious implications for the education system). This pattern of slowing population growth—which is most pronounced in Kassala, Northern, and Red Sea states—is not present in all states, however.

ANNEX 1B: ADMINISTRATIVE STRUCTURE OF THE EDUCATION SYSTEM

The Ministry of General Education (MoGE) functions according to five-year sector strategic plans. The current strategic plan runs from 2007 to 2011. The National Council for General Education approves the plans and then the Council of Ministers ratifies the strategy to be implemented by federal, state, and local governments. States develop plans that are submitted to the FMoGE for incorporation into a national strategic plan. Based on the five-year strategic plan, annual work plans and budgets are developed at the national and state levels.

STRUCTURE OF THE FEDERAL MINISTRY OF GENERAL EDUCATION[9]

As seen in figure 1B.1, there are four entities that report directly to the minister, which include the UNESCO (United Nations Educational, Scientific and Cultural Organization) National Committee, the National Center for Curricula and Educational Research (NCCER), the National Center for Languages (SELTI), and the general secretariat for the National Council of Illiteracy and Adult Education. There are nine general directorates and 49 specialist directorates under the supervision of the undersecretary. The general directorates include (a) educational planning, (b) technical education, (c) educational external relations, (d) services and administrative affairs, (e) information center, (f) media and public relations, (g) educational training and qualifications, (h) examinations, and (i) student activities. Excluding the four entities reporting directly to the minister, the total number of positions in the FMoGE administrative offices is 915.[10]

According to the recently completed organizational review (FMoGE 2010), there is considerable overlap and duplication of functional units. The review found that 70 percent of FMoGE staff members who were interviewed had not seen formal job descriptions for their respective positions (table 1B.1). Despite the small percentage of employees who

Figure 1B.1 Organizational Structure of the FMoGE

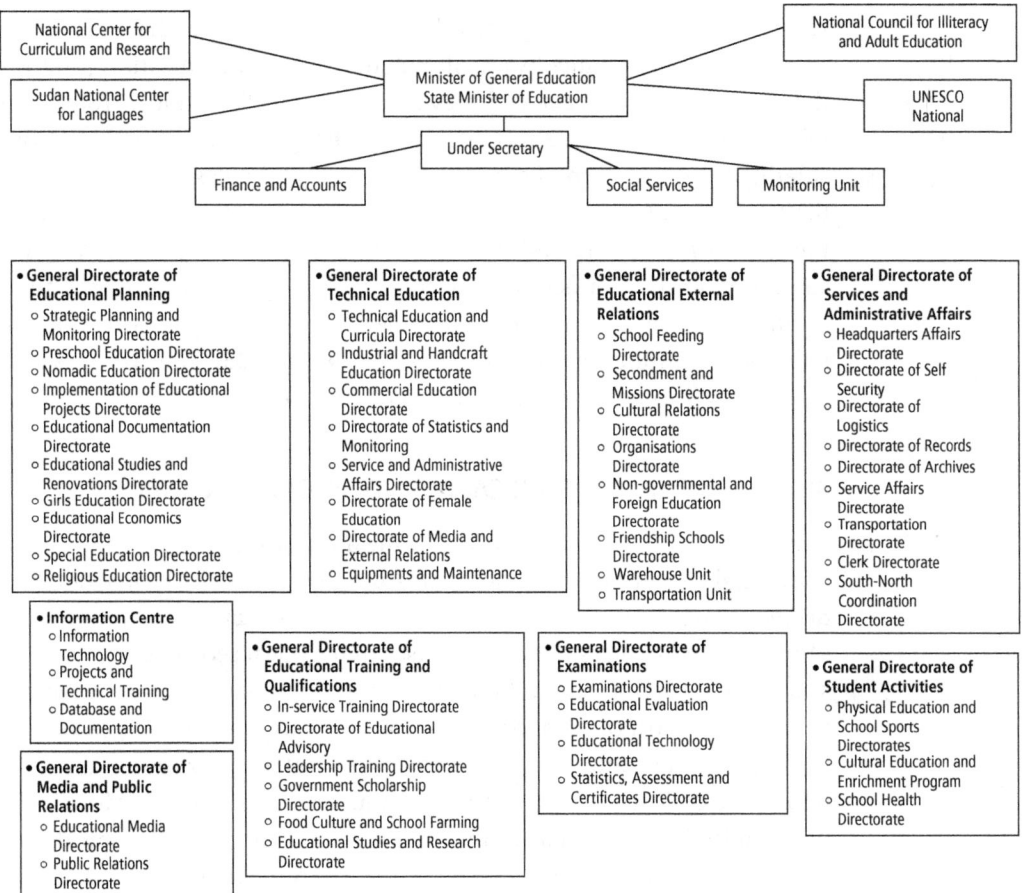

Table 1B.1 Availability of Job Descriptions in the FMoGE
percent

Question	Yes	No
Availability of formal job descriptions	17	70
Incumbent read his or her job description	17	47
Source of information and learning		
Briefed by senior staff	40	
Experience and colleagues	60	

Source: FMoGE 2010.
Note: Because job descriptions only exist for 17 percent, the rest could only be perceived roles and responsibilities and may not correspond to what is actually expected.

had seen formal job descriptions, 94 percent of respondents claimed they knew their duties and responsibilities well. When asked how they learned about their roles and responsibilities, 40 percent said they had been briefed about their duties by a senior member of the organization, whereas the remaining 60 percent said they learned about their duties, roles, and responsibilities over time and from their colleagues and senior staff. Considering the devolution of school education to the states, staffing levels in the FMoGE's administration are considered to be inflated. As a result of the CPA, a revised organizational structure for the education sector was submitted to the Council of Ministers in 2007 by the Ministry of Labor, Public Service and Human Resources Development. The revised structure reduces the number of staff members from 915 to 603. However, this proposal has yet to be formally endorsed by the council.

ADMINISTRATION OF TECHNICAL AND VOCATIONAL EDUCATION

There are three ministries involved in the administration of technical and vocational education in northern Sudan (figure 1B.2): the MoHESR offers degree courses in technical education in higher education institutions; the MoGE and state ministries offer courses in technical secondary education; and the Ministry of Labor, Public Service and Human Resource Development (MoLPSHR) offers apprenticeships and vocational training programs through private enterprises, nongovernmental organizations, and the public sector. The difference between courses offered by the MoGE and the MoLPSHR is defined by their relative proportion of technical and practical content. Technical secondary education offered by the MoGE has 50 percent theoretical and 50 percent practical courses, whereas the vocational training offered by the MoLPSHR has 30 percent theoretical and 70 percent practical courses.

Figure 1B.2 Ministries Providing Technical and Vocational Training

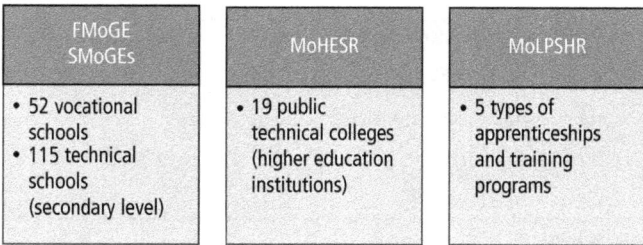

Note: FMoGE = Federal Ministry of General Education; MoHESR = Ministry of Higher Education and Scientific Research; MoLPSHR = Ministry of Labor, Public Service and Human Resource Development; SMoGE = State Ministry of General Education.

The National Council for Technical and Technological Education (NCTTE) was established in December 2005 to consolidate all programs dealing with technical and vocational education under one accreditation body. The council consists of 38 members headed by the vice president of northern Sudan. One duputy chairman represents the MoHESR and another, the MoGE. The purpose of the NCTTE is to improve the quality of technical and vocational education and to ensure that the courses and programs offered correspond with the needs of the labor market.

ADMINISTRATION OF HIGHER EDUCATION

The MoHESR has overall responsibility for higher education in the entire nation, both northern and southern Sudan. There are five types of higher education institutions in Sudan: public universities, public technical colleges, private universities, philanthropic universities, and private colleges. Universities confer degrees and colleges confer diplomas. Philanthropic universities are not-for-profit private institutions established by communities and funded by philanthropists. They differ from other private universities in that the communities that establish them actively participate in the management and the programs offered by the institutions.

NOTES

1. A parallel study was undertaken for the semiautonomous region of southern Sudan, see GoSS/World Bank (forthcoming).
2. Based on *World Development Indicators* (World Bank 1990; 2000).
3. For the purposes of this study, population data from the 2008 population census (GoNU and GoSS 2009) for the 2–24 age group were smoothed because the census data reflected an uneven population curve and underreporting of infants. Smoothing simply means that the population was redistributed across single ages while holding the total population constant (see annex 1A for details).
4. The poverty line is defined as SDG 114 per person per month.
5. Internally displaced persons are "persons or groups of persons who have been forced or obliged to flee or leave their homes or places of habitual residences, in particular as a result of or in order to avoid the effects of armed conflict, situations of generalized violence, violations of human rights or natural or human-made disasters, and who have not crossed an internationally recognized State border" (Guiding Principles of Internal Displacement 1998).
6. Preschools include *khalwas*, which are traditional Islamic schools that teach the Quran, and public and private preschools.
7. Basic education refers to primary education in Sudan.
8. During the preparation of this report, these two issues were discussed with the Central Bureau of Statistics in both Khartoum and Juba and with the counterparts in the ministries of education.
9. As a result of the Comprehensive Peace Agreement, a revised organizational structure for the education sector was submitted to the Council of Ministers in

2007 by the Ministry of Labor, Public Service and Human Resources Development. This proposal has yet to be formally endorsed by the council.

10. According to the FMoGE organizational review (2010), this includes 304 posts with shared responsibilities across units (twinning), 50 posts for the "friendship" schools in Chad, and an additional 300 posts for ancillary personnel such as drivers and cleaners.

REFERENCES

Ahmed, Awad Hag Ali. 2008. "The Fifth Population Census in Sudan: A Census with a Full Coverage and a High Accuracy." Al Neelain University, Khartoum. http://unstats.un.org/unsd/demographic/sources/census/country_impl.htm.

EIU (Economic Intelligence Unit). 2010. Available at http://country.eiu.com/Sudan.

EU (European Union). 2008. Cost and Financing Study.

FMoGE (Federal Ministry of General Education). Various years. *Statistical Yearbooks*. Khartoum.

———. 2008. "Baseline Survey on Basic Education in the Northern States of Sudan: Final Report June 2008." Khartoum. Online document available at http://planipolis.iiep.unesco.org/epiweb/E029336e.pdf

———. 2010. "Organizational Review and Training and Development Needs Assessment." Education Management Information System Project Implementation Unit, Khartoum.

GoNU (Government of National Unity). 2010. "Poverty in Northern Sudan: Estimates from the NBHS 2009." Draft, Central Bureau for Statistics, Khartoum.

GoNU (Government of National Unity) and GoSS (Government of Southern Sudan). 2006. *Sudan Household Health Survey (SHHS) 2006*. Khartoum/Juba: Central Bureau of Statistics and Southern Sudan Center for Census, Statistics and Evaluation.

———. 2009. *Fifth Sudan Population and Housing Census: 2008*. Khartoum and Juba: Central Bureau of Statistics and Southern Sudan Center for Census, Statistics, and Evaluation.

GoS (Government of Sudan), SPLM (Sudan Peoples Liberation Movement), World Bank, and UNDP (United Nations Development Programme). 2005. *Joint Assessment Mission: Framework for Sustained Peace, Development, and Poverty Eradication*. Vols. I–III. Available at http://www.unsudanig.org/docs/Joint%20Assessment%20Mission%20(JAM)%20Volume%20I.pdf.

GoSS (Government of South Sudan) and World Bank. Forthcoming. "Education in South Sudan: Status and Challenges for a New System." World Bank, Washington, DC.

Guiding Principles of Internal Displacement. 1998. Available at http://daccess-dds-ny.un.org/doc/UNDOC/GEN/G98/104/93/PDF/G9810493.pdf?OpenElement.

Interim Constitution of the Republic of Sudan. 2005. Available at http://www.sudan-embassy.de/c_Sudan.pdf.

Population Census Council/Technical Working Group. 2009. Priority results of the *Fifth Sudan Population and Housing Census: 2008* submitted to the Population Census Council by the Technical Working Group. Powerpoint presentation.

UNAIDS (Joint United Nations Programme on HIV/AIDS). 2009. Available at http://www.unaids.org/es/dataanalysis/monitoringcountryprogress/2010progressreportssubmittedbycountries/file,33666,es.pdf.

UNHCR (United Nations High Commissioner for Refugees). 2010. Available at http://www.unhcr.org/cgi-bin/texis/vtx/home/opendocPDFViewer.html?docid=4dfdbf480&query=IDPs%20Sudan%202010.

UNICEF (United Nations Children's Fund). 2009. *The State of the World's Children 2009: Maternal and Newborn Health.* New York: UNICEF. Available at http://www.unicef.org/sowc09/report/report.php.

World Bank. 1990. *World Development Indicators.* Washington, DC: World Bank.

———. 2000. *World Development Indicators.* Washington, DC: World Bank.

———. 2007. "Sudan. Public Expenditure Review. Synthesis Report." Report 41840-SD. World Bank, Washington, DC.

———. 2009. *World Development Indicators.* Washington, DC: World Bank.

———. 2010a. "Northern States Budget Review Notes." Draft. World Bank, Washington, DC.

———. 2010b. "Sudan. Country Economic Memorandum." World Bank, Washington, DC.

CHAPTER 2

Overall Enrollment Patterns

This chapter reviews the trends in student enrollments in northern Sudan over the past nine years, and contrasts these trends with the evolution in the numbers of schools and teachers. It goes on to assess the trends in coverage at the various levels of education. Finally, the chapter compares the educational coverage in northern Sudan with that of similar countries, and draws on alternative sources of data to cross-check existing estimates of the coverage of basic school education.[1]

STRUCTURE OF THE EDUCATION SYSTEM AND ENROLLMENTS

The formal education system in northern Sudan has four levels. These levels include (a) two years of preschool education in kindergartens or *khalwas*,[2] (b) eight years of basic school, (c) three years of secondary school divided into an academic and a technical track, and (d) higher education in universities and higher institutes.[3] Since 1993, teacher education has been part of higher education.

As mentioned in chapter 1, the system offers 13 years of general education. Because the formal age of entry to basic school is 6 years, it follows that preschool is targeted to 4–5-year-olds, basic school to 6–13-year-olds, and secondary school to 14–16-year-olds—thus, a total of 13 years of general education systemwide.

The federal Ministry of General Education (FMoGE) publishes statistical yearbooks with data on preschool, basic, and secondary schools. The Ministry of Higher Education and Scientific Research (MoHESR) maintains data on higher education.[4] Table 2.1 provides data on the trends in student enrollments between 2000–01 and 2008–09 based on these two data sources.

Table 2.1 Trends in Student Enrollments by Level of Education in Northern Sudan, 2000–01 to 2008–09

Education level or form	2000–01	2001–02	2002–03	2003–04	2004–05	2005–06	2006–07	2007–08	2008–09	Average annual growth (percent)
Preschool	334,655	341,655	409,092	411,681	416,050	471,189	470,928	592,399	725,113	10
Kindergarten									595,057	—
Khalwas									130,056	—
Basic	3,314,281	3,401,496	3,589,527	3,767,260	3,905,381	4,193,939	4,237,907	4,688,685	4,870,464	5
Secondary	460,605	477,174	499,363	595,362	620,347	613,863	615,534	658,842	734,859	6
Academic	429,721	446,762	476,476	572,997	594,114	569,735	585,266	628,295	707,654	6
Technical	30,884	30,412	22,887	22,365	26,233	44,128	30,268	29,507	27,205	−2
Higher			317,139					453,866		7
Other										
Secondary Islamic									1,450	—
Special education	2,073	2,000	2,000	1,763	6,821	9,966	2,105	2,360	39,752	45
Adolescents' education	2,468	2,468	5,776	11,509	19,441	161,001	24,666	36,677	13,382	24
Literacy and adult education	388,910	106,885	157,326	215,802	180,411	422,576	87,748	54,017	181,465	−9
							288,256	301,903		

Source: FMoGE statistical yearbooks for the years indicated. For higher education, data are from the MoHESR.
Note: Figures include both public and private enrollments. FMoGE = federal Ministry of General Education; MoHESR = Ministry of Higher Education and Scientific Research; — = not available.

Enrollments have greatly increased at all four levels of the system. Preschool enrollments more than doubled from 2000–01 to 2008–09; they grew from 335,000 to 725,000 students. Basic school enrollments grew from 3.3 million in 2000–01 to 4.9 million students in 2008–09. Secondary school enrollments grew from 461,000 students in 2000–01 to 735,000 in 2008–09 because of an increase in enrollments in the academic track, but enrollments in the much smaller technical track contracted.[5] Higher education enrollments grew from 317,000 students in 2002–03 to 454,000 students in 2007–08.

Few students attend adolescents' education, special education, and literacy and adult education. The yearbooks also report a small number of students attending Islamic secondary education: 1,450 in 2008–09. That same year, a fairly small number of students attended adolescents' education: about 14,000. Some 40,000 students attended special education in 2008–09, up from only about 2,000 students at the beginning of the decade. Literacy and adult education is the largest subsector outside the structure of the formal system, but enrollments fluctuate greatly from one year to the next without exhibiting a clear trend: in 2008–09, enrollments were about 180,000 students, down from 300,000 a year earlier and almost 400,000 at the beginning of the decade.

The fastest relative growth in enrollments has taken place in preschool and higher education. As shown in table 2.1, the fastest relative growth in enrollments since 2000–01 occurred in preschool (10 percent per year), higher education (7 percent per year), secondary school (6 percent per year), and basic school (5 percent per year). However, basic education is the level that accounts for the largest absolute increase in enrollments. As illustrated in figure 2.1, basic education is by far the largest subsector of education in terms of student enrollments. That is why—although basic education experienced the lowest relative growth in enrollments—basic schools still account for the largest absolute increase in student numbers since 2000–01. Enrollments in basic schools grew by almost 1.6 million students in just eight years.

Overall, growth in basic school enrollments accelerated after 2005. These enrollments increased by almost a million students between 2004–05 and 2008–09, which corresponds to an average annual growth of 5.7 percent. In comparison, there was an average annual increase of 4.2 percent between 2000–01 and 2004–05. Several events occurred in 2005 that explain this acceleration: (a) the signing of the Comprehensive Peace Agreement (CPA) between northern and southern Sudan,

Figure 2.1 Trends in Student Enrollments in Northern Sudan, 2000–01 to 2008–09

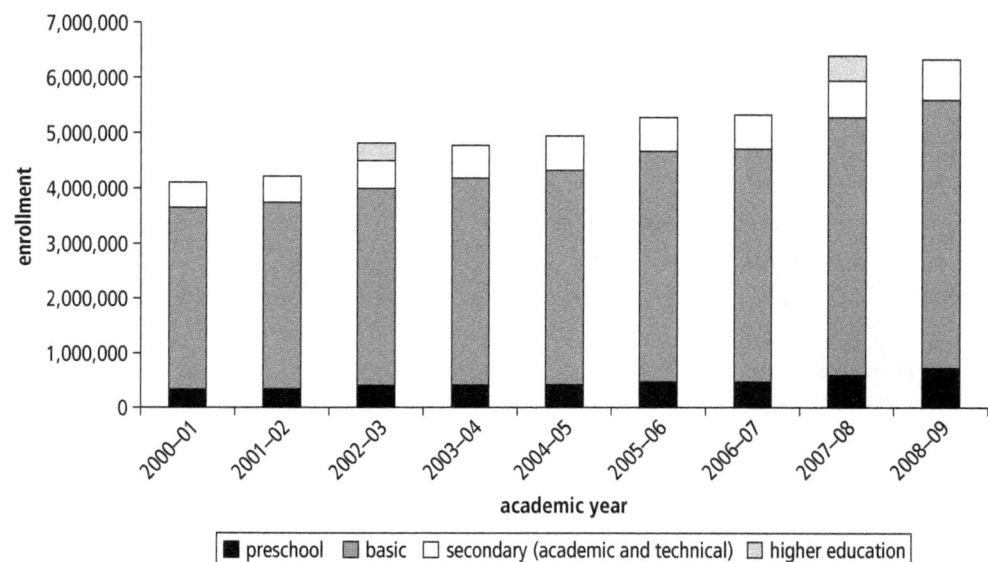

Source: Authors' calculations based on FMoGE statistical yearbooks for the years indicated.
Note: Data on aggregate higher education enrollments were available for only the two years shown.

(b) a large increase in the transfer of resources to the states, and (c) a policy declaration within the Interim Constitution of 2005 stating that basic schooling should be free. The Darfur Peace Agreement and the Eastern Sudan Peace Agreement were signed a year later, in May 2006.

Some states now have close to full enrollment in basic school. As illustrated in figure 2.2, which provides such enrollments in selected states from 2001–01 to 2008–09, Northern and River Nile enrollments were flat over this period. In these states, as we see in chapter 4, almost all children already have access to basic school, and had access even during the conflict years. Because these states are fairly close to enrolling all children in basic school, enrollment growth has slowed and is now largely driven by demographic growth. In other states, such as Southern Darfur and Western Darfur, there was a surge in enrollments after 2005. These states were more affected by conflict and are now benefiting from the more peaceful circumstances.

Thus, there is evidence of a positive impact of peace on basic school enrollments for the populations that were disadvantaged and affected by conflict prior to 2005. Figure 2.3 shows the average annual growth in basic school enrollments from the 2004–05 to the 2008–09 academic

Figure 2.2 Evolution in Basic School Enrollments in Selected States, 2000–01 to 2008–09

Source: Based on FMoGE statistical yearbooks for the years indicated.

Figure 2.3 Average Growth Rates for Basic School Enrollments, by State, 2004–05 to 2008–09

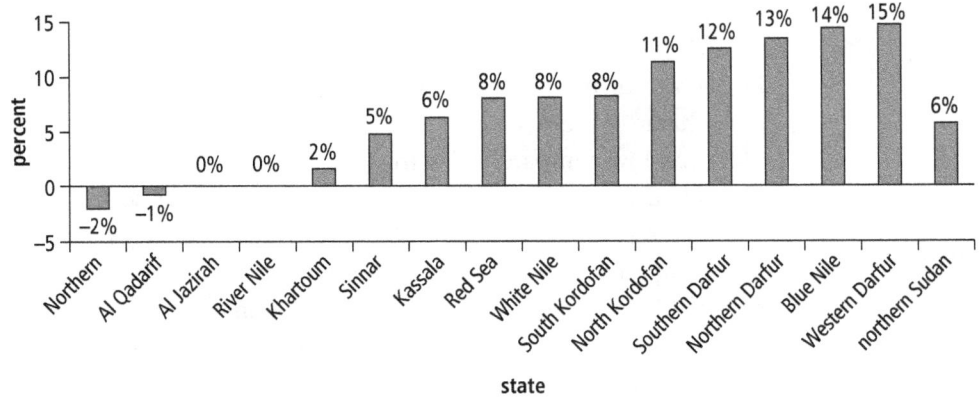

Source: Authors' calculations based on FMoGE statistical yearbooks for the years indicated.

years in each of the 15 northern states. It is noteworthy that basic school enrollments grew rapidly after 2005 in most or all of the states affected by one of the three conflicts, particularly the three Darfur states in the western part, the Kordofan states and Blue Nile in the southern part, and Kassala and Red Sea in the eastern part of Sudan.

TRENDS IN NUMBERS OF SCHOOLS AND TEACHERS

The numbers of schools, teachers, and students have increased, but not at the same pace.

Table 2.2 provides data that describe some basic characteristics of schools in northern Sudan and assess trends in school size and student-teacher ratios from 2004–05 to 2008–09. This table provides useful information about how the education system has adapted to and possibly facilitated the growth in student enrollments in recent years.

The various levels of general education have exhibited very different development trends, as follows:

- *Enrollments in preschool have outpaced the also rapid increase in the number of schools, leading to moderately larger schools and higher student-teacher ratios.* Despite a rapid expansion in the number of schools at this level, enrollments in the average preschool have grown from 49 students in 2004–05 to 53 students in 2008–09. The average national student-teacher ratio for preschool has also increased and is now 32:1.[6]

- *The number of basic schools has kept pace with basic school enrollments, but there are fewer teachers per school and higher student-teacher ratios.* Basic school enrollments and the number of basic schools have both increased by about 25 percent since 2004–05. The average school size has therefore remained about 300 students. However, the average school now has 9.1 teachers, down from 9.9 teachers in 2004–05. As a result, the student-teacher ratio has risen from 30 students per teacher in 2004–05 to 33 students per teacher in 2008–09.[7] This ratio is below the average of more than 50 students per teacher in 33 low-income Sub-Saharan African countries (Mingat, Ledoux, and Rakotomalala 2010) and low compared with the average of 40 students per teacher often cited for countries that have not yet reached universal primary completion (Bruns et al. 2003). The northern Sudan ratio is high, however, compared with the average primary education student-teacher ratio of 26:1 across middle-income Sub-Saharan African countries or of 19:1 across Middle Eastern and North African countries.[8]

- *The number of academic secondary schools has increased significantly since 2004–05, leading to smaller schools and lower student-teacher ratios.* In secondary education, the trends are very different from those of preschool and basic schools. At this level, the average school size has dropped from 269 students in 2004–05 to 212 students in 2008–09. The student-teacher ratio has also dropped from 19:1 to 17:1 over the same period. It is noteworthy that although preschools and basic schools have similar student-teacher ratios (about 33:1), the average

Table 2.2 Increase in the Number of Schools, Teachers, and Students from 2004–05 to 2008–09

Indicator	Preschool			Basic			Academic secondary			Technical secondary		
	2004–05	2008–09	Percentage change	2004–05	2008–09	Percentage change	2004–05	2008–09	Percentage change	2004–05	2008–09	Percentage change
Number of												
Schools	8,452	13,657	62	13,125	16,290	24	2,209	3,339	51	114	170	49
Teachers	14,834	22,990	55	130,048	147,833	14	31,348	41,249	32	1,363	1,915	40
Students	416,050	725,113	74	3,905,381	4,870,464	25	594,114	707,654	19	26,233	27,205	4
Average number of												
Students per school	49	53	8	298	299	0	269	212	−21	230	160	−30
Teachers per school	1.8	1.7	−6	9.9	9.1	−8	14.2	12.4	−13	12.0	11.3	40
Students per teacher	28	32	14	30	33	10	19	17	−11	19	14	−26

Source: FMoGE statistical yearbooks for the years indicated.
Note: This table is based on all schools, both government and nongovernment. Annex table 2A.1 provides data on the number of basic schools in each state by type of school.

ratio in secondary school is only about half, with 17 students per teacher. The low student-teacher ratio in secondary schools is likely a result of the greater use of specialized teachers at this level.

- *The numbers of technical secondary schools and teachers have expanded greatly, but there has been no growth in enrollments.* Although the number of schools has grown rapidly, available statistics show that student enrollments have remained flat. However, these contradictory trends suggest that data on technical secondary education may be incomplete.

PUBLIC-PRIVATE SHARES OF ENROLLMENTS

The share of students enrolled in nongovernment schools varies across levels of education. These schools include fee-charging as well as not-for-profit institutions run by religious, community, and other nongovernmental organizations (NGOs). At the preschool level, this category also includes the *khalwa* schools; and at the secondary level, it includes tutorial classes organized by the Teachers' Union. Figure 2.4 shows the proportion of students who are enrolled in nongovernment schools according to the FMoGE statistical yearbooks.

Figure 2.4 Share of Students Enrolled in Nongovernment Schools, 2008–09 or Latest Available Year

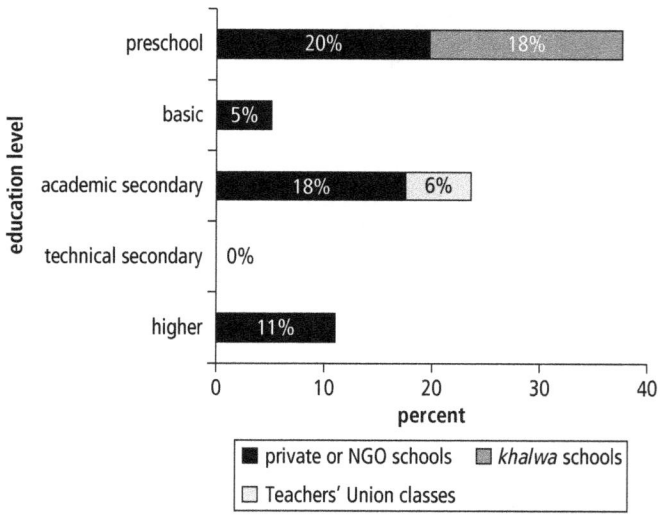

Source: FMoGE 2008–09 statistical yearbook. Data for higher education relate to the 2007–08 academic year.
Note: NGO = nongovernmental organization.

The nongovernmental sector plays an important role in providing education at the preschool and secondary education levels. Government schools account for about 95 percent of enrollments in basic schools, 100 percent of enrollments in technical secondary schools, and almost 90 percent of enrollments in higher education. This finding could indicate that federal and state governments have, to some degree, prioritized the development of these levels of education. Regarding technical secondary education, which in most countries is quite costly to provide, it may also be uneconomical for the private sector to enter this market, which could explain why there are no nongovernment technical secondary schools. At the preschool level, nongovernment schools—which include the religious *khalwa* schools as well as fee-charging private schools—enroll as many as 38 percent of all students. In academic secondary school, nongovernment schools—including Teachers' Union tutorial classes—enroll 24 percent of all students.

In some states, the nongovernment basic education schools are more prevalent. The share of enrollments in nongovernment basic schools is relatively high in four states: Khartoum (13 percent of total basic school enrollments), Red Sea (10 percent), Southern Darfur (10 percent), and Kassala (8 percent). In the remaining states, the nongovernment share is between 0 percent and 4 percent of total enrollments. In Southern Darfur, most nongovernment schools are likely NGO-run schools within camps for internally displaced persons (IDPs).

Some schools in northern Sudan may include both public and private sections within the same school. At the secondary education level in particular, the nongovernmental sector—including the Teachers' Union classes—caters to students who need or wish to repeat the last year of the cycle to improve their results on the Secondary School Certificate examination. In some of the secondary schools visited, private classes were even held within the public school building to respond to this demand.[9] This melding of public and private efforts makes it harder to analyze the secondary education level regarding aspects of student flow, student-teacher ratios, per-student cost, internal efficiency, and the like. Whenever data are presented about secondary education in the current report, this issue was addressed and adjustments were made as needed. Based on the FMoGE 2008–09 statistical yearbook, table 2.3 provides data to describe the basic characteristics of nongovernment and government schools: average school enrollments and average student-teacher ratios.

Nongovernment schools are smaller than government schools, on average. The first finding from table 2.3 is that for all three levels of general education, nongovernment schools are significantly smaller than

Table 2.3 School Size and Student-Teacher Ratios in Government and Nongovernment Schools, 2008–09

Education level	Government schools	Nongovernment schools (excluding khalwas/Teachers' Union classes)	Khalwas/Teachers' Union classes	All schools
Preschool, average number of students per			(*Khalwa*)	
Schools	54	47	56	53
Teachers	35	19	58	32
Basic, average number of students per				
Schools	309	186	n.a.	299
Teachers	33	32	n.a.	33
Academic secondary, average number of students per			(Teachers' Union)	
Schools	231	125	n.a.	212
Teachers	16	18	n.a.	17
Technical secondary, average number of students per				
Schools	160	0	n.a.	160
Teachers	14	0	n.a.	14

Source: Authors' construction based on data from the FMoGE 2008–09 statistical yearbook.
Note: Khalwa is treated as a separate category to be consistent with the FMoGE 2008–09 statistical yearbook. The Teachers' Union does not have its own schools, but organizes secondary-level classes using teachers and classrooms of the public school system in a second, private shift—hence the n.a. (not applicable) designation. Including Teachers' Union data with either public or private schools would distort the calculation of students per school and students per teacher in these two categories.

government schools. This finding is particularly pronounced at the academic secondary level, where nongovernment schools are almost half the size of government schools. Regarding student-teacher ratios, nongovernment preschools have a much lower student-teacher ratio (19:1) than do government preschools (35:1) or *khalwas* (58:1). At the basic and academic secondary levels, however, there is not a big difference between nongovernment and government schools in the statistics.

In basic and academic secondary education, enrollments in nongovernment schools are growing faster than those in government schools, albeit from a much lower base. In basic education, enrollments in nongovernment schools grew by 8 percent per year from 2000–01 to 2008–09; that figure is 3 percentage points more than the rate of growth in government school enrollments over the same period. In academic secondary education, nongovernment school enrollments grew by 7 percent per year from 2000–01 to 2008–09; that figure is 1 percentage point more than the rate of growth in government school enrollments during that time. Again, this is evidence of a strong demand for children's education—a demand that may be growing faster than the government can respond to it. In Khartoum State, which is home to most of the country's nongovernment schools, the number of nongovernment schools has grown from 140 to more than 750 over a period of eight years. In the three Darfur states again, the surge in nongovernment schools is a result of the involvement of NGOs in providing education to IDPs.

Government secondary schools have the lowest student-teacher ratios of the three levels of general education, with 16 students per teacher in academic secondary schools and 14 students per teacher in technical secondary schools. Government secondary schools in northern Sudan have low student-teacher ratios compared with the average of 27:1 across low-income Sub-Saharan African countries (Mingat, Ledoux, and Rakotomalala 2010). However, they are similar to the average student-teacher ratio of 19:1 across middle-income Sub-Saharan African countries and of 15:1 across Middle Eastern and North African countries.

SCHOOLS FOR NOMADIC AND INTERNALLY DISPLACED POPULATIONS

In 2008–09, more than 12 percent of all basic education schools in northern Sudan were either nomadic, IDP, or village schools. According to the FMoGE statistical yearbooks, government or village schools specifically serve nomadic or displaced populations. Village schools are rural multigrade schools that usually offer only the first four grades of the basic education cycle (FMoGE 2008).

Table 2.4 provides the number of schools in these three categories and their enrollments during the 2007–08 and 2008–09 academic years. In 2008–09, nomadic schools accounted for 8.7 percent, IDP schools for 1.6 percent, and village schools for 2.1 percent of 12.4 percent component of all basic education. According to the FMoGE 2008–09 statistical yearbook, these schools accounted for 8 percent of total enrollments in basic education, although this figure may have been underestimated because the FMoGE report (2008) includes a much higher number of village schools.

Nomadic schools are small, mobile, and multigrade, and they are fairly spread out across the peripheral states. During the 1990s, there was a push for the education of nomadic communities through the establishment of the mobile school system. According to the FMoGE

Table 2.4 Number of Schools and Enrollments in Government Nomadic, IDP, and Village Schools, 2007–08 and 2008–09

Schools	2007–08	2008–09	Percentage increase
Nomadic			
Number	1,431	1,422	−1
Number of students	220,535	146,826	−33
Average number of students per school	154	103	−33
IDP			
Number	339	261	−23
Number of students	109,508	212,602	94
Average number of students per school	323	815	152
Village			
Number	286	338	18
Number of students	22,644	32,757	45
Average number of students per school	79	97	23

Source: Authors' construction based on data from the FMoGE 2008–09 statistical yearbook. Annex table 2A.1 includes data on the number of nomadic, IDP, and village basic schools in each state.
Note: IDP = internally displaced person.

2007–08 and 2008–09 statistical yearbooks, there were more than 1,400 government nomadic schools, and they existed in all states except Al Jazirah and Khartoum. Almost a third of the basic schools in Kassala belonged in this category, compared with 15–20 percent of the basic schools in the three Darfur states and Red Sea. Nomadic school enrollments typically are small. With an average enrollment of 103 students in 2008–09, these schools enrolled only about 147,000 children in total, or 3 percent of basic school enrollments across northern Sudan. As may be seen in table 2.4, enrollment in nomadic schools declined in 2008–09. According to the FMoGE report (2008), nomadic schools are divided into mobile, multigrade schools for grades 1–4 and collective schools for grades 5–8.[10]

A case study of two nomadic tribes that have partially settled in Northern Darfur reported that more than 90 percent of the families in these tribes have one or more family members who are literate; thus, they have had access to some education (Al Fashir University / IOM 2010). However, the study highlighted that although these tribes are no longer practicing "whole-family" movement, one or more family members are still moving with the animals, even if only within the tribal territory. The youth are sometimes involved in this work, which potentially has negative implications for their schooling. The study also emphasized that the schools in these communities were barely functioning.

Unlike nomadic schools, IDP schools are typically large and mainly located in the three Darfur states. According to government statistics, there were 261 government IDP schools in 2008–09.[11] With the exception of three IDP schools in Northern State, all are located in the Darfurs—although in the 2007–08 school year, there were also IDP schools in Blue Nile and Kassala. IDP schools have large enrollments. With an average enrollment of 815 students in 2008–09, these schools enrolled as many as 213,000 students, or 4 percent of total basic school enrollments in northern Sudan.

Data on the school enrollment of IDP children are incomplete. However, this enrollment is quite small if we consider that there are an estimated 2.7 million IDPs in the Darfur states alone and that almost 700,000 of these, or 25.7 percent, are between the ages of 6 and 13.[12] Many IDP children could, however, be enrolled in regular schools, so it is not possible on this basis to conclude what share of IDP children have access to basic schooling. Chapter 3 in this report presents the gross enrollment rates for each state, including the three Darfur states, but it has not been possible to further break down these numbers into IDP and non-IDP schools within the states.

Finally, village schools are small, multigrade, and rural, and they are located primarily in the Kordofan states. More than 10 percent of schools in North and South Kordofan are multigrade village schools. As with nomadic schools, the average enrollment in village schools is small. With an average of just 97 students per school in 2008–09, these schools accounted for only 3 percent of basic enrollments in North Kordofan and 6 percent in South Kordofan. Village schools offer only the first grades of the basic education cycle, up to grade 4 in North Kordofan and grade 5 in South Kordofan. The number of schools and their enrollments increased between 2007–08 and 2008–09. According to the FMoGE report (2008), there were also village schools in Al Jazirah, Kassala, Red Sea, and Southern Darfur, but these schools were not captured in government statistics for that period (or reported as regular basic schools).

THE GROSS ENROLLMENT RATE

By contrasting data on enrollments with data on the population of relevant school age, we can calculate the gross enrollment rate (GER) for each level of education.[13] This calculation requires making a choice about which population data to use, and for the latest school year, 2008–09, the 2008 population census is the obvious choice.[14] The result is a GER of 37 percent for preschool, 72 percent for basic school, and 34 percent for secondary school. It is important to stress that the GER is mainly an indicator of the capacity of the education system vis-à-vis the population of school-age children, but it is inadequate for measuring the share of this population who are currently in school. For example, we can interpret the GER as showing that basic schools in northern Sudan had enough school places to enroll 72 percent of 6–13-year-olds, but not that 72 percent of 6–13-year-olds were actually in school during the 2008–09 school year.

In higher education, there were 1,500 students per 100,000 inhabitants in the 2007–08 academic year. Because higher education usually encompasses a series of degree programs of differing lengths, it is difficult to define a reference population for this level, which would be needed to calculate a GER.[15] Instead, another indicator is commonly used to measure the coverage of higher education: the number of students attending higher education (enrollments) per 100,000 inhabitants. The value of this indicator was 1,500 students per 100,000 population in the 2007–08 school year.

TRENDS IN GERs FOR GENERAL EDUCATION

Figure 2.5 shows the trends in GERs between 2000–01 and 2008–09. Because there was no population census in Sudan between 1993 and 2008, it is not obvious what population data to use for calculating the GER for the years prior to 2008. For this report, we chose to project population data backward in time (backcasting) from the 2008 population census for the best consistency of the analysis over time. Annex table 1A.1 in chapter 1 lists the population data used for this report.

Since 2000–01, the GER has increased by 17 percentage points for preschool, 15 percentage points for basic school, and 8 percentage points for secondary school. Thus, school enrollments have increased at all three levels compared with the size of the relevant age groups. The gains in the GER for secondary schools, however, are fairly modest, at only about 1 percentage point per year. The strong increase in the GER for preschool education may partly be attributed to improvements in the data on preschool enrollments, but the increase is also thought to reflect an expansion of coverage at this level.[16]

Figure 2.5 Trends in Gross Enrollment Rates for General Education in Northern Sudan, 2000–01 to 2008–09

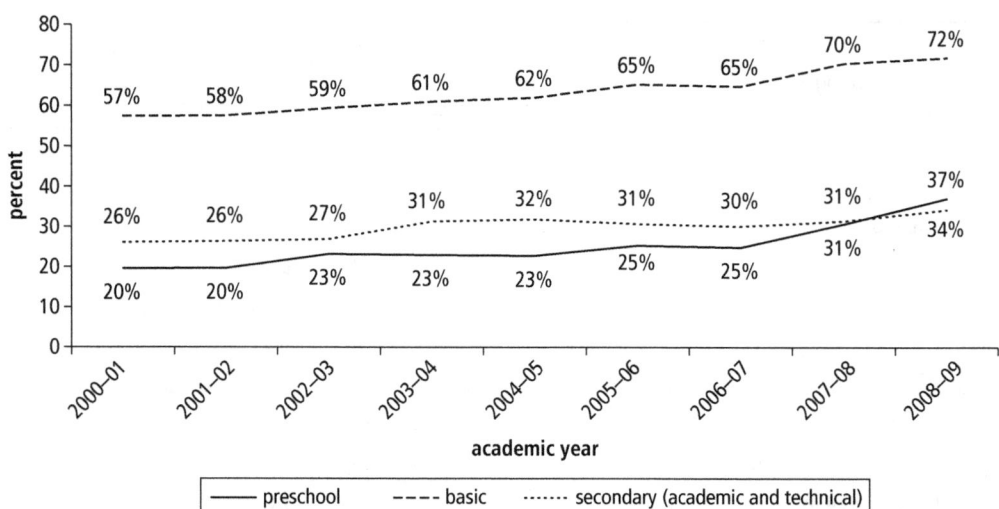

Source: Authors' construction based on enrollment data in table 2.1 and population data in annex table 1A.1.

The number of higher education students per 100,000 inhabitants increased by 5 percent per year in five years. The figures are 1,161 in 2002–03 and 1,500 in 2007–08 and reflect a very considerable gain.

INTERNATIONAL COMPARISON OF THE GER

The GER-6 is a more standardized indicator for international comparisons of primary, or basic, coverage. In the previous section, we calculated the basic school GER at 72 percent, which is the GER for the whole eight-year primary cycle. For the purpose of international comparability, however, the GER for the first six years of basic schooling is a more standardized measure. The GER-6 is 76 percent for northern Sudan.

Table 2.5 compares this value to the GERs for three groups of comparator countries. Based on its level of GDP per capita, northern Sudan is classified by the World Bank as a lower-middle-income country for operational purposes; therefore, table 2.5 lists the primary education GERs for a number of lower-middle-income countries in Sub-Saharan Africa as well as the Middle East and North Africa. The table also compares the primary school GER with those of northern Sudan's immediate neighbors, which are typically low-income countries.

Table 2.5 Primary Education GERs in Northern Sudan and Comparator Countries, 2008 or Latest Available Year
percent

Selected neighboring countries[a]	GER	Lower-middle-income countries			
		Sub-Saharan Africa	GER	Middle East and North Africa	GER
Central African Republic	77	Cameroon	111	Egypt, Arab Rep.	100
Chad	75	Cape Verde	101	Iran, Islamic Rep.	128
Congo, Dem. Rep.	90	Congo, Rep.	114	Jordan	96
Eritrea	57	Côte d'Ivoire	74	Morocco	107
Ethiopia	98	Lesotho	108	Syrian Arab Republic	124
Kenya	112	Nigeria	93	Tunisia	108
Uganda	117	São Tomé and Principe	130	West Bank and Gaza	80
		Swaziland	108		
Average	89		105		106
northern Sudan (GER-6)			76		
southern Sudan (GER-6)			76		
All of Sudan (GER-6)			76		

Source: World Bank EdStats database, which draws on data from the UNESCO (United Nations Educational, Scientific, and Cultural Organization) Institute of Statistics and other agencies.
Note: The GERs shown in this table are all based on primary cycles standardized to 5, 6, or 7 years. GER = gross enrollment rate.
a. Egypt is not included here because it is included in the group of lower-middle-income countries.

The basic school GER for northern Sudan is considerably lower than those for the chosen comparator countries.

Table 2.5 indicates that northern Sudan's GER-6 of 76 percent exceeds the GER only of Eritrea and is comparable to the GERs for countries such as the Central African Republic, Chad, and Côte d'Ivoire. All other countries in the table have higher primary GERs. The GER-6 in south Sudan is also 76 percent.

The secondary school GER for northern Sudan is similar to those for comparator countries. Table 2.6 indicates that northern Sudan's secondary school GER of 34 percent is comparatively high, although—as we see in chapter 3—this is the result of a large number of repeaters. The GER is higher than those for most of northern Sudan's neighbors, except Kenya, and is comparable to those for other lower-middle-income countries in Sub-Saharan Africa. Its secondary school GER is also similar to those for countries such as Morocco and the Syrian Arab Republic but lower than the average for countries in the Middle East and North Africa.

Table 2.6 Upper Secondary Education GERs in Northern Sudan and Comparator Countries, 2008 or Latest Available Year
percent

Selected neighboring countries[a]	GER	Lower-middle-income countries			
		Sub-Saharan Africa	GER	Middle East and North Africa	GER
Central African Republic	—	Cameroon	28	Egypt, Arab Rep.	69
Chad	12	Cape Verde	53	Iran, Islamic Rep.	69
Congo, Dem. Rep.	29	Congo, Rep.	22	Jordan	74
Eritrea	20	Côte d'Ivoire	—	Morocco	37
Ethiopia	12	Lesotho	23	Syrian Arab Republic	35
Kenya	40	Nigeria	26	Tunisia	72
Uganda	14	São Tomé and Principe	20	West Bank and Gaza	75
		Swaziland	37		
Average	21		30		62
northern Sudan			34		
southern Sudan			4		
All of Sudan			28		

Source: World Bank EdStats database, which draws on data from the UNESCO Institute of Statistics and other agencies.
Note: GER = gross enrollment rate; — = not available.
a. Egypt is not included here because it is included in the group of lower-middle-income countries.

The higher education gross enrollment in northern Sudan is high from an international comparative perspective. Table 2.7 shows this figure to be 1,500 students per 100,000 inhabitants, which is higher than the same statistics in most of Sudan's neighboring countries (except Egypt) and also higher than those in the lower-middle-income countries of Sub-Saharan Africa. The higher education gross enrollment in northern Sudan is lower, however, than those figures for almost all of the lower-middle-income countries in the Middle East and North Africa Region (except Morocco).

MEASURING EDUCATION COVERAGE MORE PRECISELY

Other sources of data are needed for an added perspective and to correct for multicohort effects. Gross enrollment rates (GERs) calculated using the administrative enrollment data from the federal Ministry of General Education (FMoGE) statistical yearbooks have limitations. First, they may be inflated by multicohort effects that are present when children of different ages gain access to school at the same time, which is common in

Table 2.7 Higher Education Enrollments in Northern Sudan and Comparator Countries, 2008 or Latest Available Year
number of students per 100,000 people

Selected neighboring countries[a]	GER	Lower-middle-income countries			
		Sub-Saharan Africa	GER	Middle East and North Africa	GER
Central African Republic	218	Cameroon	780	Egypt, Arab Rep.	3,362
Chad	171	Cape Verde	1,335	Iran, Islamic Rep.	4,698
Congo, Dem. Rep.	379	Congo, Rep.	—	Jordan	4,000
Eritrea	193	Côte d'Ivoire	779	Morocco	1,274
Ethiopia	328	Lesotho	426	Syrian Arab Republic	—
Kenya	424	Nigeria	984	Tunisia	3,190
Uganda	340	São Tomé and Principe	—	West Bank and Gaza	4,714
		Swaziland	501		
Average	293		801		3,540
northern Sudan					1,500
southern Sudan					258
All of Sudan					1,233

Source: World Bank EdStats database, which draws on data from the UNESCO Institute of Statistics and other agencies.
Note: GER = gross enrollment rate; — = not available.
a. Egypt is not included here because it is included in the group of lower-middle-income countries.

rapidly expanding school systems. This situation can occur when new schools are opened in places where there were none before or when school fees are eliminated.[17] It is reasonable to believe that there is some multicohort effect in Sudan, a postconflict country with a rapidly growing number of schools.[18] Second, if the administrative data are not complete or if the population data used in the denominator have a large margin of error, then the GER will also be inaccurate. To improve the measurement of access and retention, it is helpful to compare administrative enrollment data with other sources of data. An alternative is provided by household surveys that include questions on the schooling status of all children, both those currently in school and those out of school.

Enrollment indicators based on statistical yearbook data may be underestimated. Household survey data can also be used to calculate a measure of the gross enrollment rate for basic school. Figure 2.6 compares GERs based on different data sources and finds that in recent years, household surveys have generally produced higher estimates of basic school coverage than have data from FMoGE statistical yearbooks and the population census. This finding underlines the need to improve data on

Figure 2.6 Comparing the Gross Enrollment Rate Calculated from Different Sources, 2005–06 to 2008–09

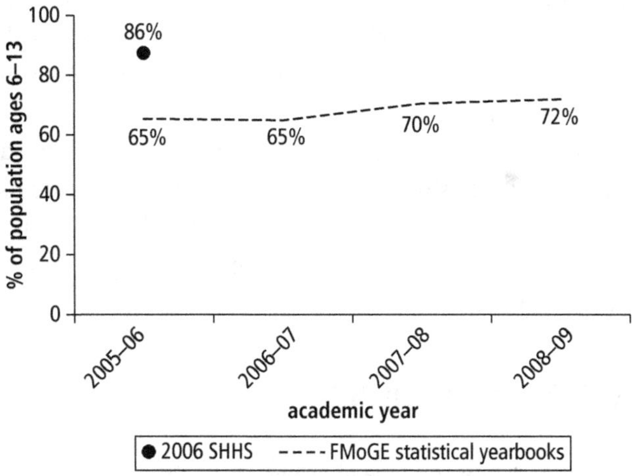

[Chart: % of population ages 6–13 by academic year. 2006 SHHS: 86% (2005–06). FMoGE statistical yearbooks: 65% (2005–06), 65% (2006–07), 70% (2007–08), 72% (2008–09).]

Source: Analysis of the 2006 Sudan Household Health Survey (GoNU and GoSS 2006); FMoGE statistical yearbook for the years indicated.

school enrollments, a process that is under way with the implementation of a comprehensive Education Management Information System.

SUMMARY

- Overall, student enrollments have grown rapidly from 2000 to 2009 at all four levels of the formal education system preschool, basic, secondary, and higher education. This growth demonstrates both a significant government commitment to the development of the sector and a significant demand for education among its citizens.
- The private provision of education is fairly large at some levels, particularly in preschool and academic secondary education. In basic education, where private provision is still rare, it is generally growing faster than public provision.
- In the peripheral states of northern Sudan, basic school enrollments accelerated rapidly after the peace agreements of 2005 and 2006. In the central states, growth in basic school enrollments is leveling off because these states are edging closer to universal primary education.
- As a result of these positive trends, the coverage of basic education has increased significantly, although the eight-year basic school GER—at 72 percent in 2008–09—was still low from an international comparative perspective. This situation may partly be explained by data issues, however. Household surveys suggest that the conventional GER based on

relating enrollment data to population figures may be underestimated. More work is therefore needed to improve the reliability of education sector statistics and their comparability to population data. In states that have experienced large changes in population size, new household surveys may need to be analyzed to appropriately determine actual levels of school participation.
- From a comparative perspective, participation in secondary education is close to the average of similar countries. However, enrollments in higher education are high in northern Sudan compared with those in African countries, although they are comparable with Middle East and North African (MENA) countries.

ANNEX: NUMBER OF BASIC SCHOOLS

Table 2A.1 Number of Basic Schools by State and Type of School, 2008–09

State	Government schools					Private schools	Government and private schools
	Regular	Village[a]	IDP	Nomadic	Total		
Northern	445	0	3	16	464	3	467
River Nile	689	0	0	65	754	14	768
Khartoum	1,583	0	0	0	1,583	753	2,336
Al Jazirah	1,891	0	0	0	1,891	31	1,922
Blue Nile	381	0	0	39	420	2	422
Sinar	627	0	0	50	677	14	691
White Nile	874	0	0	49	923	57	980
North Kordofan	1,524	213	0	126	1,863	64	1,927
South Kordofan	844	125	0	108	1,077	23	1,100
Northern Darfur	837	0	65	164	1,066	36	1,102
Southern Darfur	997	0	135	252	1,384	207	1,591
Western Darfur	877	0	58	213	1,148	21	1,169
Red Sea	348	0	0	69	417	42	459
Kassala	422	0	0	208	630	47	677
Al Qadarif	595	0	0	63	658	21	679
Percentage of all schools	79	2	2	9	92	8	100
Total	12,934	338	261	1,422	14,955	1,335	16,290

Source: FMoGE 2008–09 statistical yearbooks.
Note: IDP = internally displaced person.
a. Village school is a school for grades 1–4 with a multigrade teacher.

NOTES

1. This chapter includes only aggregate data on higher education enrollments because a World Bank–sponsored study on higher education was being developed at the same time as this report.

2. *Khalwas* are traditional Islamic schools that teach the Quran. They enroll children of all ages, but the FMoGE 2008–09 statistical yearbook reports enrollments only in the preschool section of *khalwas*.

3. There are other public schools and institutes that are not part of this hierarchy: religious institutes, vocational institutes, national industries institutes, and vocational training centers, which are all under the Ministry of Public Service and Administrative Reform. The current study does not include information on these schools.

4. Their website, www.mohe.gov.sd, includes data on university enrollments, personnel, number of graduates, and so on.

5. However, the year-on-year fluctuations in technical secondary enrollments are so large as to suggest that these enrollment data may not be comparable over time, possibly because of the incompleteness of the data or a redefinition of what constitutes technical secondary versus academic secondary education.

6. The student-teacher ratios (STRs) in table 2.2 include teachers not on the government payroll—for example, volunteer teachers financed by communities. If these teachers are excluded, the average STRs remain virtually the same for all subsectors except preschool, where volunteer teachers account for a large share of teachers in certain states. See annex table 7A.3 for preschool STRs that exclude teachers not on the government payroll by state.

7. As discussed in chapter 6, because of subject specialization of teachers from grade 3 onward, student-teacher ratios do not translate directly to class sizes.

8. These ratios were calculated based on data from the World Bank EdStats database.

9. The observation is based on a field visit to Red Sea State in February 2010.

10. The collective schools for older children are possibly recorded in government statistics as regular basic schools.

11. This figure does not include the nongovernment IDP schools. The FMoGE 2008–09 statistical yearbook reports more than 250 nongovernment schools in the Darfurs. It is likely that many of these schools are also IDP schools.

12. This observation is made according to the population structure for the three Darfur states, as reported by the 2008 population census.

13. The gross enrollment rate is calculated as total enrollments in the level of education divided by the population of relevant age for that level. The relevant age groups are 4–5 for preschool, 6–13 for basic school, and 14–16 for secondary school.

14. See annex table 1A.1 in chapter 1 for the population data used in this report.

15. If we insist on calculating a GER for higher education, we may use the 17–20-year-olds as the reference population, and assuming that the average duration is about four years, this results in a GER of 18 percent for 2007–08.

16. Since 2008, the FMoGE statistical yearbooks also report the enrollment in religious preschools, *khalwas*, in addition to government and nongovernment kindergarten.

17. See, for example, Avenstrup, Liang, and Nellemann (2004) for a description of the surges in enrollments in Kenya, Lesotho, Malawi, and Uganda, when school fees were eliminated.

18. The number of basic schools increased by 24 percent from 2004–05 to 2008–09 (see table 2.2).

REFERENCES

Al Fashir University/IOM (International Organization for Migration). 2010. "Nomadic Population Baseline Survey. Case of Kuma and Malha Localities, North Darfur, Sudan. Analysis, Results and Recommendations." Al Fashir University, Faculty of Environmental Sciences and Natural Resources, in collaboration with the IOM.

Avenstrup, R., X. Liang, and S. Nellemann. 2004. "Kenya, Lesotho, Malawi, and Uganda: Universal Primary Education and Poverty Reduction." *Scaling Up Poverty Reduction: A Global Learning Process and Conference.* Shanghai: World Bank.

Bruns, Barbara, Alain Mingat, and Ramahatra Rakotomalala. 2003. *Achieving Universal Primary Education by 2015: A Chance for Every Child.* Washington, DC: World Bank.

FMoGE (Federal Ministry of General Education). 2008. "Baseline Survey on Basic Education in the Northern States of Sudan: Final Report June 2008." Khartoum. Online document available at http://planipolis.iiep.unesco.org/epiweb/E029336e.pdf

GoNU (Government of National Unity) and GoSS (Government of Southern Sudan). 2006. *Sudan Household Health Survey (SHHS) 2006.* Khartoum/Juba: Central Bureau of Statistics and Southern Sudan Center for Census, Statistics and Evaluation.

Mingat, A., B. Ledoux, and R. Rakotomalala. 2010. *Developing Post-Primary Education in Sub-Saharan Africa: Assessing the Financial Sustainability of Alternative Pathways.* Africa Human Development Series. Washington, DC: World Bank.

CHAPTER

Patterns of Student Flow

This chapter presents a more detailed analysis of student enrollment patterns than does chapter 2 by focusing on student flow through the four levels of the education system. However, the analysis gives most attention to basic and secondary schooling, as these are the levels for which data on student flow are most readily available.[1]

The chapter opens with a presentation and discussion of the schooling profile by grade and the education pyramid. It then provides an assessment of the distance from attaining the goal of universal primary completion, which is a Millennium Development Goal, and of the pace of progress toward this goal in recent years. The chapter also looks at the schooling status of individuals of different ages to offer a better understanding of issues such as under- and overage enrollment, dropout, and out-of-school children.

SCHOOLING PROFILE AND DISTANCE FROM UNIVERSAL PRIMARY COMPLETION

THE SCHOOLING PROFILE AND EDUCATION PYRAMID

Figure 3.1 shows the schooling profile for northern Sudan from grade 1 of basic school to the last grade of secondary school, which is based on student enrollment data from the federal Ministry of General Education (FMoGE). The profile illustrates the progression of students through the grades and the transition between basic and secondary education (in the following discussion, *secondary* refers to both the academic and the technical tracks). Unlike the gross enrollment rate, the profile is calculated based on the number of nonrepeaters in each grade and is therefore not inflated by repetition.

Figure 3.1 Schooling Profile for the Primary and Secondary Levels, 2008–09

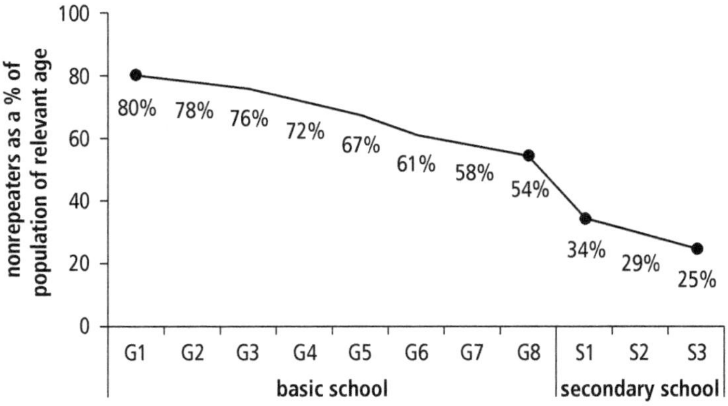

[Chart: nonrepeaters as a % of population of relevant age]
- G1: 80%
- G2: 78%
- G3: 76%
- G4: 72%
- G5: 67%
- G6: 61%
- G7: 58%
- G8: 54%
(basic school)
- S1: 34%
- S2: 29%
- S3: 25%
(secondary school)

Source: Authors' calculations using data on the enrollment of nonrepeaters from the FMoGE 2008–09 statistical yearbook and smoothed population data from the 2008 census; see also annex table 3A.1. For secondary school, the share of nonrepeaters in total enrollments was estimated by the authors.
Note: The figure is based on the enrollment patterns in a single year (cross-sectional method) and therefore does not depict the progression of a single generation through the grades (longitudinal).

The schooling profile shows that it is common for students to drop out of both basic school and secondary school. It illustrates a fairly high intake rate of new students to grade 1 of basic school but also a much lower completion rate for that level of education, indicating a high dropout rate as well. The schooling profile also reveals considerable dropout from secondary school. The first data point of the schooling profile is the gross intake rate (GIR) to basic education, which is 80 percent (although 80 percent is very likely underestimated, as discussed in chapter 2).[2] The figure also shows the primary completion rate (PCR) (54 percent), the GIR to the secondary level (34 percent), and the completion rate of the secondary level (25 percent).[3]

The educational pyramid in figure 3.2 illustrates the high rates of transition between basic and secondary education and between secondary and higher education. It displays the coverage at the beginning and end of each level of education from preschool to higher education.[4] The rate of transition between basic and secondary education is 74 percent, and the rate between secondary and higher education is estimated at 87 percent (both rates were calculated by comparing two years of enrollments). Taken together, figures 3.1 and 3.2 indicate that most dropout from the education system happens within levels rather than between levels. With such high transition rates, the current expansion in basic school enrollments is likely to result in considerable pressure on secondary education to accommodate a rapidly increasing

Figure 3.2 Educational Pyramid for Northern Sudan, 2008–09

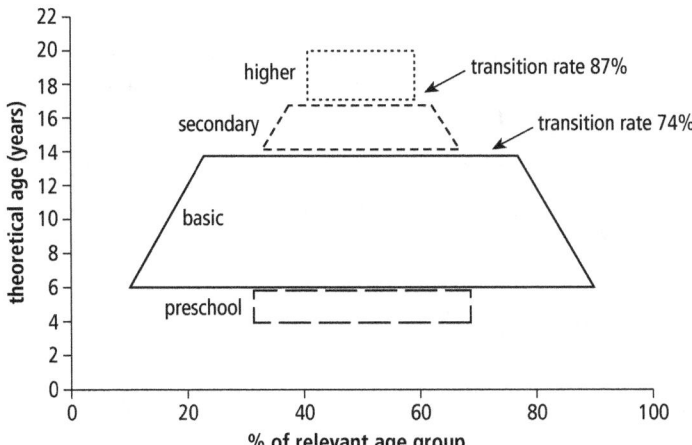

Source: Authors' construction using enrollment data from the FMoGE 2008–09 statistical yearbook and population data from the 2008 census.
Note: The pyramid is based on the enrollment patterns in a single year. The transition rates, however, are based on comparing enrollments in two different years.

number of basic school graduates seeking to continue their studies. Whether the system is able to respond to this increased pressure will determine whether the transition rates remain at these high levels in the years ahead.

INTAKE, COMPLETION, AND DISTANCE TO UNIVERSAL PRIMARY COMPLETION

Only about 54 percent of children attain the last grade of basic education. Table 3.1 summarizes the intake and completion rates for basic and secondary education. A measure of access to grade 1, the basic education GIR is 80 percent. The PCR, 54 percent, measures the access to grade 8 of basic school (not actual graduation or completion of the grade 8 year, simply enrollment in the grade). Similarly for secondary education, the GIR to the secondary level is 34 percent, and the completion rate is 25 percent. The PCR is an important indicator of the share of children completing primary, or basic, education. The globally agreed-upon Millennium Development Goals call for a full course of schooling for all children. In most countries, this goal is interpreted as six years of primary schooling. Table 3.1 also shows the completion rate for the first six years of basic school in northern Sudan, which is 61 percent or 7 percentage points higher than the PCR, but still far from 100 percent. For a country to achieve a PCR of 100 percent,

Table 3.1 Gross Intake Rate and Primary Completion Rate, 2008–09
percent

Education level	Gross intake rate	Completion rate for six years	Primary completion rate	Completion rate
Basic	80	61	54	
Secondary	34			25

Source: Authors' construction using enrollment data from the FMoGE 2008–09 statistical yearbook and population data from the 2008 census.

all children must enter grade 1 and all children must remain in school until the end of grade 8.

Household survey data can provide an added perspective and correct for multicohort effects. The GIR calculated in table 3.1 is a commonly used measure of access to schooling but is often inflated by multicohort effects (which were briefly discussed in chapter 2). Because the number of basic schools across northern Sudan has increased by about 25 percent in the past four years, it is likely that several age cohorts of children are now entering first grade at the same time and creating a bulge in new enrollments. For example, if a school is opened in a village that did not have a school earlier, children of many ages may enroll in grade 1 in the same year; the number of new enrollees may even exceed the population of 6-year-olds, even if some children remain unenrolled (this situation would give a GIR above 100 percent although access is less than complete). To improve our measurement of the actual rate of access to schooling, we therefore turn to household survey data, which can give a more accurate estimate of access to schooling within each age cohort.

In 2005–06, about 15 percent of children were excluded from formal schooling. Figure 3.3 shows the share of children and youth, by age, who reported ever having attended school in the latest available household survey, the Sudan Household Health Survey (SHHS) 2006. The probability of ever having been in school (access) reached its maximum about ages 11–13, at which age 85 percent of children were or had been enrolled in school. Thus, the probabilistic (cohort) rate of access was 85 percent in 2005–06. This, in turn, means that 15 percent of children had never had any access to formal schooling at the time.

In 2010, an estimated 10 percent of children did not have access to formal school. Table 3.2 shows that the probability of having been in school has been increasing over time, because it differs for different age groups in the table: from about 75 percent of the 25–30-year-olds and 80 percent of the 20–25-year-olds to about 83 percent of the 15–20-year-olds

Figure 3.3 Access to Grade 1: Share of Population between Ages 5 and 29 Who Had Ever Accessed Basic School, 2005–06

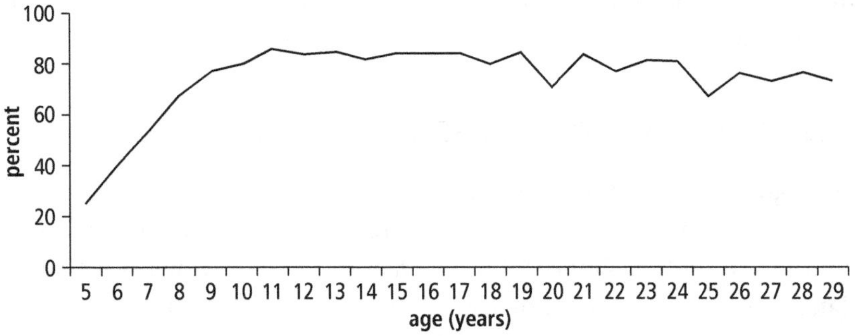

Source: Authors' analysis of the 2006 Sudan Household Health Survey (GoNU and GoSS 2006).

Table 3.2 Basic School Intake and Completion Rates Based on Two Data Sources, 2005–06
percent

Household survey data[a]		Administrative data[b]	
Cohort access to grade 1[c]	Cohort attainment of grade 8[d]	Gross intake rate	Primary completion rate
85	46	79	47

Source: Cohort measures are based on the authors' analysis of the 2006 Sudan Household Health Survey (GoNU and GoSS 2006). The gross intake rate and primary completion rate were calculated based on enrollment data from the FMoGE statistical yearbook for the year indicated and population data shown in annex table 1A.1 in chapter 1.
a. Data are cohort measures for 2005–06.
b. Data are cross-sectional measures for the 2005–06 school year.
c. Share of respondents ages 11–13 who report having ever attended basic education.
d. This figure is based on the responses of children ages 15–19.

and 85 percent of the 10–15-year-olds. This finding means that the cohort access rate has been improving at a rate of between 0.5 and 1 percentage point per year over the past 20 years. It is therefore reasonable to expect a value of about 90 percent for a 10-year-old in 2010, which would mean that 10 percent of children did not receive formal schooling at that time.

The GIR is underestimated in northern Sudan. Table 3.2 compares the cohort measure of access to grade 1 and attainment of grade 8 based on household survey data with the corresponding measures calculated from yearbook enrollment data for the same year. The two measures of completion of the basic education level are almost identical, at 46 percent and 47 percent, respectively. Surprisingly, the GIR, which was only 79 percent in 2005–06, is actually lower than the cohort measure of access, 85 percent (in most countries, the GIR is much higher than the cohort access rate because of multicohort effects). This finding means that the actual rate of access to grade 1 is indeed underestimated in northern Sudan. Various reasons may account for this result: incompleteness of the enrollment data published in the FMoGE yearbooks or an overestimation of the school-age population in the population census data.

LATE ENROLLMENT AND OUT-OF-SCHOOL CHILDREN

Most grade 1 students are between 6 and 8 years old, but children also begin school when they are much older. Figure 3.4 shows the ages of children attending grade 1 based on the 2005–06 household survey data. According to the household survey, many children are either younger or older than the official age for attending grade 1, which is 6–7 years (6 years on entry and turning 7 during the school year). More

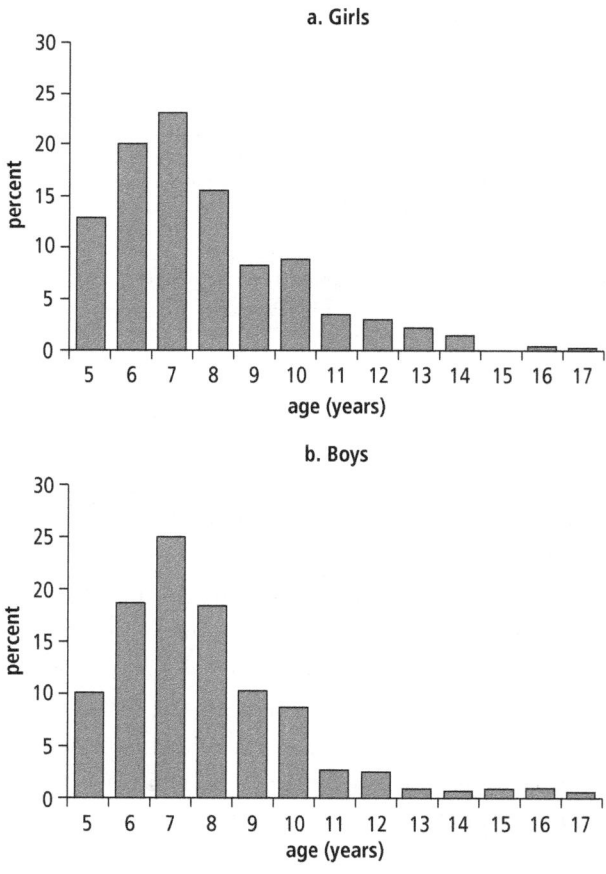

Figure 3.4 Ages of Girls and Boys Attending Grade 1, 2005–06

Source: Analysis of the 2006 Sudan Household Health Survey (GoNU and GoSS 2006).

than 10 percent were only 5 years old, whereas more than 40 percent were 8 years or older. Girls tend to be a little younger than boys when attending grade 1, but the difference is not very large. Once they are 15, girls no longer enroll in first grade, whereas some boys enroll even at 16 and 17. This pattern may start to change, however, once the expansion of access to schooling is complete. Based on experience from other countries, once all children have access to a school in their village or neighborhood, they tend to enroll closer to the correct age.

With so many children entering school late, the age-based net intake rate and net enrollment rate are not good measures of access and coverage in Sudan.[5,6] The net intake rate, which is calculated as the number of new entrants in grade 1 who are age 6 divided by the age 6 population, would clearly underestimate the extent of access to schooling in Sudan.

In the 8–15 age group, an estimated 30 percent of girls and 22 percent of boys were out of school in 2005–06. Figure 3.5 presents the schooling status, by age and gender, of all individuals between the ages of 5 and 24 years at a given time (2005–06, when the SHHS was conducted). In particular, it shows the proportion of each age group that is enrolled in education (any level) and, inversely, the proportion of each age group that is out of school. There are clearly many more girls than boys not in school. For both girls and boys, school participation peaks at age 11, at 78 percent for girls and 84 percent for boys. This finding, however, means that 22 percent of 11-year-old girls and 16 percent of 11-year-olds boys are not in school (any level). For other ages, this proportion is higher. On the whole, 30 percent of girls and 22 percent of boys would be considered out of school.[7] The chart also distinguishes between two groups of out-of-school children: (a) those who have never attended school and (b) those who have attended school in the past. This distinction is important because these two groups may need different types of support to enroll and remain in school.

The pattern of late enrollment is prevalent throughout the education system, particularly for boys.

Figure 3.6 focuses on the children and youth who are enrolled and distinguishes between the levels of education in which they are enrolled. As discussed earlier, it is clear that many children access basic school at a relatively late age. This is also the case for secondary school. Interestingly, secondary school enrollment peaks at age 17 for girls (32 percent of the age group) and age 19 for boys (30 percent of the age group), and girls tend to be a little younger than boys in higher education. Thus, the age gap between girls and boys that starts in basic school persists through secondary and into higher education.

Figure 3.5 Enrollment Status of Girls and Boys by Age, 2005–06

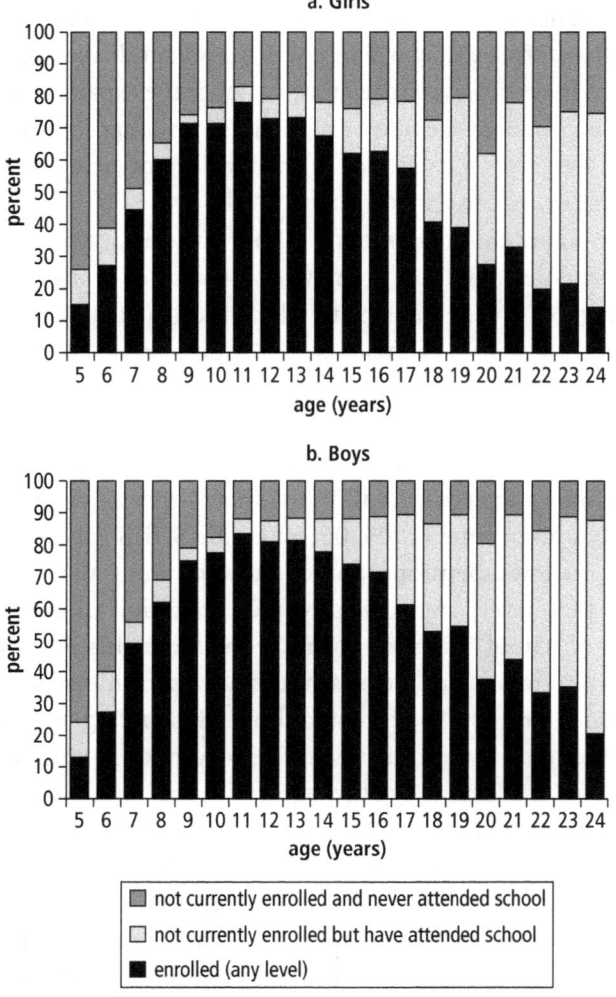

Source: Authors' analysis of the 2006 Sudan Household Health Survey (GoNU and GoSS 2006).

SCHOOL LIFE EXPECTANCY

This section summarizes school participation patterns by looking at school life expectancy (SLE), a systemwide indicator of educational coverage that includes all of basic, secondary, and higher education. A northern Sudanese child can expect to receive an average of 7.0 years of schooling. The SLE, or average schooling duration, is the total number of years of schooling that a child can expect to receive given the current enrollment

Figure 3.6 Schooling Status and Level of Education of Girls and Boys by Age, 2005–06

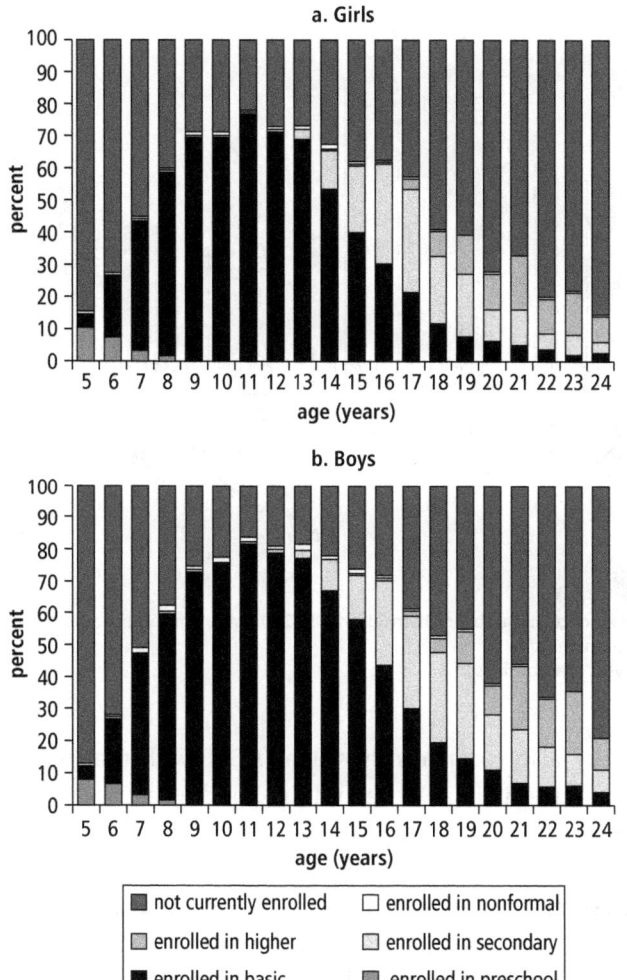

Source: Authors' analysis of the 2006 Sudan Household Health Survey (GoNU and GoSS 2006).
Note: For this figure, *nonformal* combines all other types of education not captured in the other categories.

rates across the system of education. In 2008–09, a child in northern Sudan (15 states) could expect to receive an average of 7.0 years of schooling (see figure 3.7). This number is considerably higher than that recorded by the UNESCO (United Nations Educational, Scientific, and Cultural Organization) Institute for Statistics for the year 2000, which was 4.4 years for all of Sudan (25 states), and is evidence of strong expansion in educational coverage in recent years.

Figure 3.7 School Life Expectancy in Sudan and Comparator Countries, Latest Available Year

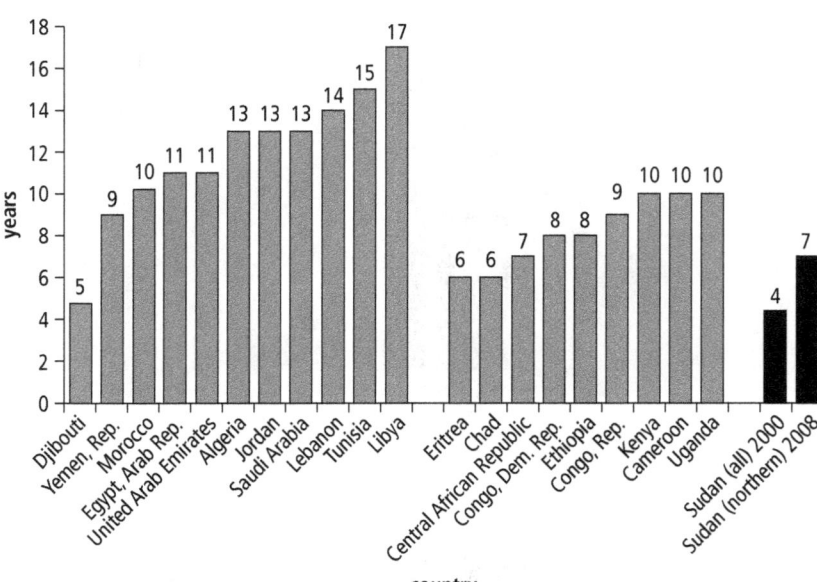

Source: Authors' calculations for northern Sudan; UNESCO Institute for Statistics database (various years) for all other countries.
Note: Latest year available is as of 2011.

Figure 3.7 also compares the Sudan's SLE with that of a number of countries in Sub-Saharan Africa and the Middle East and North Africa. It is evident that despite recent progress, northern Sudan's SLE is still low from an international perspective. For example, the indicator is about 10 years in several neighboring or comparator countries (Arab Republic of Egypt, Kenya, Morocco, and Uganda). The gap with comparator countries, however, may partly be explained by the fact that some of the enrollment indicators—and therefore also the SLE—for northern Sudan appear to be somewhat underestimated, as discussed earlier.

OTHER ASPECTS OF STUDENT FLOW EFFICIENCY AND PROJECTIONS

REPETITION

Repetition in basic schools was fairly low in 2008–09. Three sources of information on repetition in basic schools are compared in Table 3.3. The FMoGE's administrative data (statistical yearbooks) suggest that the share of repeaters is between 4 percent and 7 percent—a fairly low level

Table 3.3 Share of Repeaters in Basic Schools from Different Sources, 2005–06 to 2008–09
percent

Source	Year	G1	G2	G3	G4	G5	G6	G7	G8	Total
FMoGE statistical yearbooks	2008–09	5.1	4.4	5.0	4.9	4.3	4.7	4.2	3.2	**4.6**
	2007–08	5.3	5.1	6.1	6.0	5.9	7.1	5.8	4.5	**5.7**
	2006–07	6.6	6.7	6.7	7.3	7.2	7.7	7.1	5.3	**6.8**
	2005–06	6.3	6.4	7.2	7.3	7.5	8.3	7.3	5.3	**6.9**
FMoGE baseline survey	2007–08	8.0	6.9	7.0	7.1	6.8	6.7	6.2	5.3	**6.9**
	2006–07	6.9	7.7	7.7	8.1	7.7	7.2	6.8	5.5	**7.3**
SHHS 2006	2005–06	7.1	4.7	3.3	3.1	4.7	3.9	2.9	4.8	**4.4**

Sources: Excel tables prepared as part of the FMoGE baseline survey on basic education (FMoGE 2008); authors' analysis of the 2006 Sudan Household Health Survey (GoNU and GoSS 2006).

but not negligible. No major difference is observed across grade levels. The low level of repetition is confirmed by the two other sources provided in the table: (a) the 2008 baseline survey on basic education (FMoGE 2008), in which the share of repeaters was about 7 percent, and (b) the 2006 Sudan Health Household Survey (GoNU and GoSS 2006), in which about 4 percent of those enrolled reported being repeaters. The yearbook data indicate that the level of repetition has been declining since 2005–06.

Repetition is very high in secondary education, particularly in the final year. The FMoGE yearbooks provide information on secondary school enrollments by grade, but do not include the proportion of repeaters. The structure of enrollments by grade, however, is such that it is apparent that many students repeat the final grade of the cycle. It is also apparent that the repeat year is often taken in a nongovernment school, including Teachers' Union classes. Table 3.4 estimates the breakdown of academic secondary school enrollments by repeaters and nonrepeaters.

A third of students in the final year of academic secondary school are repeaters. Table 3.4. shows that only a few percent of students in S1 and S2 are repeaters but that as many as 36 percent in S3 are likely to be repeaters. The total level of repetition is 15 percent across the three-year cycle. It is also estimated that 40 percent of all repeaters attend Teachers' Union classes. The remaining 60 percent are most likely to be repeating in a nongovernment school other than the Teachers' Union. As a result, more than half of students in nongovernment secondary schools are in fact repeaters who came from government schools.

Table 3.4 Estimation of Repetition in Government and Nongovernment Academic Secondary Schools, 2008–09

Grade	Government		Nongovernment		Total share of repeaters in secondary enrollments (percent)	Share of all repeaters who attend Teachers' Union classes (percent)
	Nonrepeaters	Repeaters	Nonrepeaters	Repeaters		
S1	214,709	4,382	24,062	491	2	n.a.
S2	175,799	3,588	23,581	3,718	4	n.a.
S3	140,798	1,422	23,109	91,995	36	n.a.
Total	531,306	9,392	70,752	96,204	15	40

Source: Authors' construction based on data from the FMoGE 2008–09 statistical yearbook and the database of secondary schools from Khartoum State that includes information on enrollments and repeaters.
Note: n.a. = not applicable.

Repetition in technical secondary schools appears to be low. These schools have a very different pattern of student flow. This pattern does not indicate the presence of a high rate of repetition but rather a high number of dropouts, because S3 enrollments are less than half of S1 enrollments.

From a comparative perspective, northern Sudan has a low level of repetition in basic schools but a high level of repetition in secondary schools. When compared to selected countries in Sub-Saharan Africa and the Middle East and North Africa (figure 3.8), the level of repetition in basic schools in northern Sudan is similar to the levels in countries such as Egypt, Mauritius, Botswana, and the Republic of Yemen but significantly lower than the levels found in Djibouti, Morocco, Swaziland, and Namibia. For secondary education, however, northern Sudan is among the countries in the selected group with the highest rate of repetition.

In basic education, we are concerned with repetition because it is a costly practice that does not usually provide substantial benefits. Children who repeat grades are at risk of dropping out of school entirely, and if they stay in school, generally do not benefit much from the additional year of schooling. To lower repetition rates, some Sub-Saharan African countries have been successful in putting into practice automatic promotion between grades. In secondary school, if repetition occurs in the final year to improve the result on the final exam, as is the case in northern Sudan, and the cost of repeating is borne by the parents, then the issues are different. There may be governance issues if public school teachers earn an additional salary from teaching private shifts of repeaters and are then more frequently absent, tired, or unprepared during their regular shifts. Also, this system may not be satisfactory to students; and there could be equity issues if not all students who need it can pay for the extra year.

Patterns of Student Flow • 71

Figure 3.8 International Comparison of the Share of Repeaters in Primary and Secondary Schools, Latest Available Year

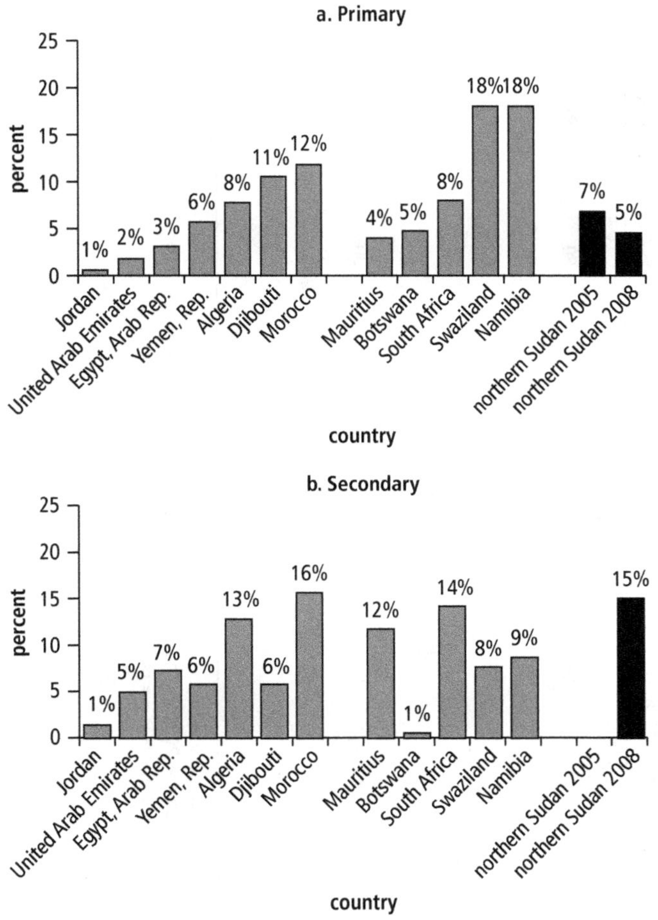

a. Primary

Jordan 1%, United Arab Emirates 2%, Egypt, Arab Rep. 3%, Yemen, Rep. 6%, Algeria 8%, Djibouti 11%, Morocco 12%, Mauritius 4%, Botswana 5%, South Africa 8%, Swaziland 18%, Namibia 18%, northern Sudan 2005 7%, northern Sudan 2008 5%

b. Secondary

Jordan 1%, United Arab Emirates 5%, Egypt, Arab Rep. 7%, Yemen, Rep. 6%, Algeria 13%, Djibouti 6%, Morocco 16%, Mauritius 12%, Botswana 1%, South Africa 14%, Swaziland 8%, Namibia 9%, northern Sudan 2008 15%

Source: UNESCO Institute for Statistics database for all countries other than Sudan.
Note: Latest year available is as of 2011.

RETENTION

Retention to grade 8 of basic education was only about 57 percent in 2008–09. Table 3.5 shows the evolution in the gross intake and primary completion rates from 2000–01 to 2008–09 in basic education, and calculates a simple measure of retention by dividing the PCR by the GIR each year (*transversal method*). The transversal retention rate oscillated between a high of about 70 percent and a low of 53 percent in 2007–08. These large fluctuations are, in part, evidence of weaknesses in the educational statistics.

Table 3.5 Retention and Other Indicators for Basic and Secondary Education, 2000–01 to 2008–09

Education level	2000–01	2001–02	2002–03	2003–04	2004–05	2005–06	2006–07	2007–08	2008–09
Basic									
GIR	66	68	—	66	67	79	80	88	80
PCR	49	46	—	46	49	47	44	46	54
Retention (transversal)	73	68		69	73	59	54	53	68
Retention (longitudinal)								57	
Secondary									
GIR						29	30	31	34
CR						21	21	22	25
Retention (transversal)						72	71	72	72
Retention (longitudinal)								74	

Source: FMoGE statistical yearbooks for the years indicated and authors' calculations.
Note: The transversal retention rate is based on a single year and calculated as PCR/GIR. The longitudinal retention rate is calculated by dividing nonrepeaters in grade 8 in 2007–08 by nonrepeaters in grade 1 in 2000–01. CR = completion rate; GIR = gross intake rate; PCR = primary completion rate; — = not available.

Table 3.5 also provides a *longitudinal* retention rate by following the cohort that enrolled in grade 1 in 2000–01 until they reached grade 8 in 2007–08. This retention rate is 57 percent, so it is within the range indicated by the transversal retention rate. A retention rate of 57 percent indicates that only 57 of every 100 students who enroll in grade 1 are still in school by grade 8. This means that the probability of dropping out before grade 8 is about 43 percent, indicating a dropout rate of 6 percent per grade for grades 1–7. Student dropout is therefore a serious concern in basic education.

Students are at risk of dropping out of school when parents and students do not perceive that additional schooling is worth the investment of time and money—when the costs of schooling exceed the expected benefits. A high rate of dropout could indicate that students are not learning enough, that is, that the quality of schooling is simply too low to justify students' time and the direct cost in terms of parental contributions. Other factors can also put children at risk of dropping out of schools. For example, when schools do not offer all the grades of the basic cycle and children have to change schools to reach the higher grades, thereby likely increasing their travel time to school, there is an increased risk of dropout. More research is needed to understand the main causes and risk factors for dropout in northern Sudan so that appropriate measures to improve retention can be put into place.

Retention is lower in secondary than in basic education when adjusted for the length of the cycles. Similarly, Table 3.5 presents the transversal retention rate for secondary education, 72 percent, and the longitudinal retention rate, 74 percent. A retention rate of 74 percent means that 26 percent of those who enrolled in the first year have dropped out before reaching the final year, corresponding to a dropout rate of 13 percent per year in the first two years of the secondary cycle. Thus, retention appears to be very low in secondary education, and dropout is a very serious issue. It should be noted, however, that these results assume that the enrollment data in the yearbooks are correct, but the analysis indicates even more weaknesses in the secondary school enrollment data than in the basic school data.[8]

INTERNAL EFFICIENCY COEFFICIENT

Table 3.6 calculates an index of the internal efficiency in basic and secondary education. As a function of the pattern of repetition and dropout, the index measures the efficiency of the system in terms of

Table 3.6 Internal Efficiency Coefficients in Basic and Secondary Education, 2005–06 to 2008–09

Education level	2005–06	2006–07	2007–08	2008–09
Basic				
IEC (percent)	72	68	67	76
Student years to produce one completer	11.2	11.7	12.0	10.5
Secondary				
IEC (percent)	76	74	74	71
Student years to produce one completer	3.9	4.1	4.1	4.2

Source: Authors' calculations based on information about repetition and retention by grade from the FMoGE statistical yearbooks for the years indicated.
Note: IEC = internal efficiency coefficient.

producing completers using as few inputs, or student years, as possible. This efficiency is calculated by comparing the number of student years it actually takes to produce one completer as a result of dropout and repetition patterns to the number of student years needed if there were no dropout or repetition (eight years for basic and three for secondary). An education system with no dropout and no repetition would have a coefficient of 100 percent.

It took 10.5 student years to produce a basic school completer and 4.2 student years to produce a secondary school completer in 2008–09. In basic education, the internal efficiency coefficient (IEC) was 76 percent in 2008–09; and, on average, it took 10.5 student years, instead of 8, to produce one completer. An IEC of 76 percent implies that 23 percent of the inputs, or student years, are used on students who do not complete the cycle. In secondary education, the IEC was 71 percent in 2008–09; and, on average, it took 4.2 student years, instead of 3, to produce a completer.

Compared with many Sub-Saharan African countries, the internal efficiency in basic education in northern Sudan is higher. Table 3.7 compares the IEC for basic education with that statistic for selected countries in Sub-Saharan Africa and finds that northern Sudan is performing quite well, although not as well as Kenya and Tanzania. This mostly positive result stems from the comparatively low rate of repetition in northern Sudan. Still, there is room for improvement in both dropout and repetition rates.

Table 3.7 International Comparison of Internal Efficiency Coefficients in Basic Education

Country	Year	IEC
Tanzania	2006	0.85
Kenya	2005	0.83
Sudan (northern)	**2008**	**0.76**
Eritrea	2006	0.74
Ethiopia	2006	0.71
Uganda	2005	0.61
Central African Republic	2006	0.40
Chad	2005	0.35
Malawi	2006	0.35

Source: UNESCO Pôle de Dakar database for the years indicated.
Note: IEC = internal efficiency coefficient.

PROJECTION OF ACCESS AND COMPLETION RATES FOR BASIC EDUCATION

The GIR has grown fast since 2004–05, but the PCR has improved more slowly. Table 3.8 presents the average rates of increase in the GIR and PCR for basic education from 2000–01 to 2008–09. The GIR has grown at 1.7 percentage points per year, and the PCR, at 0.7 percentage point per year. Focusing on 2004–05 to 2008–09, although both indicators increased their pace of growth, the GIR has still been growing much faster (3.2 percentage points per year) than the PCR (1.3 percentage points per year).

This pattern will most likely change in coming years. As northern Sudan gets closer to universal access to basic education, the growth in the GIR will slow down. Further growth in this indicator is not possible once all children are in school. However, as the many new students move through the grades of basic school and begin to reach the last grades, growth in the PCR is likely to pick up. Figure 3.9 illustrates what might happen in the coming years, based on a continuation of the recent improvement trend. The figure uses the data in table 3.8 and depicts the evolution in the GIR and PCR over time. It shows a third indicator, the cohort access rate, which is our best estimate from table 3.8 of the actual extent of access to basic school It is constructed by moving the GIR upward to reach a value of 85 percent in 2005–06.

In an optimistic scenario, 80 percent of children could complete the basic education cycle by 2015. As shown in figure 3.9, if the past trend

Table 3.8 Gross Intake and Primary Completion Rates for Basic Education, 2000–01 to 2008–09

Indicator	Average annual percentage-point increase		
	2000–01 to 2008–09	2000–01 to 2004–05	2004–05 to 2008–09
Gross intake rate	1.7	0.2	3.2
Primary completion rate	0.7	0.2	1.3

Source: Based on data in table 3.5.

Figure 3.9 Projection of the Rate of Access and Completion of Basic Education to 2015

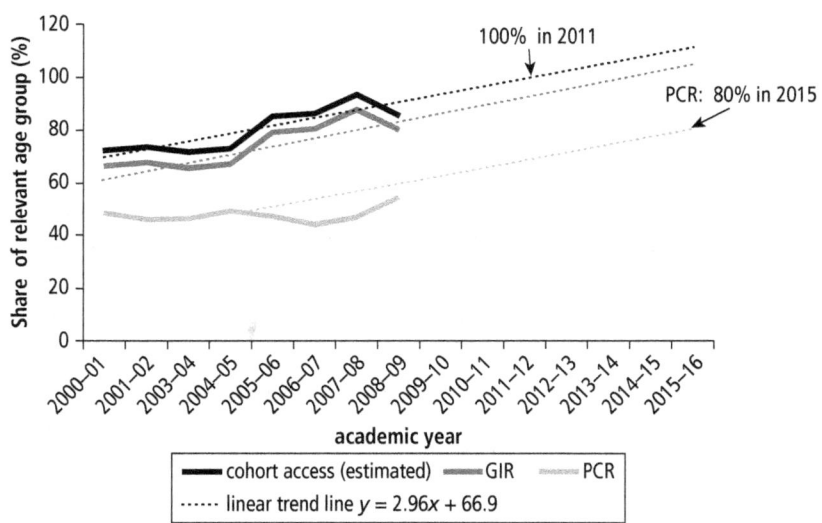

Source: Authors' construction from data in table 3.8.

in the GIR (as indicated by the linear trend line) continues, then the cohort access rate will reach 100 about 2012—that is, all, or almost all, children will at least enroll in grade 1. If that same trend is applied to the PCR, then that rate will reach 80 percent in 2015—that is, four out of five children will complete the basic cycle. In this scenario, northern Sudan is thus not on track to reach universal primary completion by 2015, but providing access to all children is within reach. If current trends continue, reaching universal primary completion will likely take almost another decade.

Despite reason for optimism, there is a risk that indicators will stagnate. There is no guarantee, however, that the trends shown in figure 3.9 can be accomplished in the years ahead. First, as shown in the figure, the GIR actually declined in 2008–09, the latest year.[9] Second, figure 3.9 shows that there has not been any improvement in boys' access rate in many years. This finding could indicate that there are population groups in northern Sudan who remain largely excluded from the education system. These groups could be hard to reach using traditional measures such as merely making schools available, because this measure has clearly not worked so far. Other measures may be needed, such as adjusting schools better to the needs of the population groups or providing more incentives to increase their demand for schooling.

SUMMARY

The analysis of student flow patterns in northern Sudan resulted in the following findings:

- According to our best estimate, about 90 percent of children currently access grade 1 of basic education (2010 estimate). However, many of them enter school early or late: more than 10 percent were only 5 years old, whereas more than 40 percent were 8 years or older.
- On average, a child can expect 7.0 years of basic schooling. Despite recent growth in school life expectancy, northern Sudan is behind many comparator countries with regard to this indicator. Also, given that the basic cycle is eight years, a school life expectancy of only 7 years is clearly insufficient.
- There is a fairly low level of repetition in basic schools—only about 4–5 percent—but 36 percent of students repeat the final year of secondary school.
- There is considerable student dropout from the basic and secondary education cycles. Dropping out from a cycle before obtaining a diploma or certificate seems to be the most common way of exiting the education system. As a result, in the 8–15 age group, an estimated 30 percent of girls and 22 percent of boys were out of school in 2005–06.
- Also, as a result of repetition and dropout patterns, an input of 10.5 student years (instead of 8) is required to produce one basic school completer and 4.2 student years (instead of 3) is required to produce a secondary school completer.

- Transition rates between the cycles are very high: about 74 percent of basic school completers continue on to secondary education, and about 87 percent of secondary school completers continue on to higher education. Thus, relatively few students complete a cycle without continuing on to the next cycle.
- In 2008–09, only about 54 percent of children completed the basic cycle (61 percent completed the first six years). In an optimistic scenario, if recent years' strong pace of improvement in basic school enrollments continues, almost all children may access at least grade 1 by about 2012, and 80 percent of children may complete basic school by 2015. There are risks, however, and accomplishing these results will require sustained efforts to continue improvements in basic school access and retention.

ANNEX: BASIC AND SECONDARY EDUCATION ENROLLMENTS

Table 3A.1 Enrollments by Grade in Basic and Secondary Education, Northern Sudan, 2008–09

Grade	School-age population	Enrollment	Repeaters (estimated)	Nonrepeaters (estimated)	Schooling profile/access[a] (percent)	Retention within cycle
G1	934,516	785,777	39,196	746,581	80	100
G2	905,574	736,540	31,107	705,433	78	98
G3	881,916	701,368	33,745	667,623	76	95
G4	857,918	645,384	30,561	614,823	72	90
G5	833,680	584,953	24,764	560,189	67	84
G6	809,303	516,718	23,712	493,006	61	76
G7	784,884	474,225	19,422	454,803	58	73
G8	760,525	425,499	13,359	412,140	54	68
All basic	6,768,317	4,870,464	215,866	4,654,598	n.a.	n.a.
S1	736,325	255,939	5,119	250,820	34	100
S2	712,384	217,286	7,518	209,768	29	86
S3	688,801	263,084	93,475	169,609	25	72
All secondary	2,137,510	736,309	106,112	630,197	n.a.	n.a.

Source: FMoGE 2008–09 statistical yearbook.
Note: n.a. = not applicable.
a. Rate was determined by enrollment excluding repeaters divided by the population of relevant ages for that grade.

NOTES

1. The main sources of data are the yearbooks of educational statistics prepared by the federal Ministry of General Education (FMoGE) and when indicated, the 2006 Sudan Health Household Survey (SHHS) (GoNU and GoSS 2006).
2. The gross intake rate is calculated as the nonrepeaters in grade 1 divided by the age 6 population.
3. The primary completion rate is calculated as the nonrepeaters in grade 8 divided by the age 13 population.
4. Preschool and higher education are shown as rectangular shapes because we have no information on their intake and completion rates, only their total enrollments.
5. The net intake rate is calculated as the nonrepeaters in grade 1 who are age 6 divided by the age 6 population.
6. The net enrollment rate is calculated as the enrollment of 6–13-year-olds in basic school divided by the population of 6–13-year-olds.
7. These data are based on 8–15-year-olds, which is the eight-year-long cohort with the highest rate of school participation; an eight-year cohort was chosen because the basic education cycle is eight years.
8. In particular, as discussed in chapter 2, the fact that secondary school enrollments increased little from 2004 to 2009, even though the number of schools grew by 50 percent, suggests a problem with the enrollment data.
9. In 2007–08, there was a government campaign informing parents of the importance of sending their children to school, and grade 1 enrollments increased. The following year, there was no campaign, and grade 1 enrollments decreased.

REFERENCES

FMoGE (Federal Ministry of General Education). 2008. "Baseline Survey on Basic Education in the Northern States of Sudan: Final Report June 2008." Khartoum. Online document available at http://planipolis.iiep.unesco.org/epiweb/E029336e.pdf
———. Various years. "Statistical Yearbooks." Khartoum.
GoNU (Government of National Unity) and GoSS (Government of Southern Sudan). 2006. *Sudan Household Health Survey (SHHS) 2006*. Khartoum/Juba: Central Bureau of Statistics and Southern Sudan Center for Census, Statistics and Evaluation.

CHAPTER

Disparities

This chapter investigates three types of disparities in the rates of schooling across the 15 states of northern Sudan. It first examines *regional* disparities in the indicators of school enrollment and then turns to various *social* disparities. Finally, the chapter looks into the extent of *structural* disparities in the distribution of public spending on education across individuals of the same generation. Wherever relevant, the extent of the disparities in school participation in northern Sudan is placed in an international comparative context.

REGIONAL DISPARITIES

GROSS ENROLLMENT RATE

Because general education is managed by the states, the analysis of regional disparities necessarily involves examining the disparities across all 15. We start by comparing the gross enrollment rates (GERs) of preschool, basic, and secondary education, as shown in table 4.1.[1]

There are large disparities in the GER across states at all three levels of education. The GER spans 13–65 percent for preschool, 65–94 percent for basic school, and 15–61 percent for secondary school.[2] The wide bands in these ranges, particularly the one for basic school—which is supposed to be free and compulsory and therefore should not have such a large variation—indicates that some states have quite advanced education systems and others are far behind in terms of even enrolling children in basic school.

However, there are also considerable inconsistencies in the data. As mentioned in chapter 2, the basic school GER based on yearbook data is low compared with the same indicator based on the 2006 Sudan Household Health Survey. Not surprisingly, this is also the case when

Table 4.1 Comparison of GERs in Preschool, Basic, and Secondary Schools across States, 2008–09
percent

Enrollment level	Preschool		Basic		Secondary (academic and technical)	
	Gross enrollment rate	Average annual percentage-point change since 2005–06	Gross enrollment rate	Average annual percentage-point change since 2005–06	Gross enrollment rate	Average annual percentage-point change since 2005–06
High						
Khartoum	43	1	94	5	61	7
River Nile	65	6	89	−1	7	1
Al Jazirah	44	3	90	0	57	3
Northern	64	4	85	−3	50	2
White Nile	43	5	85	5	37	1
5-state average	52	4	89	1	50	3
Medium						
South Kordofan	52	9	82	2	32	3
Western Darfur	26	5	88	2	25	3
Sinnar	13	0	80	3	31	1
North Kordofan	23	—	78	4	23	0
Al Qadarif	36	6	70	3	31	1
5-state average	30	5	80	3	28	2
Low						
Northern Darfur	32	4	67	4	21	−2
Red Sea	64	—	—	1	17	−1
Blue Nile	20	0	65	4	20	1
Southern Darfur	38	8	—	1	17	−1
Kassala	17	0	—	−2	15	0
5-state average	34	3	66	2	18	0
15-state average	37	4	72	2	34	2

Source: Authors' construction based on enrollment data from the FMoGE statistical yearbooks from 2005–06 to 2008–09.
Note: The states are listed in order of their weighted average GERs across the three education levels using the cycle lengths as weights (two, eight, and three years, respectively, for preschool, basic school, and secondary school). — = not available.

comparing the same two statistics by state, but the discrepancy between the two sources of data is much larger for some states than for others. For Kassala, Red Sea, and Southern Darfur states, in particular, the discrepancies are so large that we cannot easily reconcile the numbers; therefore, they are not shown in table 4.1, although the table does place these three states among those with comparatively low school enrollment.[3]

Khartoum State has the highest GER overall, as shown in table 4.1. When the states are ordered in terms of their average GERs across the three levels of general education, Khartoum State is at the top of the list. It has very strong GERs in preschool (43 percent), basic school (94 percent), and secondary school (61 percent). The five states with the highest levels of school enrollment—Khartoum, River Nile, Al Jazirah, Northern, and White Nile—are, not surprisingly, the states with the highest levels of economic development in northern Sudan. The five states with the lowest levels of school enrollment—Northern Darfur, Red Sea, Blue Nile, Southern Darfur, and Kassala—were all affected by conflict and presumably have a ways to go to "catch up" with the other states.

States with low GERs are falling even further behind. Table 4.1 also provides the average percentage-point increase in the GER across the three levels of education between 2005 and 2009. On average across all 15 states, the GER increased by 2 percentage points per year in both basic and secondary schools (and 4 percentage points per year in preschool). In the five states with low GERs, however, the basic school GER grew by 2 percentage points per year, but the secondary school GER did not increase over the three years. This finding suggests on the one hand, that these states prioritize expanding basic schooling coverage at this moment in time, which is appropriate given their low coverage, but on the other hand, that their overall coverage of schooling is growing slower than other states' coverage. These states may need additional assistance to increase the pace of growth in school enrollments, as detailed in chapter 7, on education finance.

The higher the basic school GER is, the faster the growth in the secondary school GER. The GERs are generally growing fast in the groups designated high and medium in table 4.1. In the intermediate-GER group, coverage is expanding rapidly in both basic schools (3 percentage points per year) and secondary schools (2 percentage points per year). In the high-GER group, coverage in basic schools is expanding at a slower pace (1 percentage point per year) than in secondary schools (3 percentage points per year) for an obvious reason: these states are closer to full basic education coverage.

ACCESS TO GRADE 1 OF BASIC SCHOOL

Household surveys provide another source of data on the regional disparities in school enrollment.[4] For selected states, figure 4.1 depicts the

Figure 4.1 Access: Regional Disparities in the Share of Children between Ages 5 and 17 Who Had Ever Accessed Basic School, 2005–06

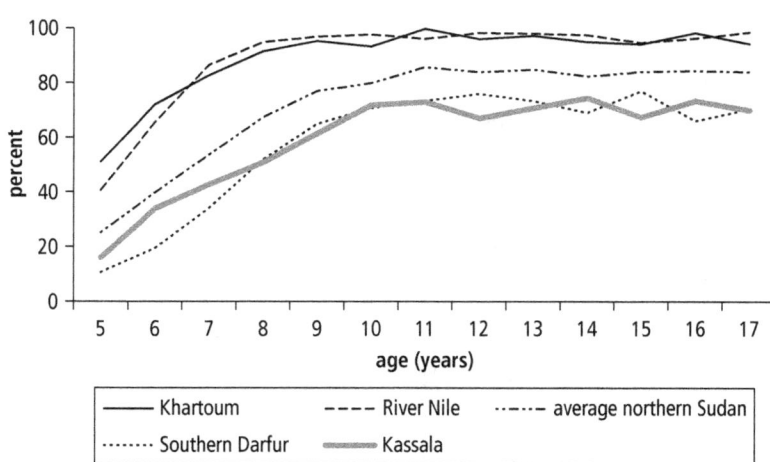

Source: Authors' analysis of the 2006 Sudan Household Health Survey (GoNU and GoSS 2006).

share of children ages 5–17 who reported in the 2006 Sudan Household Health Survey having ever been enrolled in basic school (whether they were still enrolled or not).

In Khartoum and River Nile states, almost all children access school at some point, although not at age 6 for most of them. For these top two states in table 4.1, the share of children enrolled or having been enrolled in school rose from 40–50 percent of 5-year-olds and 65–70 percent of 6-year-olds to 80–85 percent of 7-year-olds and 90–95 percent of 8-year-olds only to level out around 95–99 percent for children ages 9 and up. Thus, some 95–99 percent of children reportedly entered basic school at some point in their lives. This statistic is also known as the *cohort access rate*. However, only about 10–20 percent of children entered school at the exact age of 6, the official age of entry to grade 1.

In Southern Darfur and Kassala, about 70 percent of children gained access to school in 2006, but most did so after age 6. Similarly, for Southern Darfur and Kassala, the bottom two states in table 4.1, the cohort access rate can be estimated as the share of children in the 10–13 age group who have ever accessed school. In these two states, the value of this statistic is about 70 percent based on household survey data. It is noteworthy that it is much less common in these two states for 5-year-olds to be enrolled in school but more common to enter school late.

SOCIAL DISPARITIES

This section looks at social disparities in the rates of school participation. It is severely limited by the availability of data, and therefore considers only three dimensions: boys versus girls, urban versus rural children, and rich versus poor children.

Statistical information is missing about vulnerable groups. First, there is insufficient information to assess the school enrollment (and nonenrollment) rates of internally displaced persons (IDPs) and nomads, who make up two of the most vulnerable groups in northern Sudan.[5] Second, there are no available data on orphans, neither on the number of orphans, potentially high given that it is a postconflict country, nor on their rates of school participation or barriers to their access to schooling. These are areas that need further research.

GENDER DISPARITIES

We start the analysis of social disparities by looking at the effect of gender on school enrollments. Based on data from the yearbooks, table 4.2 provides information on the share of girls in total enrollments by level of education.

In the formal system, the share of girls increases with rising levels of schooling. In 2008–09, girls made up 47 percent of enrollments in preschool, 46 percent in basic school, 49 percent in academic secondary school, and 56 percent in higher education (and 25 percent in technical secondary school), according to table 4.2. Thus, with the exception of the technical track of secondary school, the proportion of girls increases with rising levels of education, indicating better retention of girls than boys in the system. The table also shows that the proportion of girls in total enrollments has fluctuated only slightly since the 2000–01 academic year.

Table 4.3 shows nomadic and village schools have higher gender gaps than do other basic schools. Government schools that are not nomadic,

Table 4.2 Share of Girls in Enrollments by Level of Education, 2000–01 and 2008–09

| Academic year | Preschool | Basic | Secondary | | Higher |
			Academic	Technical	
2000–01	50	46	52	36	52
2008–09	47	46	49	25	56

Source: FMoGE statistical yearbooks for years indicated.

Table 4.3 Share of Girls in Enrollments by Type of Basic School, 2008–09
percent

Academic year	Government school				Nongovernment school
	Nomadic	IDP	Village	Other	
2008–09	38	44	41	47	44

Source: FMoGE 2008–09 statistical yearbook.
Note: IDP = internally displaced person.

IDP, or village schools have higher shares of girls (47 percent) than do nomadic schools (38 percent), IDP schools (44 percent), multigrade village schools (41 percent), or even nongovernment schools (44 percent). This finding suggests that girls are at a greater disadvantage among marginalized or vulnerable population groups than in the population as a whole.

More adult women than men attend literacy education. In special education, girls make up 36 percent of enrollments, whereas girls make up 57 percent of enrollments in adolescents education and 76 percent of enrollments in literacy and adult education. The higher enrollment of women in literacy education may be explained by a greater need for catch-up education for women as a result of lower rates of schooling for girls in past generations, as indicated by the lower literacy rates for women (52 percent) than for men (71 percent).[6]

In order to assess the extent of gender disparities in education more precisely, adjustments are needed in the population data for girls and boys. Specifically, it is necessary to calculate the GER for girls and boys separately to take into account that the population may not include equal numbers of girls and boys. This calculation is not simple for northern Sudan, however, because 4 out of the 15 states have gender ratios far outside the natural range, according to data from the 2008 census.[7] As shown in figure 4.2, Northern Darfur, Southern Darfur, Kassala, and Red Sea have between 113 and 146 boys per 100 girls in the 6–13 age groups, numbers normally seen only in countries with a strong preference for sons, such as China and parts of India (Das Gupta and others 2002). For the calculation of separate GERs for girls and boys, the breakdown of the population by gender is therefore adjusted to reflect the average ratios for northern Sudan (when excluding the four states) for the age group, which are 104 boys per 100 girls in the 4–5 age group, 106 boys per 100 girls in the 6–13 age group, and finally, 100 boys per 100 girls in the 14–16 age group.

Overall, the slight advantage for boys in preschool and basic school is no longer present by secondary school. Table 4.4 compares the GER for girls with that of boys and calculates the gender parity index (GPI) by level of education.[8] Both preschool and basic school have GPIs of

Figure 4.2 Ratio of Boys to Girls in the Basic School-Age Population, by State, 2008

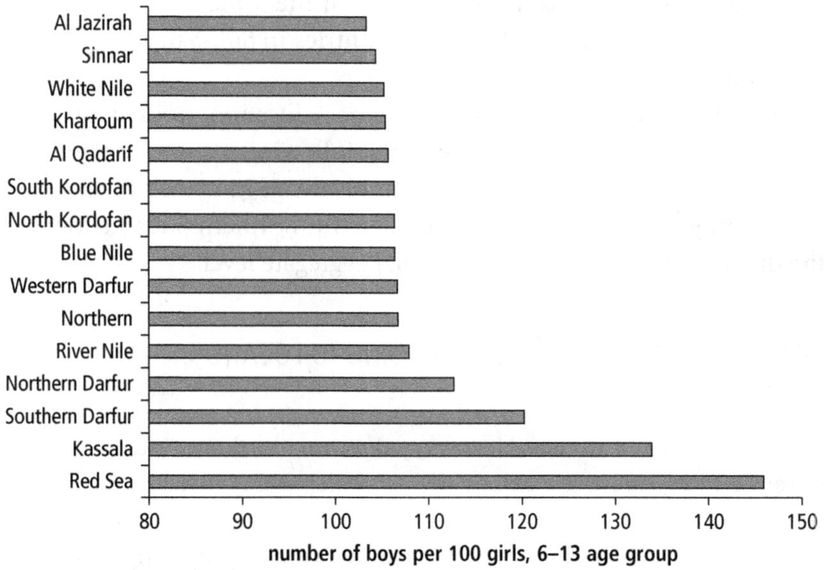

State	number of boys per 100 girls, 6–13 age group
Al Jazirah	~102
Sinnar	~103
White Nile	~104
Khartoum	~104
Al Qadarif	~105
South Kordofan	~106
North Kordofan	~106
Blue Nile	~106
Western Darfur	~106
Northern	~106
River Nile	~108
Northern Darfur	~112
Southern Darfur	~120
Kassala	~133
Red Sea	~146

Source: Authors' analysis of the 2008 population census data.

Table 4.4 Gender Disparities at All Levels of Education, 2008–09

Indicator	Preschool	Basic	Secondary Academic	Secondary Technical	Higher
Gross enrollment rate (percent)					
Girls	35	68	33	0.6	20
Boys	39	76	34	1.9	16
Gender parity index	0.90	0.90	0.97	0.33	1.27

Source: FMoGE 2008–09 statistical yearbook.

0.90, which indicates that slight disadvantages are present for girls at these education levels. In academic secondary school, the GPI is almost 1.00 (and the GER for girls, 33 percent, is almost equal to that for boys, 34 percent).

Interestingly, by the time they enter higher education, boys are at a considerable disadvantage. This reversal is indicated by the GPI of 1.27 in table 4.4. The better retention of girls in the system may be explained by greater incentives for girls to stay in school to delay marriage and to delay entrance into an uncertain labor market. However, boys may have better opportunities in the labor market and therefore fewer incentives to stay in school. In secondary and higher education, the GPI for northern Sudan is closer to the GPI for countries in the Middle East and North Africa than it is to the GPI for most countries in Sub-Saharan Africa, as shown in Table 4.5.

In spite of promising statistics for girls' education, pockets of disadvantage for girls persist. As we see in the following section, some groups of girls may still be at a considerable disadvantage in terms of their access to schooling, although the aggregate data for northern Sudan show that the differences are small at the national aggregate level.

COMPARISON OF DISPARITIES ACCORDING TO LOCATION, INCOME, AND GENDER

The availability of household survey data for northern Sudan makes it possible to compare the extent of social disparities in education across several social dimensions. The 2006 Sudan Household Health Survey was the most recent survey available at the time of preparing this report and thus the source of the data (GoNU and GoSS 2006). Figure 4.3 presents the probability of a child's ever enrolling in basic school based on the following variables: urban or rural location, level of household income, and gender. However, because the survey was conducted in

Table 4.5 International Comparison of Gender Parity Index by Level of Education, Latest Available Year

Country	Preschool	Basic	Academic secondary	Higher
Northern Sudan	**0.90**	**0.90**	**0.97**	**1.27**
Cameroon	1.02	0.86	0.80	0.79
Kenya	0.96	0.98	0.92	0.70
Nigeria	0.99	0.88	0.77	0.70
Uganda	1.05	1.01	0.85	0.80
Four-country average (SSA)	1.01	0.93	0.84	0.74
Egypt, Arab Rep.	0.94	0.95	0.94	—
Iran, Islamic Rep.	0.96	1.40	0.98	1.14
Jordan	0.94	1.02	1.04	1.11
Tunisia	0.99	0.97	1.10	1.50
Four-country average (MENA)	0.96	1.09	1.02	1.25

Source: World Bank EdStats database.
Note: MENA = Middle East and North Africa; SSA = Sub-Saharan Africa.

Figure 4.3 Access: Probability of Ever Enrolling in Basic School (Grade 1) according to Location, Income, and Gender, circa 2005

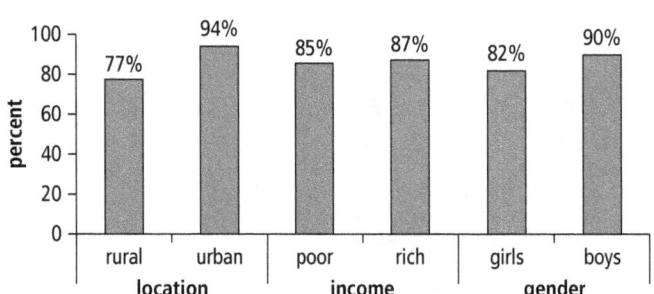

Source: Authors' analysis of the 2006 Sudan Household Health Survey (GoNU and GoSS 2006). The figure is based on responses of children ages 11–15. Annex table 4B.1 provides the details of the regression analysis on which this chart is based.
Note: For this figure, *poor* means belonging to the lowest income quintile and *rich* means belonging to the two richest quintiles of the population.

2006 and because the probabilities were computed based on the responses of children a few years after they enrolled (or not) in basic school, the figures may be taken as indicative of the social disparities in the system around 2000–05.

The urban or rural location is the best predictor of a child's chance of ever going to school, but gender and poverty also matter. Figure 4.3 clearly shows that children in rural areas, children from poorer households, and girls are at a disadvantage in terms of access to schooling. Of the three variables, the strongest predictor of access to schooling is location. Urban children are 17 percentage points more likely than rural children to access school. Overall, boys are 8 percentage points more likely than girls to access school, and rich children are 2 percentage points more likely than poor children to access school.

Gender matters even more for children in rural areas. Table 4.6 goes a step further by illustrating the total disadvantage resulting from all the possible combinations of rich-poor, urban-rural, and boy-girl. It shows that there are compounding effects from gender and rurality, so that being a girl is more of a disadvantage in a rural than in an urban setting: girls are 4 percentage points less likely than boys to attend school in urban areas but 11–12 percentage points less likely than boys to attend school in rural areas. Therefore, the poor rural girl is the most disadvantaged of all. She is about 25 percentage points less likely to ever access basic school than the rich urban boy.

More child-friendly schools can attract more girls. A joint Government of Southern Sudan (GoSS) and UNICEF study conducted in southern

Table 4.6   Access: Interaction of Gender with Poverty and Rurality

Indicator	Rich		Poor	
	Urban	Rural	Urban	Rural
Boy (percent)	96	84	95	82
Girl (percent)	92	72	91	70
Gap (percentage points)	4	11	4	12

Source: Regression analysis of the 2006 Sudan Household Health Survey (GoNU and GoSS 2006). The figure is based on responses of children ages 11–15. Annex table 4B.1 provides the details of the regression analysis on which this chart is based.
Note: The table gives the probability of still being in school by the final grade (for those who have attended grade 1).

Sudan in 2008 may provide insights into why some girls are being held back in rural areas of northern Sudan (MoEST/GoSS 2009).[9] One of the main conclusions of the study was that parents generally do want to educate their daughters, but many are not sending them to school out of concern for their safety on the way to and from school or even in the school itself. The study concludes that safer and more child-friendly school environments—for girls as well as for boys—can be achieved by making fairly modest changes, such as increasing parent involvement in school management or providing tuition waivers for girls, and that these changes are likely to be enough to persuade parents to send their daughters to school. The study also emphasizes the need for teaching life skills in schools and in the community.

Longer distances to schools in rural areas may be more of a problem for girls than for boys. The 2008 baseline survey (FMoGE 2008) found a declining GPI with increasing distance to school: 0.84 for students with a school less than 1 km from home, 0.78 for students with 1–3 km between school and home, and 0.66 for students with more than 3 km between home and school. Because of the correlations in the data between rurality and distance to school, the results may just be showing that rural girls have less access to school than do urban girls, confirming what was discussed previously. However, they may also indicate that distance to school can explain a part of the problem of girls' low access to school in rural areas.

Girls are almost as likely as boys to stay in school once enrolled. Figure 4.4 shows a similar analysis of the probability of staying in school until the final grade for those who enrolled in grade 1 (retention). Again, location is the best predictor of retention in basic school, with urban children having a 20 percentage-point higher chance than rural children of still being in school by grade 8. However, even for

Figure 4.4 Retention: Probability of Still Being in School by Grade 8, by Location, Income, and Gender, circa 2005

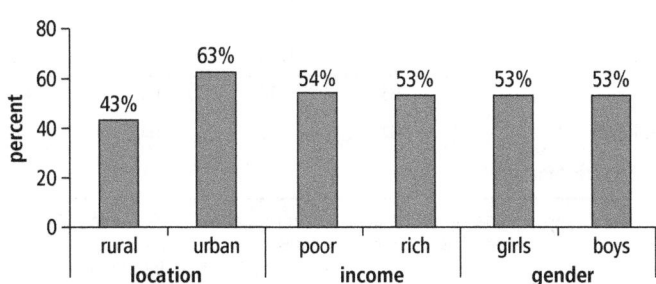

Source: Authors' analysis of the 2006 Sudan Household Health Survey (GoNU and GoSS 2006). The figure is based on the responses of children ages 15–19.
Note: The figure covers only those who attended grade 1. For this figure, *poor* means belonging to the lowest income quintile, and *rich* means belonging to the two richest quintiles of the population.

urban children, retention is no more than 63 percent. Girls are about as likely as boys to remain in school.[10]

Girls and boys have similar rates of retention in both urban and rural areas, as shown in table 4.7. Retention rates are also similar for rich and poor children. There is no compounding effect of gender with urban-rural location. Thus, the difference between boys' and girls' participation in basic education is only related to access to grade 1 (not retention once in school), and this result applies to both urban and rural children.

In urban areas, the problem is mainly retention; in rural areas, the focus must be on both access and retention. To improve access to education, more research is needed to determine whether the weak access of rural children to school is mostly a question of improving—and possibly adapting—the supply of schooling, that is, by providing schooling that is free of charge, that is close to where children live, that has acceptable school hours and curriculum, and so on. Or it could be a question of raising the demand for schooling, that is, by running campaigns informing parents about the benefits of schooling and possibly compensating families for the opportunity cost of schooling (rural children are often engaged in productive activities in the field or in the home). The retention of children in school may also be affected by both characteristics of the supply of schooling and factors affecting the demand. More data are required to understand the relative magnitude of demand and supply factors. These data will potentially be available through the 2009 Household Survey and long form of the 2008 census (demand factors) and the Education Management Information System data (supply factors).

Table 4.7 Retention: Interaction of Gender with Poverty and Rurality

Indicator	Rich		Poor	
	Urban	Rural	Urban	Rural
Boy (percent)	63	44	64	45
Girl (percent)	62	43	64	44
Gap (percentage point)	1	1	1	1

Source: Regression analysis of the 2006 Sudan Household Health Survey (GoNU and GoSS 2006). The table is based on the responses of children ages 15–19.
Note: The table gives the probability of still being in school by the final grade (for those who have attended grade 1).

OUT-OF-SCHOOL CHILDREN IN URBAN AND RURAL AREAS

Overall, all of the access and student flow issues are magnified in the rural areas. Figure 4.5 provides an illustration of the schooling status for urban and rural children and youth in northern Sudan around 2005–06.[11] The two panels confirm many of the findings that have been discussed in this and previous chapters: (a) the relatively late (or in some cases, early) age at which many children enter basic school, (b) the low level of retention from one grade to the next throughout basic and secondary education, and (c) the fact that enrollment in school seems to peak about ages 10–11. Although these basic patterns appear to be the same for urban and rural children, a comparison of the two panels also shows that these issues are, for the most part, much more severe in rural areas.

Not surprisingly, the share of out-of-school children is higher in rural than in urban areas. The two panels also show the proportion of children who are out of school by single age from 5 to 24 years, and provide a breakdown of the out-of-school children into two groups: (a) those who have never had access to school and (b) those who have been enrolled but are no longer in school. Clearly, there are many more out-of-school children in rural areas; and in particular, the share of children who have never had access to schooling is relatively much larger in rural than in urban areas (this "never access" group appears at the top of each panel).

An estimated 1 million children and youth between the ages of 10 and 17 have never been to formal school (and likely never will). For the education policy makers and planners, it is important to know how many children and youth belong to this particular group because they will likely need other forms of education in the years to come if they are to become literate adults. For the 10–17 age range, the number is

Figure 4.5 Schooling Status of Urban and Rural Children by Age, 2005–06

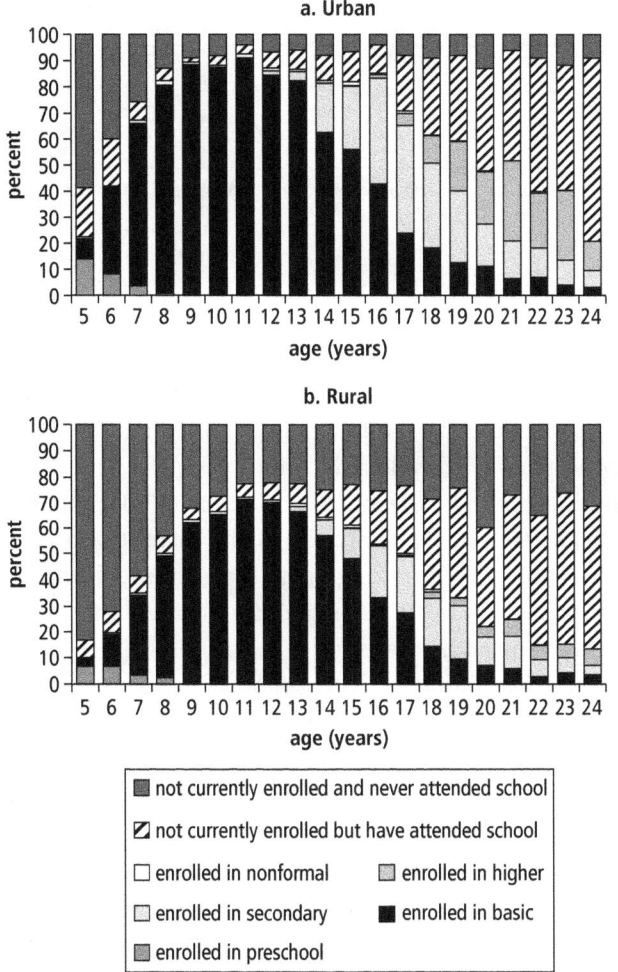

Source: Authors' analysis of the 2006 Sudan Household Health Survey (GoNU and GoSS 2006).
Note: For this figure, nonformal combines all other types of education not captured in the other categories.

estimated in table 4.8 by combining the cohort access rates provided in table 4.6 with the total 10–17 population in northern Sudan. Table 4.8 provides a breakdown of this group by gender and urban-rural location. More than 800,000 are in rural areas, and more than 500,000 are rural girls.

STRUCTURAL DISPARITIES

Structural disparities refer to the way in which educational resources are distributed among people belonging to the same generation. Children

Table 4.8 Estimated Number of 10- to 17-Year-Olds in Northern Sudan Who Have Never Been in School, by Gender, 2008

Indicator	Urban	Rural	Total
Boy	55,090	313,520	368,610
Girl	99,660	507,740	607,400
Total	154,750	821,260	976,010

Source: Authors' construction based on a combination of table 4.6 and 2008 population data.

who never access school do not consume any public educational resources, whereas those who advance all the way to higher education absorb significant public resources over the course of their school careers. Furthermore, because the level of per-student spending rises with each level of education, a considerable proportion of educational resources tends to be consumed by the 10–20 percent most educated within a generation. This section analyzes aspects of the distribution of educational resources among people belonging to the same cohort. The analysis excludes preschool for better comparability with data for other countries provided at the end of this section.

Structural disparities are a function of the schooling profile and per-student spending levels. Based on the schooling profile in northern Sudan, table 4.9 calculates the distribution of a cohort of children by the highest level of education attained (column A1): 15 percent of the cohort do not attend any schooling whatsoever, whereas 2 percent attain grade 1 as their highest level, another 2 percent attain grade 2, and so on per table 4.9, until the last row, which shows that 20 percent of the cohort attain higher education. The table also calculates the total amount of education spending absorbed by members of a cohort over their entire schooling career by the highest level attained (column B1): although the 15 percent with no schooling consume no resources, the 20 percent who attain the higher education level consume 62 percent of total education spending. Figure 4.6 plots the cumulative distribution of a cohort of children by highest education level attained by the cumulative distribution of spending (A2 against B2)—also known as the Lorenz curve.

The 10 percent most educated consume 32 percent of educational resources. Based on the Lorenz curve, it is possible to determine the value of two indicators that are commonly used to measure the extent of structural inequalities within the education system. The first indicator, the Gini coefficient for the distribution of educational resources, is

Table 4.9 Distribution of Public Education Spending among Members of the Same Cohort, 2008–09

Education level	Basic data		Distribution of cohort by highest level attained		Public spending by highest level attained			
	Schooling profile of cohort[a] (percent)	Public per student spending by level (SDG/year)	A1: percentage of total	A2: Cumulative distribution of cohort (percent)	Per student (SDG)	Per cohort[b] (SDG)	B1: Distribution (percent)	B2: Cumulative distribution of spending (percent)
No school	n.a.	0	15	15	0	0	0	0
Basic								
G1	85	260	2	17	260	553	0	0
G2	83	260	2	19	520	1,217	0	0
G3	81	260	4	24	780	3,319	1	1
G4	76	260	5	29	1,040	4,979	1	3
G5	71	260	7	35	1,300	8,713	2	5
G6	65	260	3	38	1,560	4,979	1	7
G7	62	260	4	42	1,820	7,164	2	9
G8	58	260	21	64	2,080	44,477	12	21
Secondary								
S1	36	756	5	69	2,836	14,180	4	25
S2	31	756	5	74	3,592	18,342	5	30
S3	26	756	7	80	4,348	28,678	8	38
Higher (four years)	20	1,730	20	100	11,268	220,565	62	100

Source: Authors' calculations based on the FMoGE 2008–09 statistical yearbook.

a. The "schooling profile" was calculated in chapter 2: in each grade, it is the enrollment excluding repeaters divided by the population of relevant age. Because the schooling profile based on yearbook data is likely to be underestimated in northern Sudan, the schooling profile shown in this table was adjusted upward by about 5 percentage points to match the higher cohort access rate from the SHHS 2006.
b. This value was calculated for a hypothetical cohort of 100 children.

Figure 4.6 Lorenz Curve for the Distribution of Public Education Spending, 2008–09

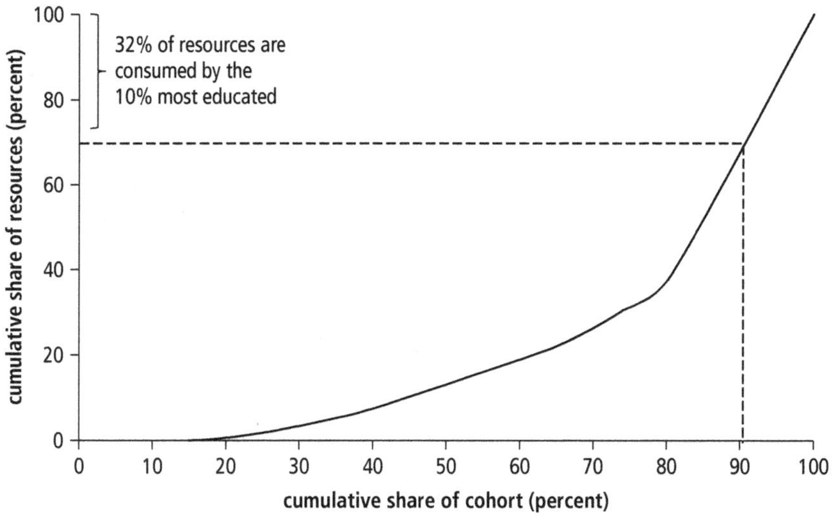

Source: Data are taken from table 4.9.

0.55 for northern Sudan. The second indicator, the share of resources consumed by the 10 percent most educated, is 32 percent.[12]

Overall, the distribution of educational resources is inequitable in comparison with other countries because of northern Sudan's low basic education coverage and retention, as well as low per-student spending at that level. Its Gini coefficient for education spending is more similar to the low-income than the middle-income countries in Sub-Saharan Africa. This finding shows that a sizeable share of a generation is excluded from any education at all or receives just a few years of schooling, and that per-student spending for basic education is comparatively low. Structural disparities could be reduced by improving access and completion rates in basic school (all other things being equal, 100 percent access and completion of basic school would reduce the Gini coefficient of education spending from 0.55 to 0.38) and by raising per-student spending at this leve.

The upper part of the education system is comparatively equitable in northern Sudan because of its high coverage and moderate per-student spending. However, table 4.10 compares these values to those for low- and middle-income Sub-Saharan African countries. Although the share of resources consumed by the 10 percent most educated (32 percent)

Table 4.10 Distribution of Public Spending on Education within a Cohort of Children, Northern Sudan Compared to Sub-Saharan Africa, 2008–09

Country	Gini coefficient	Percentage of public spending to 10 percent most educated
Northern Sudan (2008–09)	0.55	32
Cape Verde	—	25
Chad	—	67
Congo, Rep.	—	46
Ethiopia	—	65
Kenya	—	34
Morocco	—	26
Low-income-country average (2003)	0.52	43
Middle-income-country average (2003)	0.30	25

Source: Mingat and Majgaard 2010; UNESCO BREDA 2007.
Note: — = not available.

compares favorably to the average for low-income African countries (43 percent), it does not quite meet the mark of the middle-income countries (25 percent). This finding shows that secondary schooling and particularly higher education enjoy fairly high levels of coverage and that per-student spending is fairly moderate at these levels.

SUMMARY

The education system in northern Sudan is characterized by considerable disparities, although there are also encouraging signs that these gaps are diminishing. The following list summarizes, by order of importance, this chapter's analysis of regional, social, and structural disparities in the system:

- Very large gaps in school enrollment exist between rural and urban children. For example, urban children are 17 percentage points more likely than rural children to ever enroll in basic school. Within the rural segment of the population, girls are less likely than boys to enroll in school.
- Overall, more research is needed to identify the main barriers to access to schooling—whether they are associated with characteristics of the

- supply of schooling (such as distance to school, school fees, quality and relevance of schooling) or with weak demand for schooling related to poverty and opportunity costs.
- An estimated 1 million youth between ages 10 and 17 in northern Sudan have never attended basic school. This group needs support in the form of literacy programs if they are to become literate adults.
- The data on school performance of girls—after enrollment, are encouraging. The share of girls in school enrollments increases with rising levels of education, which indicates a better retention for girls once they are enrolled. This result holds even in rural areas.
- The 15 states can be divided into three groups based on their GERs across the three levels of general education. The five states with intermediate levels of GER are experiencing very strong growth in enrollments and schooling coverage. However, the five low-GER states—which are all postconflict states—are not seeing the same rapid progress and may need additional support. These states are Northern Darfur, Red Sea, Blue Nile, Southern Darfur, and Kassala.
- There is a need for more research about the rates of school enrollment of vulnerable groups—particularly nomads, IDPs, and orphans—and of the barriers to their school participation. The regional analysis, which shows that postconflict states are lagging behind other states, indicates that some of the vulnerable groups, particularly IDPs, are potentially at a serious disadvantage.
- All across northern Sudan, children access grade 1 at different ages, not necessarily at the prescribed age of 6. In Khartoum and River Nile states, they often access school before age 6, and in the more peripheral, postconflict states, most children access school after age 6.
- The education system in northern Sudan is more inequitable than the education systems in comparator countries, which are the middle-income countries of Sub-Saharan Africa and the Middle East and North Africa. Too many children within a cohort benefit minimally from public education spending in northern Sudan, whereas the 20 percent most educated within a cohort—which are essentially those who attain a university-level education—consume more than 60 percent of public education spending. Improving access to and completion of basic education would significantly reduce the inequality in the use of education resources and thereby close the gap in this indicator between northern Sudan and other middle-income countries.

ANNEX 4A: ENROLLMENT OF GIRLS IN EDUCATION IN NORTHERN SUDAN

Table 4A.1 Share of Girls in Total Enrollments, by State and Level of Education, 2008–09

State	Preschool	Basic	Secondary Academic	Secondary Technical	Higher
Northern	51	49	54	9	47
River Nile	51	47	55	20	62
Khartoum	49	50	52	22	55
Al Jazirah	51	47	53	15	68
Blue Nile	50	44	37	34	42
Sinnar	41	46	49	37	53
White Nile	49	46	49	37	52
North Kordofan	51	45	49	30	55
South Kordofan	45	45	42	0	58
Northern Darfur	52	46	42	39	69
Southern Darfur	36	43	41	7	51
Western Darfur	50	44	36	27	54
Red Sea	40	44	48	26	53
Kassala	51	42	49	30	60
Al Qadarif	46	45	47	33	60
All states	47	46	49	25	56

Source: FMoGE 2008–09 statistical yearbook.

ANNEX 4B: PROBABILITY OF CHILDREN EVER ENROLLING IN BASIC SCHOOL

Table 4B.1 Logistic Regression Results: Probability of Ever Enrolling in Basic School (Grade 1), by Location, Income, and Gender, circa 2005

Dependent variable	Probability of ever enrolling in school (access)
Constant	0.8278
Boy	0.6661***
Urban	1.5032***

(continued next page)

Table 4B.1 *(continued)*

Dependent variable	Probability of ever enrolling in school (access)
Wealth quintile 2 and 3 (second-poorest and middle quintile)	0.0647***
Wealth quintile 4 and 5 (richest two quintiles)	0.1133***
Memo items:	
Age group	Ages 11–15
Number of observations	10,959
"R^2" (Sommer'D statistic)	0.34

Source: Authors' analysis of the Sudan Household Health Survey 2006 (GoNU 2006).
*** Statistically significant at the 1% level.

NOTES

1. As in chapter 2, the GER is calculated by contrasting enrollment data from the 2008–09 school year with population data from the 2008 population census.

2. The range for basic school excludes those states for which it has not been possible to determine a realistic GER, because of problems with either enrollment or population data.

3. In table 4.1, Red Sea State and Southern Darfur State have been placed among the states with low schooling coverage based on a low basic school GER (about 40 percent) according to the yearbook data, although the 2006 Sudan Household Health Survey suggests that their schooling coverage is considerably higher (in the 70–90 percent range).

4. As mentioned earlier, household surveys are often more reliable sources of data on the effective rate of schooling coverage because they are not affected by multicohort effects or measurement errors in the school census or population data.

5. Although, as reported in chapter 2 and as follows, some data on enrollments in so-called IDP and nomadic schools are available; however, this information is not enough to determine rates of schooling coverage for these two groups because we don't have their population data and because some IDP children and nomadic children may be attending regular schools.

6. These data are from 2000 and were found in the World Bank EdStats database. The data are for a population of 15 years and older.

7. At birth, the natural range for the gender ratio is 100–106 boys per 100 girls. Among teens, the ratio of boys to girls is close to 100:100 in most populations, according to Das Gupta and others (2002).

8. The GPI is here calculated as GER girls/GER boys.

9. A rights-based, child-friendly school has two basic characteristics:
- It is child seeking—actively identifying excluded children to get them enrolled in school and included in learning; treating children as subjects with rights that the states are duty-bound to fulfill; and demonstrating, promoting, and helping to monitor the rights and well-being of all children in the community.
- It is child centered—acting in the best interests of the individual child, leading to the realization of the child's full potential, and concerned both

about the "whole" child (including her health, nutritional status, and well-being) and about what happens to that child (in her family and community) before she enters school and after she leaves it.

10. Poor children are as likely as rich children to remain in school once enrolled; this surprising result again suggests that income may be poorly determined in the survey.

11. A similar figure that shows the average for all of northern Sudan was provided in chapter 3 (figure 3.5).

12. The Gini coefficient is a measure of the inequality of distribution. It is calculated as the ratio of the area between the diagonal and the Lorenz curve to the area of the triangle beneath the diagonal. A value of zero expresses total equality and a value of one expresses maximum inequality.

REFERENCES

Das Gupta, M., World Bank Development Research Group, Public Services, and Rural Development. 2002. *Why Is Son Preference So Persistent in East and South Asia? A Cross-Country Study of China, India, and the Republic of Korea.* Policy Research Working Paper 2942. Washington, DC: World Bank.

FMoGE (Federal Ministry of General Education). 2008. "Baseline Survey on Basic Education in the Northern States of Sudan: Final Report June 2008." Khartoum. Online document available at http://planipolis.iiep.unesco.org/epiweb/E029336e.pdf

———. Various years. "Statistical Yearbooks." Khartoum.

GoNU (Government of National Unity) and GoSS (Government of Southern Sudan). 2006. *Sudan Household Health Survey (SHHS) 2006.* Khartoum/Juba: Central Bureau of Statistics and Southern Sudan Center for Census, Statistics and Evaluation.

Mingat, A., and Majgaard, K. 2010. *Education in Sub-Saharan Africa: A Comparative Analysis.* Washington, DC: World Bank.

MoEST/GoSS (Ministry of Education, Science, and Technology/Government of Southern Sudan). 2009. *A Report of the Study on Socio-Economic and Cultural Barriers to Schooling in South Sudan.* Juba: MoEST/GoSS & United Nations Children's Fund.

UNESCO BREDA (United Nations Educational, Scientific, and Cultural Organization Regional Office for Education in Africa). 2007. *Education for All in Africa 2007: Top Priority for Integrated Sector-Wide Policies.* Dakar + 7 Report. Dakar, Senegal: UNESCO BREDA. Available at http://www.poledakar.org/spip.php?article255.

CHAPTER 5

Service Delivery and Learning Outcomes in Basic Schools in Three States

This chapter focuses on the delivery of basic education services by the government and on student learning outcomes in government basic schools in Kassala, North Kordofan, and River Nile states. These three states were surveyed for this chapter, or more commonly known as the service delivery survey (SDS) in 2009, as part of the current report on the status of the education sector in northern Sudan. Both supply and demand factors affect student learning outcomes. On the supply side, school and classroom resources such as textbooks, chalkboards, class size, and teachers are necessary but not sufficient for student learning (Case and Deaton 1999; Das and others 2007). The effectiveness of service delivery—that is, how available resources are used—is also crucial to student learning outcomes (Mingat and Majgaard 2010). On the demand side, parental education and income and individual student characteristics affect learning outcomes (Glewwe and Jacoby 1994). Therefore, this chapter examines several specific issues: school and classroom resources and their use plus school management, which are all part of service delivery; student learning achievement, the ultimate objective of education systems; and selected factors outside of school that affect learning outcomes.[1]

The main purposes of the SDS are to gain an understanding of student learning outcomes, provide insights into education service delivery, and complement and add to existing studies on basic education in northern Sudan. Previous studies on basic education in this area provide useful information on the education system, but they do not assess student learning outcomes within the existing education system (EU 2008; FMoGE 2008).[2] Moreover, northern Sudan currently does not have an institutionalized learning assessment through which to monitor student learning.

Regular assessments of student learning levels are a useful tool for policy makers. Such assessments provide a guide both to how well the system is doing in promoting learning and, when coupled with a service delivery component, to factors that may contribute to or hinder the student learning process. Assessments can also be used to compare learning performance over time, across schools within a country, and internationally to inform priority setting and investment in education to ensure maximum learning outcomes in a climate of limited resources. The SDS conducted a learning assessment comprising both a mathematics and a reading component for grade 5 students in the three states to provide a snapshot of grade 5 student learning levels in the sample schools. (For details on the learning assessment, see the Student Learning Outcomes section later in this chapter.)

The three survey states were chosen to provide examples of states with high, intermediate, and low performance levels on the selected basic education indicators shown in table 5.1. For basic education, River Nile State has a high gross enrollment rate (GER), gross intake rate (GIR), primary completion rate (PCR), and retention rate; spends significantly more on

Table 5.1 Basic Education Indicators for the Three Surveyed States and the Northern Sudan Average, 2008–09

Indicator	Kassala	North Kordofan	River Nile	Northern Sudan average
Number of students enrolled	182,372	529,762	183,605	n.a.
Gross enrollment rate (percent)	46	78	89	72
Gross intake rate in grade 1 (percent)	80	76	92	80
Grade 8 completion rate (percent)	25	54	70	54
Retention rate (percent)	31	72	76	68
Percentage of girls in total enrollment	42	45	47	46
Percentage of students enrolled in nomadic schools	17	2	4	3
Per-student spending (SDG)	298	174	426	240
Student-teacher ratio	31	42	22	33

Source: FMoGE 2008–09 statistical yearbook; staff estimates.
Note: n.a. = not applicable; SDG = Sudanese pounds.

education per student; and has a lower student-teacher ratio (STR) than the national average. By comparison, for North Kordofan State, the selected education indicators are quite similar to the national average. In Kassala State, the gross enrollment, completion, and retention rates are all much lower than the national average and those of the two other states. The share of students enrolled in nomadic schools in Kassala is notably larger (17 percent), which may partly explain the relatively low retention rate and high per-student spending.

The rest of the chapter unfolds in logical order. It begins by describing the sample. Because the school and classroom environment provides the context for student learning, the subsequent section describes and discusses the results for this indicator based on the data collected by the SDS, and when possible, the findings are compared with those of previous studies. Then student learning outcomes across the three states, internationally, and for rural/peri-urban and urban schools are examined and compared before a discussion of the potential reasons for differences in student performance, in addition to school and classroom factors, begins. The penultimate section provides a brief review of student performance in secondary education, which was not covered by the SDS because the United Nations Educational, Scientific, and Cultural Organization (UNESCO) and the United Nations Children's Fund (UNICEF) are currently conducting a similar study of this subsector. Finally, the main findings are summarized.

SAMPLE DESCRIPTION

After the three states were chosen, 195 government basic schools were selected for the sample, equivalent to 5–7 percent of government schools in each state. Cost and time constraints dictated the use of a convenience sample, and mainly single-sex schools were included, which means that it is not possible to generalize the survey findings outside the schools and grade 5 students in the sample.

To collect the data, the SDS used five questionnaires. A head teacher questionnaire contained school-level questions. A classroom questionnaire was based on enumerators' observations of one grade 3, one grade 4, and one grade 5 classroom in each school. A teacher questionnaire asked three to six teachers in each school about their backgrounds and teaching. And a student background questionnaire and learning assessment consisted of one mathematics and one reading component, and was administered to 20 students in each school.

Table 5.2 presents the sample information. Of the 195 basic schools surveyed, 44 were in Kassala, 99 in North Kordofan, and 52 in River Nile. The head teacher in each school was interviewed to collect school-level data. In addition, 232 teachers in Kassala, 484 teachers in North Kordofan, and 296 teachers in River Nile were interviewed. The final student sample consisted of 3,893 students, and all of these students completed the background questionnaire and learning assessment.[3] Finally, three classrooms (one grade 3, one grade 4, and one grade 5) were observed by the enumerators in each of the 195 schools for a total of 585 observed classrooms.

Table 5.3 shows the shares of rural/peri-urban and urban schools in the sample. In Kassala, 43 percent of sample schools are rural or peri-urban and 57 percent are urban. The corresponding shares for North Kordofan are 42 percent rural or peri-urban and 58 percent urban, and for River Nile, 52 percent rural or peri-urban and 48 percent urban. The rural/peri-urban and urban classifications are based on the interviewed head teachers' categorizations of their schools. Urban schools are those reported as being located in an urban area (that is, in the main locality). For the purposes of the analysis in this chapter, the peri-urban and rural

Table 5.2 Sample Information for the Three Northern Sudan States Chosen, 2009

Basic education[a]	Kassala	North Kordofan	River Nile	Three states (average)
Number of schools				
Total for state	630	1,863	754	3,247
Sample	44	99	52	195
Sample as percentage of total	7.0	5.3	6.9	(6.0)
Number of teachers				
Total for state	5,468	12,445	8,404	26,317
Sample	232	484	296	1,012
Sample as percentage of total	4.2	3.9	3.5	(3.8)
Tested	88	198	103	389
Number of grade 5 students				
Total for state	16,943	62,887	21,840	101,670
Sample	878	1,977	1,038	3,893
Sample as percentage of total	5.2	3.1	4.8	(3.8)
Number of observed classrooms[b]	132	297	156	585

Source: Service delivery survey; FMoGE 2008–09 statistical yearbook.
a. Government schools only.
b. One grade 3, one grade 4, and one grade 5 classroom were observed in each school.

Table 5.3 Rural/Peri-urban and Urban Composition of the School Sample, 2009

State	Percentage of schools		Total number of schools
	Rural/peri-urban	Urban	
Kassala	43	57	44
North Kordofan	42	58	99
River Nile	52	48	52

Source: Service delivery survey.

schools (located outside of the locality center) were grouped together because they are very similar in terms of school characteristics and student learning outcomes.[4]

CHARACTERISTICS OF GOVERNMENT BASIC SCHOOLS IN THE SAMPLE

The characteristics of schools and the classroom environment influence student learning. If schools and classrooms do not have certain minimum resources—for example, a teacher present in the classroom and textbooks available—little or no learning will take place. However, even when resources are available, little learning may occur if these are not used effectively. Thus, this section describes the characteristics of the schools and classrooms in the sample schools to provide a picture of resource availability and use across rural/peri-urban and urban schools and across the three surveyed states. Throughout this section, to capture the variation in basic school characteristics and given the nature of the sample, the results are presented separately for each state because direct comparisons across states are not appropriate, and they are presented for rural/peri-urban and urban schools within each state.

SCHOOL INFRASTRUCTURE

The SDS focused on classroom resources directly related to the learning process. However, the 2008 baseline survey (FMoGE 2008) provides insights into school infrastructure, such as access to water and toilets, which also affect learning, even if indirectly. A total of 54 percent of basic schools in Kassala, 24 percent in North Kordofan, and 76 percent in River Nile received their drinking water from taps; and 11 percent, 32 percent, and 6 percent, respectively, received drinking water from wells. Most schools had toilets, but a large share of these toilets were in need of repair or replacement, and a large number were only temporary (FMoGE 2008). In basic schools in North Kordofan and River Nile, for example, more than 40 percent of toilets were in need of repair or replacement (FMoGE 2008).

SCHOOL AND CLASSROOM ENVIRONMENT

As already noted, the classroom environment directly influences student learning. Therefore, the SDS collected data on equipment and learning materials based on classroom observations in each sample school, where three classrooms (one grade 3, one grade 4, and one grade 5) were observed by the enumerators, who then recorded the information.

Availability of Equipment and Learning Materials. The chalkboard remains one of the most important tools for teaching in northern Sudan, especially given the lack of textbooks. Table 5.4 presents data on the availability of chalkboards and desks and the condition of the chalkboards. Among the urban sample schools, almost all classrooms had chalkboards: 100 percent in Kassala and River Nile and 97 percent in North Kordofan, but many of these chalkboards were not in usable condition. In Kassala, 9 percent of chalkboards were not usable; in North Kordofan 21 percent and in River Nile 16 percent were not usable.

The situation is generally worse in rural and peri-urban schools. Of the observed classrooms, 89 percent in Kassala, 94 percent in North

Table 5.4 Availability of Chalkboards and Desks in Observed Classrooms, 2009
percent

State/location	Classrooms with chalkboard	Chalkboards in usable condition[a]	Students with desk
Kassala			
Urban	100	91	83
Rural/peri-urban	89	83	73
North Kordofan			
Urban	97	79	34
Rural/peri-urban	94	78	17
River Nile			
Urban	100	84	64
Rural/peri-urban	98	77	38

Source: Service delivery survey.
Note: These data are averages based on observations of one grade 3, one grade 4, and one grade 5 classroom in each school.
a. This category is the percentage of chalkboards in usable condition in classrooms that have a chalkboard.

Kordofan, and 98 percent in River Nile had chalkboards, but of these chalkboards, 17 percent, 22 percent, and 23 percent, respectively, were not in usable condition. The findings are similar to those of the 2008 baseline survey, which did not distinguish between rural and urban schools but found that more than 40 percent of chalkboards were in need of repair or replacement (FMoGE 2008).

Based on the 2009 SDS, on average, 83 percent, 34 percent, and 64 percent of students in urban schools in Kassala, North Kordofan, and River Nile, respectively, had a desk. The shares of students with a desk were lower in rural and peri-urban schools, that is, 73 percent, 17 percent, and 38 percent, respectively. This finding means, for instance, that less than one in five students in the rural/peri-urban sample schools in North Kordofan had a desk and the remaining students sat on a chair without a desk, or on the floor or ground. These results are in line with the 2008 baseline survey, which found that more than 40 percent of students in North Kordofan were seated on the ground (FMoGE 2008).

In addition to a usable chalkboard and desks for students, a classroom conducive to learning needs to have textbooks. The official policy on the student–textbook ratio is 2:1 (FMoGE 2008). However, the share of students with textbooks in the observed classrooms in the three surveyed states was generally small. Students in observed classrooms in River Nile were more likely to have textbooks, with the average student–textbook ratio close to 2:1 for mathematics and 1.6:1 for reading, which is in line with or better than the official policy. The average student–textbook ratio in Kassala was 3:1 for mathematics and 2.5:1 for reading, which is higher than the official policy. Students in observed classrooms in North Kordofan had it the worst: the average student–textbook ratio in rural/peri-urban classrooms was 9:1 and in urban classrooms was 5:1. Considering that education councils also provided textbooks for students in several of these schools (see table 5.5), the higher-than-recommended average student–textbook ratios in Kassala and the very high ratios in North Kordofan point to a serious failure of the public education system, with negative consequences for student learning.

Another study, based on visits to 71 government basic schools in seven states also documents the lack of textbooks when it found an average student–textbook ratio of 4:1 (EU 2008). That study also discovered significant differences in textbook availability across states, with basic schools in River Nile being particularly well provided for in terms of textbooks, similar to the findings of the SDS.

In contrast, the vast majority of students in the observed classrooms had other learning materials. In each of the three states and in both

Table 5.5 Availability of Textbooks in Observed Classrooms
percent

State/location	Students in grade 3, 4, and 5 classrooms with textbooks	
	Mathematics	Reading
Kassala		
Urban	33	43
Rural/peri-urban	32	39
North Kordofan		
Urban	11	21
Rural/peri-urban	11	18
River Nile		
Urban	56	64
Rural	58	61

Source: Service delivery survey.
Note: These data are averages based on observations of one grade 3, one grade 4, and one grade 5 classroom in each school.

rural/peri-urban and urban schools, between 90 and 99 percent of students had notebooks for mathematics and reading and had pens and pencils. Unlike textbooks, these learning materials are generally provided by families or education councils.

Instruction Characteristics. It is difficult for students to learn without access to textbooks and more challenging for teachers to teach the required syllabus. To gauge syllabus coverage, the enumerators recorded approximately how much of the syllabus had been covered at the time of their visit, which was at a point about 80 percent into the school year. Thus, 80 percent of the syllabus should have been covered by then. However, teachers in North Kordofan were on strike during the month before the SDS was conducted, which implies a loss of instruction time to be considered when comparing the findings presented in table 5.6. In addition, eight of the sample schools in Kassala started their school year in April rather than June, so were potentially even further behind in terms of syllabus coverage.

Average syllabus coverage in mathematics for grade 3, 4, and 5 classrooms was 76 percent in sample schools in Kassala, 67 percent in North Kordofan, and 78 percent in River Nile. For reading, average syllabus coverage was generally somewhat higher but followed the same state and rural/peri-urban versus urban patterns.

Going beyond averages reveals notable variations in syllabus coverage across schools. In about half of the schools in Kassala and River Nile,

Table 5.6 Syllabus Coverage in Observed Classrooms, 2009

State/location	Percentage of schools for which average share of mathematics syllabus coverage is			Average mathematics syllabus coverage	Percentage of schools for which average share of reading syllabus coverage is			Average reading syllabus coverage
	40–59	60–79	>80		40–59	60–79	>80	
Kassala								
Urban	4	52	44	78	4	40	56	79
Rural/peri-urban	11	37	53	74	0	33	67	80
North Kordofan[a]								
Urban	9	71	18	70	6	59	33	73
Rural/peri-urban	37	51	12	64	33	50	17	66
River Nile[b]								
Urban	0	29	67	79	0	16	80	81
Rural/peri-urban	0	48	52	78	7	44	48	78

Source: Service delivery survey.
Note: These data are averages based on observations of one grade 3, one grade 4, and one grade 5 classroom in each school.
a. In 2 percent of observed classrooms in urban schools in North Kordofan, less than 40 percent of the syllabus had been covered, which is not shown in the table.
b. In 4 percent of observed classrooms in urban schools in River Nile, less than 40 percent of the syllabus had been covered, which is not shown in the table.

80 percent or more of the syllabus had been covered at the time of the visits, both in mathematics and in reading (table 5.6). The vast majority of the remaining schools had covered 60–79 percent of the syllabus. Syllabus coverage was generally lower in rural and peri-urban classrooms than in urban classrooms. For example, 4 percent of urban schools in Kassala had covered only 40–59 percent of the syllabus compared with 11 percent of rural and peri-urban schools. These schools in North Kordofan did even less well, with 37 percent and 33 percent, respectively, having covered only 40–59 percent of the syllabus for mathematics and reading, which is low even after taking into account teaching time lost because of the teacher strike. Rural and peri-urban schools are of particular concern because a complete catch-up in terms of syllabus coverage would be nearly impossible.

Both the lack of textbooks and the failure to cover the complete syllabus affect the amount of instruction to which students are exposed.[5] Two other factors that also influence exposure to instruction are average class size and student attendance. The average student–teacher ratio for basic education was 31:1 in Kassala, 42:1 in North Kordofan, and 22:1 in River Nile (see chapter 7, on finance). These ratios are below or close to the benchmark of 40:1 for basic education prescribed by the Education for All Fast-Track Initiative, and they are much lower than the average student–teacher ratios for neighboring countries such as Ethiopia and Kenya (also see chapter 6, on teacher management). However, in many of the sample schools, although student–teacher ratios were relatively low, class sizes tended to be fairly large.

The data on class size presented in table 5.7 are based on the enumerators' recording of the number of students present in the three classrooms observed in each sample school on the day of the school visit. Therefore, if many students were absent on the day of the school visit, these class sizes would be smaller than true class sizes. However, the majority of students were present in the majority of schools on the day of the visit, which suggests that the class size data provide a fair approximation of actual class size.

Generally, class sizes are larger in urban than in rural schools, which makes sense given the lower population density in rural areas. The average class size in the observed classrooms was 55 students in urban sample schools compared with 44 in rural/peri-urban schools in Kassala, 50 in urban schools compared with only 28 in rural/peri-urban sample schools in North Kordofan, and 48 in urban schools and 38 in rural/peri-urban schools in River Nile (table 5.7).

That rural class sizes tend to be smaller than urban class sizes is also supported by the findings in the 2008 baseline survey (FMoGE 2008). To

Table 5.7   Class Size in Observed Classrooms, 2009

State/location	Percentage of observed classrooms with class size of				Average class size
	15–34	35–50	51–65	>65	
Kassala					
Urban	0	36	44	20	55
Rural/peri-urban	47	11	21	21	44
North Kordofan					
Urban	26	25	26	23	50
Rural/peri-urban	71	19	10	0	28
River Nile					
Urban	20	32	32	16	48
Rural/peri-urban	41	44	15	0	38

Source: Service delivery survey.
Note: These data are averages based on observations of one grade 3, one grade 4, and one grade 5 classroom in each school.

take two extreme examples, no urban sample schools in Kassala had class sizes smaller than 34 students, whereas 47 percent of rural schools did; and in River Nile, 16 percent of urban sample schools had class sizes larger than 65 students, whereas no rural schools did.

Student absenteeism reduces the amount of student-teacher contact time, which in turn affects learning (the issue of school functional days is discussed below, and teacher attendance is discussed in chapter 6, on teacher management). Based on the classroom observations, student attendance in the sample schools was high in Kassala and River Nile but lower in North Kordofan, and it was similar across rural/peri-urban and urban schools (table 5.8). Between 92 and 95 percent of students in both rural/peri-urban and urban schools were present on the day of the school visits in Kassala, 84–85 percent were present in North Kordofan, and 98 percent were present in River Nile. Again, the teacher strike in North Kordofan the month before the SDS might have affected attendance if students and parents were uncertain as to whether the schools were open again after the strike.

The 2008 baseline survey investigated student absenteeism by asking teachers what they considered the main reasons for students not coming to school. The most frequently cited reasons were health, bad weather, lack of textbooks, teacher absenteeism, and lack of school uniforms (FMoGE 2008). This finding relates to the issue of the quality of education. If parents think their children are unlikely to learn while in school (for example, because of the lack of textbooks and teachers being absent), then arguably they are less likely to send them to school. Further study is needed to understand if the observed higher student absenteeism in

Table 5.8 Average Student Attendance in Observed Classrooms, 2009
percent

State/location	Students present in observed classrooms on day of school visit
Kassala	
Urban	95
Rural/peri-urban	92
North Kordofan	
Urban	84
Rural/peri-urban	85
River Nile	
Urban	98
Rural/peri-urban	98

Source: Service delivery survey.
Note: These data are averages based on observations of one grade 3, one grade 4, and one grade 5 classroom in each school.

North Kordofan may be because of the lower, or perceived lower, quality of education in these schools.

SCHOOL MANAGEMENT

The previous sections examined the availability of resources in the sample schools, whereas this section examines how the existing resources are used. The data presented here are based on interviews with the head teacher at each of the 195 sample schools.

School Functional Days. Directly related to resource management is the number of days a school operates in a year. If a school is closed when it should be open, then students receive fewer teaching hours, with detrimental results for learning outcomes.[6] The official school year in northern Sudan is 210 days per year (FMoGE 2008). For reference, the average official school year in primary education across countries is 200 days, with a range of 175–210 days (UNESCO 2007). The average length of the official school year reported by head teachers in the sample schools in the three states lies within the range of 200–214 days. However, these are averages, which means that some head teachers report a notably shorter and others a notably longer school year than the official 210 days. This finding suggests that many school heads are not aware of the official policy of 210 school days per year.

In the sample schools, the average length of the actual school year is shorter than the official school year in each state. The final column in table 5.9 shows the difference between the official school year of 210 days and the average actual school year. In River Nile, the average number of actual school days is close to the official number of days in both rural/peri-urban schools and urban schools (7 and 5 days' difference, respectively). But for Kassala and North Kordofan, the average actual school year is substantially shorter than the official school year—about 26 days shorter in Kassala and North Kordofan.[7] The 2008 baseline survey also found that the actual school year was shorter than the official school year in the majority of basic schools (FMoGE 2008).

Overall, this finding implies that students are missing, on average, more than one month of teaching each year, which has notable implications for student learning outcomes. To ameliorate this situation, policies need to be put into place that clearly communicate official policy on the length of the official school year, make up for lost days, and enable schools to be open as intended.

School Record Keeping: Student Enrollment and Performance. To assess resource needs and effectively manage these resources, schools need to

Table 5.9 Official and Actual Number of School Days in the Academic Year, State Averages, 2009

	Reported number of school days		
State/location	Official	Actual	Difference in average official (210 days) and actual
Kassala			
Urban	208	186	24
Rural/peri-urban	202	182	28
North Kordofan			
Urban	211	184	26
Rural/peri-urban	212	184	26
River Nile			
Urban	210	203	7
Rural/peri-urban	212	205	5

Source: Service delivery survey.
Note: These data are based on the responses by the head teachers interviewed in each sample school.

have up-to-date information on students (record keeping on teacher-related issues is discussed in the chapter 6, on teacher management). The majority of sample schools (80–84 percent) were able to show their student enrollment records to the enumerators during the school visits, and there was no notable difference between rural/peri-urban and urban schools in Kassala and River Nile (table 5.10).[8] In North Kordofan, 98 percent of rural and peri-urban sample schools could show their records of student enrollment compared with 91 percent of urban sample schools.

Many schools also keep records of student performance based on their own continuous assessment of student learning throughout the academic year. School record keeping on student performance was weaker than record keeping on enrollments in North Kordofan and River Nile, and was much weaker in Kassala. In River Nile and North Kordofan, the majority of rural/peri-urban and urban schools (89–95 percent) were able to show their student performance records on the day of the school visits. In Kassala, only 58 percent of the rural/peri-urban sample schools and 76 percent of the urban schools could show their student performance records to the enumerators.

Education Councils. The participation of communities and parents in providing support to schools, often through education councils, is strongly

Table 5.10 School Record Keeping on Student Enrollment and Performance, State Averages, 2009
percent

State/location	Schools able to show records of student	
	Enrollment	Performance
Kassala		
Urban	84	76
Rural/peri-urban	84	58
North Kordofan		
Urban	91	88
Rural/peri-urban	98	95
River Nile		
Urban	80	92
Rural/peri-urban	81	89

Source: Service delivery survey.
Note: These data are based on the head teacher in each school showing the relevant records to the enumerator.

encouraged by the government. Typically, education councils consist of elected parents, the head teacher, teachers, and selected members from the local community. The main tasks of education councils are to raise and provide funds for school construction and maintenance, teacher housing and supplementary payments, and learning materials, and to determine fees (EU 2008).

Table 5.11 presents the main characteristics of education councils in the sample schools. In the three states, 95–100 percent of the sample schools had education councils. Of these education councils, 84–96 percent had an executive committee. Most of the committees held one or more meetings during the previous month, indicating that they are very active. This information is further corroborated by the 2008 baseline survey, in which 90 percent of the schools reported that there was cooperation between the school and the education council, and 85 percent reported that the education council was effective (FMoGE 2008). Between 50 percent and 75 percent of the sample schools also received financial or in-kind support from the education councils (table 5.11).

Education councils buy textbooks and learning materials and help teachers in the classroom. In 15–23 percent of the sample schools, the education council helped teachers in the classroom; in 4–24 percent of schools, the council purchased textbooks; and in 32–72 percent of

Table 5.11 Characteristics of Education Councils, State Averages, 2009
percent

State/location	Schools that receive support from education council	Schools with education council	Education councils with executive committee	Executive committees that held one or more meetings last month
Kassala				
Urban	68	100	84	72
Rural/peri-urban	53	100	84	79
North Kordofan				
Urban	60	98	90	56
Rural/peri-urban	74	95	93	86
River Nile				
Urban	56	96	88	64
Rural/peri-urban	63	96	96	67

Source: Service delivery survey.
Note: These data are based on the responses from the head teachers interviewed in each school.

schools, it bought learning materials (table 5.12). This suggests that in many schools, education councils are complementing insufficient government education spending (also see chapter 7, on education finance).

In many of the sample schools, education councils supplement teacher salaries. For instance, in North Kordofan, the executive committees helped to pay teacher salaries in 20 percent of the rural/peri-urban sample schools, and in River Nile, it was 15 percent of salaries in rural/peri-urban schools. It is noteworthy that North Kordofan also has a large share of volunteer teachers (see chapter 6, on teacher management), implying that there may be a teacher shortage in rural schools that is being met by education councils' paying volunteer teachers to fill the gaps. Education councils may also be topping off salaries to attract teachers to schools in remote areas, but more evidence is needed to better understand exactly which types of teachers education councils are paying for and why.

However, not only do school and classroom resources and their use affect student learning outcomes, but also family background and household characteristics matter. The next section examines household characteristics and learning outcomes based on the data collected by the SDS.

Table 5.12 School Support Provided by Educational Councils, State Averages, 2009
percent

	Schools in which the education councils			
State/location	Help teachers in the classroom	Buy textbooks	Buy learning materials	Pay teacher salaries
Kassala				
Urban	16	16	72	4
Rural/peri-urban	16	11	32	0
North Kordofan				
Urban	23	14	40	0
Rural/peri-urban	21	24	67	21
River Nile				
Urban	16	4	44	0
Rural/peri-urban	15	7	56	15

Source: Service delivery survey.
Note: These data are based on the responses from the head teachers interviewed in each school.

STUDENT LEARNING OUTCOMES

The findings in this section are based on the data collected by the student background questionnaire and the learning assessment completed by 20 grade 5 students in each sample school. The section begins by describing the two learning assessments used to test student learning outcomes in the three states. It then presents the findings on learning outcomes for the sample of students before providing an international comparison and examining differences in learning outcomes among boys and girls, respectively, in rural/peri-urban and urban schools. Finally, potential reasons at the household level for differences in learning outcomes are explored.

ASSESSMENTS AND FINDINGS

The learning assessment administered to the students consisted of a mathematics component with 30 questions and a reading component with 25 questions, which the students were given 90 minutes to complete.[9] The mathematics questions were selected from the 1995 and 2003 Trends in International Mathematics and Science Study (TIMSS) grade 4 assessment, and the reading questions were taken from the 1991 and 2001 Progress in International Reading Literacy Study (PIRLS) grade 4 assessment. All questions included in the assessment were reviewed by the SDS Steering Committee to ensure suitability given the national curriculum. An advantage of using questions from the TIMSS and PIRLS is the potential for international comparisons of student learning achievements. However, students in northern Sudan were assessed in grade 5 instead of grade 4 because the SDS Steering Committee considered it more appropriate given the post-conflict situation, which needs to be taken into account for the purpose of the international comparisons.

The average student in the sample for the three states only answered 34 percent of the mathematics and 39 percent of the reading questions correctly (figure 5.1). This is low, especially considering that the questions are multiple choice. With four answer options, if a student simply guessed, he or she would respond correctly 25 percent of the time.[10] The lowest scores in both mathematics and reading were zero, and no student answered all questions on either component correctly. Of the 3,893 students who took the learning assessment, the vast majority of students (84 percent for mathematics and 72 percent for reading) answered less than half the questions correctly, further underlining the fact that student learning outcomes are very weak. Finally, in general, students performed better on the reading than on the mathematics component of the learning assessment.

Figure 5.1 Grade 5 Student Learning Assessment Scores in Mathematics and Reading in Kassala, North Kordofan, and River Nile, 2009
percent

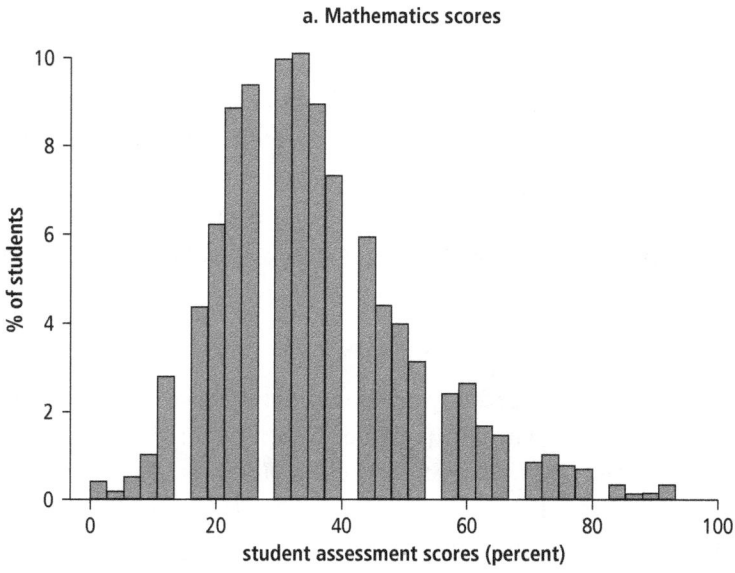

a. Mathematics scores

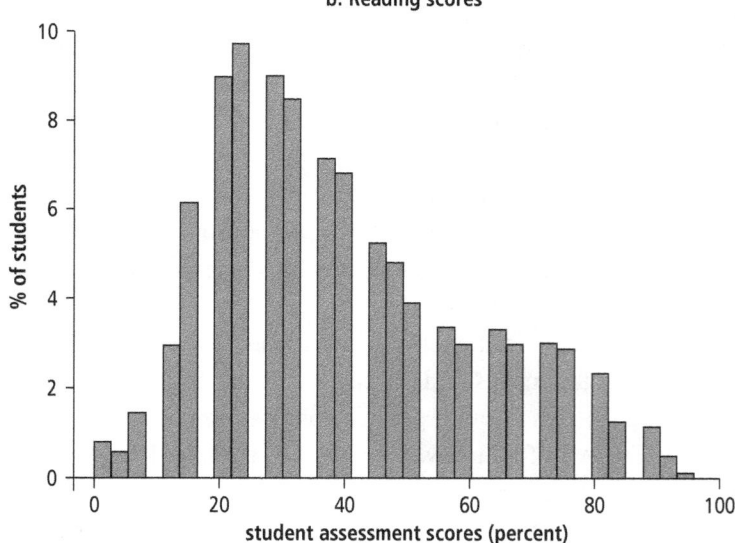

b. Reading scores

Source: Service delivery survey.

Table 5.13 shows the summary statistics for the grade 5 student scores on the learning assessment for the each of the three surveyed states. Although the student scores lie within roughly the same 0–96 percent range for all the states, the average scores were highest in Kassala, with

Table 5.13 Grade 5 Student Learning Assessment Scores in Mathematics and Reading, 2009
percent

	Student learning assessment scores							
	Mathematics				Reading			
State	Average	Standard deviation	Lowest	Highest	Average	Standard deviation	Lowest	Highest
Kassala	45	17	3	93	53	21	4	96
North Kordofan	31	13	0	90	31	15	0	92
River Nile	39	15	0	93	45	21	0	96

Source: Service delivery survey.
Note: The maximum score is 100 percent (all questions answered correctly).

45 percent for mathematics and 53 percent for reading. These scores compare to 39 percent for mathematics and 45 percent for reading in River Nile, and 31 percent for both mathematics and reading in North Kordofan. However, these scores are simple averages, which do not account for differences in school and classroom resources or for student background.

INTERNATIONAL COMPARISON OF STUDENT PERFORMANCE

The learning assessment scores for students in northern Sudan cannot be compared directly with those of students in other countries because the former were assessed using a subset of questions from the full versions of the TIMSS and PIRLS. Instead, to enable an international comparison, the shares of students in northern Sudan that answered each question on the mathematics component correctly are compared with the corresponding shares of students in Morocco, Singapore, and Tunisia, and on the reading component, compared with the corresponding shares in Benin and Singapore. Not all 30 mathematics questions and all 25 reading questions were used in the learning assessments in these countries. Therefore, figure 5.2 shows only the 24 questions of the mathematics assessment that were asked in Morocco, Northern Sudan, Singapore, and Tunisia; and figure 5.3 shows only the 24 questions of the reading assessment that were asked in Benin, northern Sudan, and Singapore.

Figure 5.2 illustrates that students in northern Sudan performed similarly to their counterparts in Morocco and Tunisia in terms of the relative number of mathematics questions students answered correctly. However, compared with Singapore, one of the top-performing TIMSS countries,

Figure 5.2 International Comparison of Student Performance in Mathematics between Morocco, Northern Sudan, Singapore, and Tunisia, 2008–09

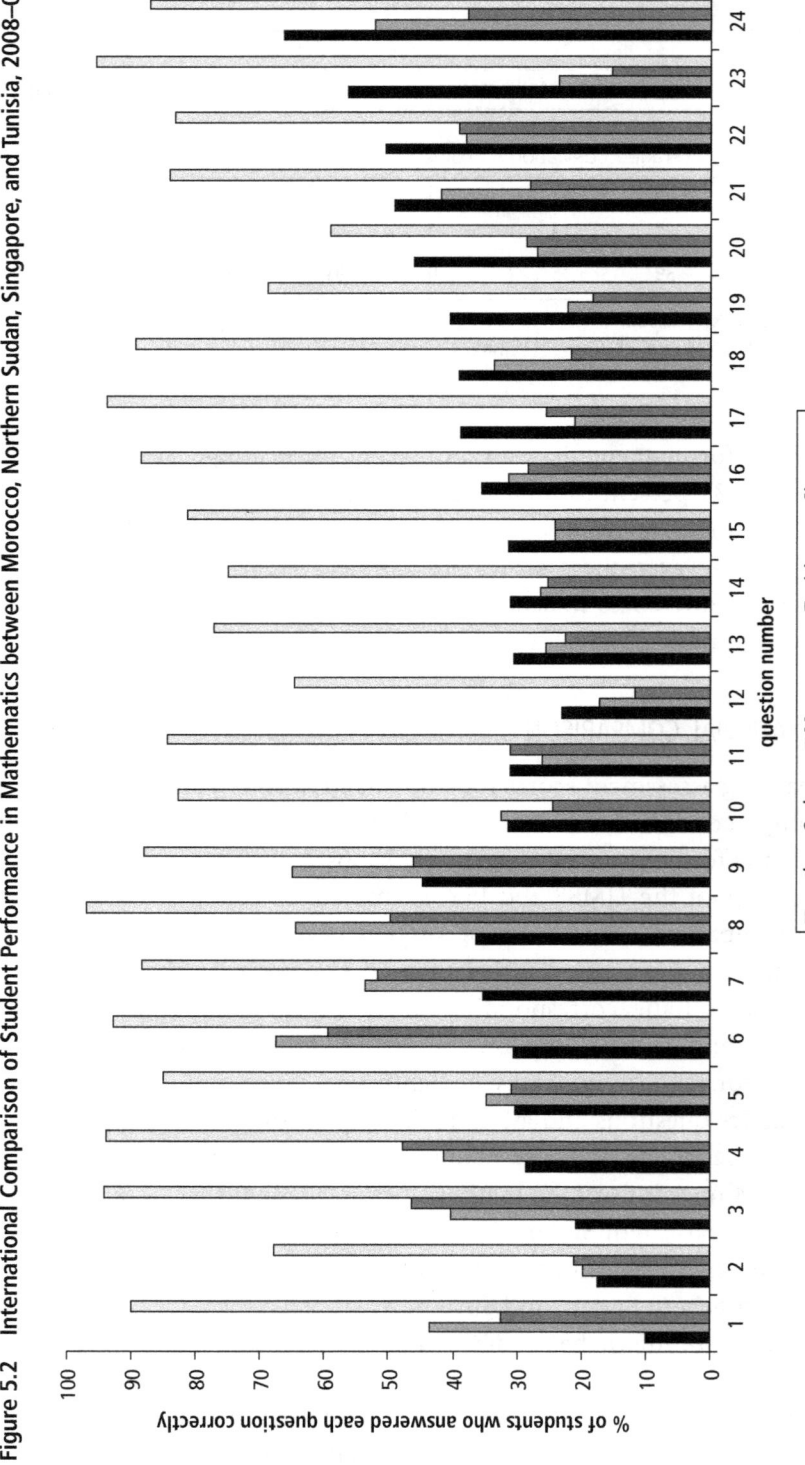

Source: IAEEA 2008; service delivery survey.

Figure 5.3 International Comparison of Student Performance in Reading between Benin, Northern Sudan, and Singapore, 2008–09

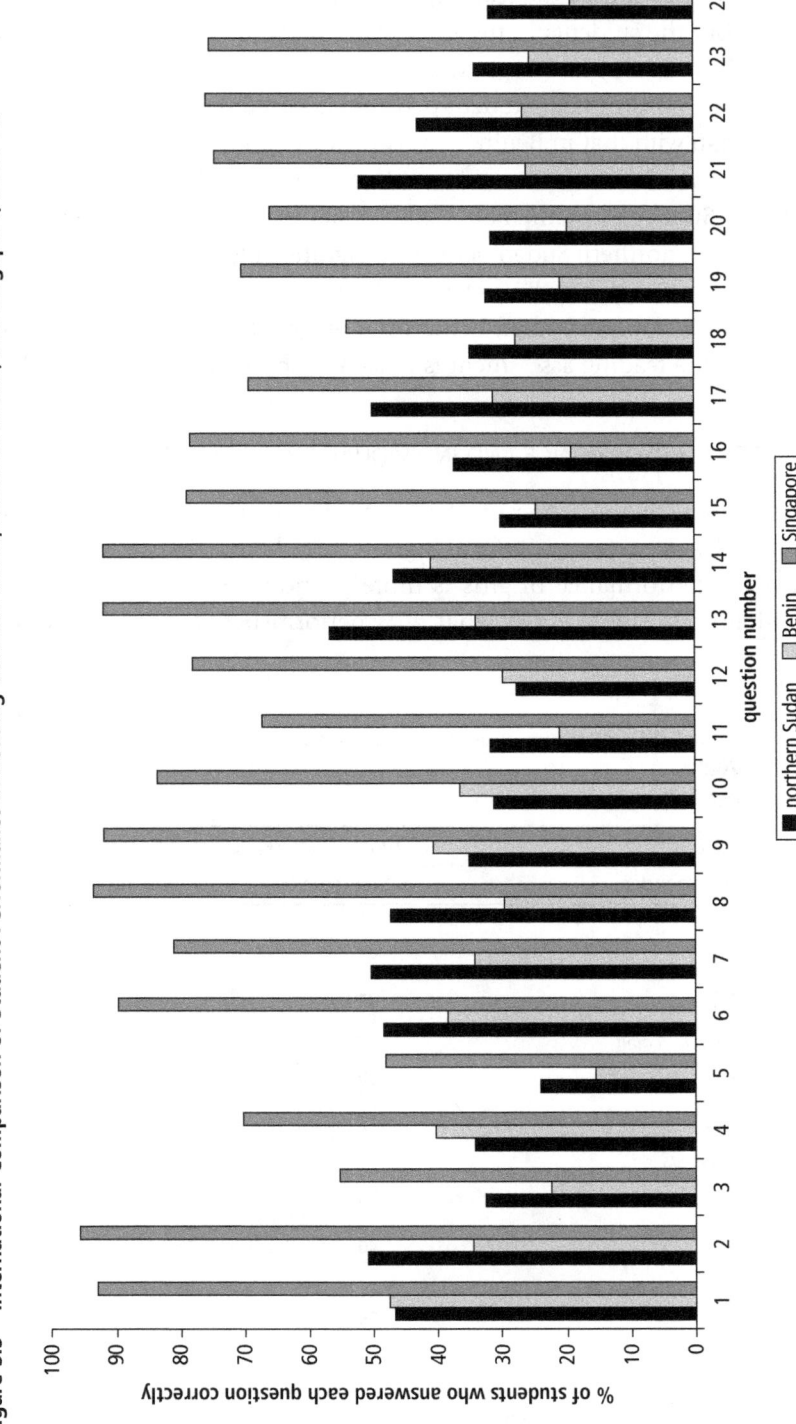

Source: IAEEA 2008; service delivery survey.

students in northern Sudan performed significantly worse. Moreover, as discussed previously, the learning assessments are geared to grade 4 students, but the students in the three states in northern Sudan were tested in grade 5, so they had approximately one additional year of schooling.

Figure 5.3 compares student performance in the three states of northern Sudan with that in Benin, a low-income country, which administered the same reading component to students also in grade 5, and again, Singapore. Similar to mathematics, the results for reading show that tested students in northern Sudan performed significantly worse compared with students in Singapore. But relative to students in Benin, the students in northern Sudan performed better on average. Overall, student performance on the reading assessment is weak and shows low learning levels.

STUDENT PERFORMANCE AND INDIVIDUAL CHARACTERISTICS

Examining student scores on the learning assessment by gender, we see that girls, on average, perform significantly better than boys, and the stronger performance of girls is more pronounced in reading than in mathematics (table 5.14). That girls perform better than boys (when

Table 5.14 Average Student Learning Assessment Scores, by Gender, 2009
percent

State/gender	Student learning assessment scores	
	Mathematics	Reading
Kassala		
Boys	43	51
Girls	47	54
North Kordofan		
Boys	30	29
Girls	32	33
River Nile		
Boys	38	43
Girls	40	48
Three-state average		
Boys	35	38
Girls	37	41

Source: Service delivery survey.
Note: The maximum score is 100 percent (all questions answered correctly).

they have equal access to education) is a general finding across both developing and developed countries and is generally linked to attitudes toward learning (EFA 2006).

To capture the relative wealth of the assessed students' families, an asset index was constructed based on the students' responses to which of the following assets were present in their homes: refrigerator, electricity, tap water, TV, radio, computer, mobile phone, gas or electric cooker, and car.[11] Figure 5.4 shows the average student scores on the mathematics and reading components of the learning assessment by wealth as measured by the asset index. For both components, students among the richest 20 percent performed better on average than students in the middle 60 percent, who in turn performed better than students among the poorest 20 percent. That is, students from richer households on average tend to perform better in both mathematics and reading than students from poorer households.

Another main determinant of student learning is parents' education. Average student mathematics and reading scores and the education level of fathers are presented in figure 5.5.[12] On average, students whose fathers have completed higher education scored better on both the mathematics and reading components, but there is no significant difference in performance between students whose fathers have some or have completed basic education and those whose fathers have completed secondary education, except in River Nile State. The results for mothers' education level are highly similar to those for fathers' education level, so they are not shown here.[13]

Thus, in line with existing studies on learning achievement, the SDS findings indicate that family background variables such as wealth and parental education and household characteristics including location are related to student learning outcomes.

SECONDARY EDUCATION EXAMINATION RESULTS

This final section of the chapter provides only a brief overview of pass rates for secondary school examinations (which leads to the Sudan Secondary School Certificate) because UNESCO and UNICEF are currently conducting a study on secondary education in northern Sudan. Their results should be able to complement these findings and enable further analysis of this subsector.

The total number of candidates from general, vocational, and religious secondary schools sitting for the Secondary School Certificate examinations increased from about 260,000 in 2004 to 363,000 in 2008 (BoSE 2009). In

Figure 5.4 Average Student Performance in Mathematics and Reading, by Household Wealth, 2009

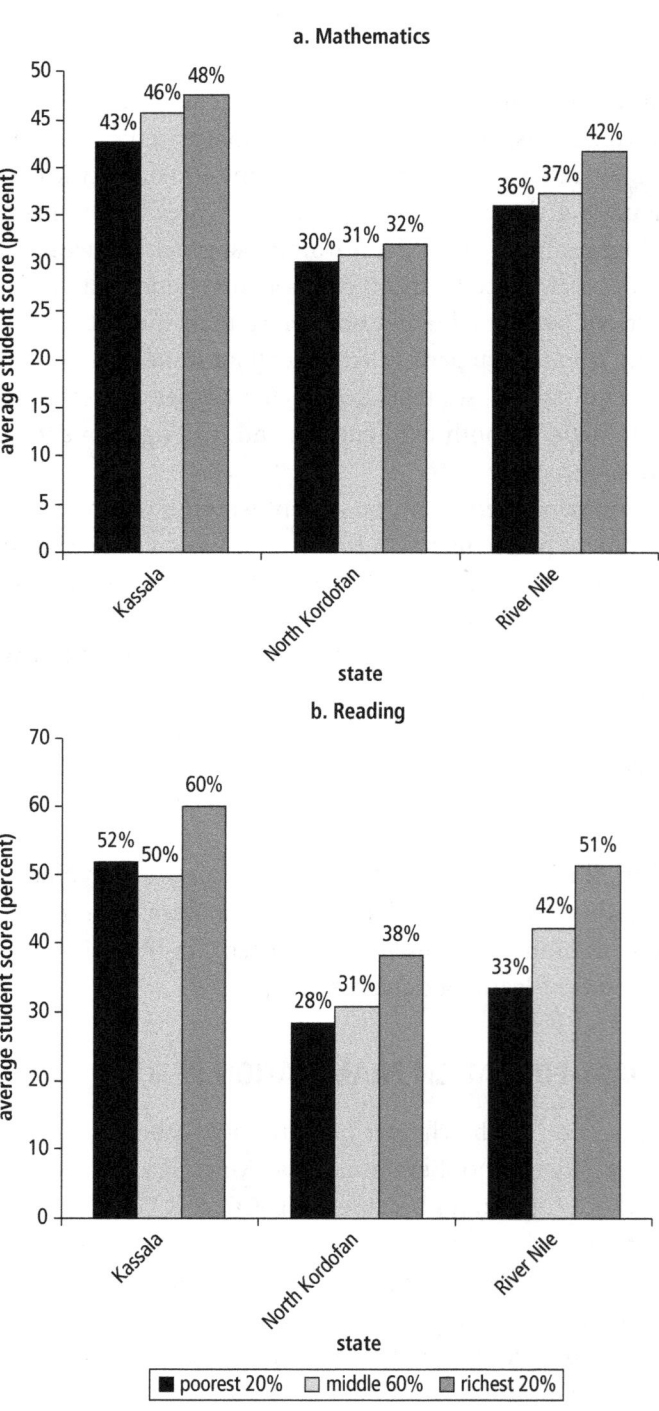

Source: Service delivery survey.

Figure 5.5 Average Student Performance in Mathematics and Reading, by Father's Education Level, 2009

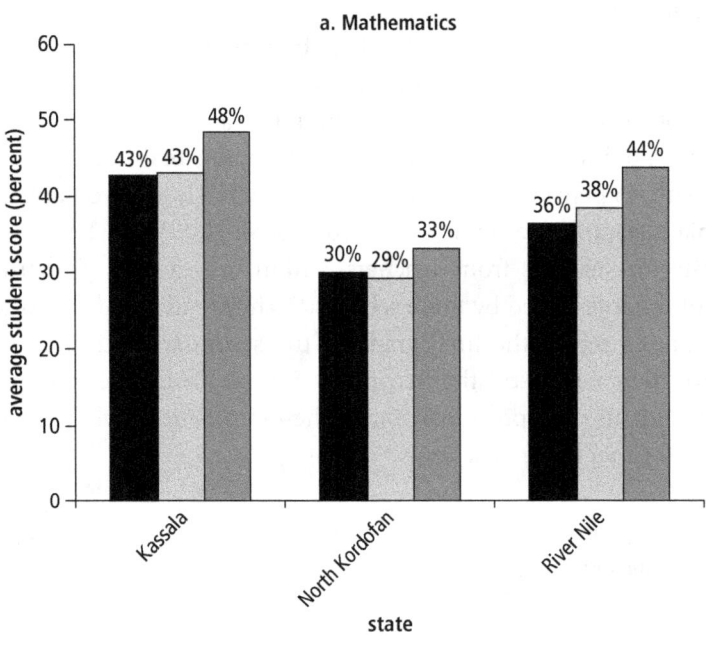

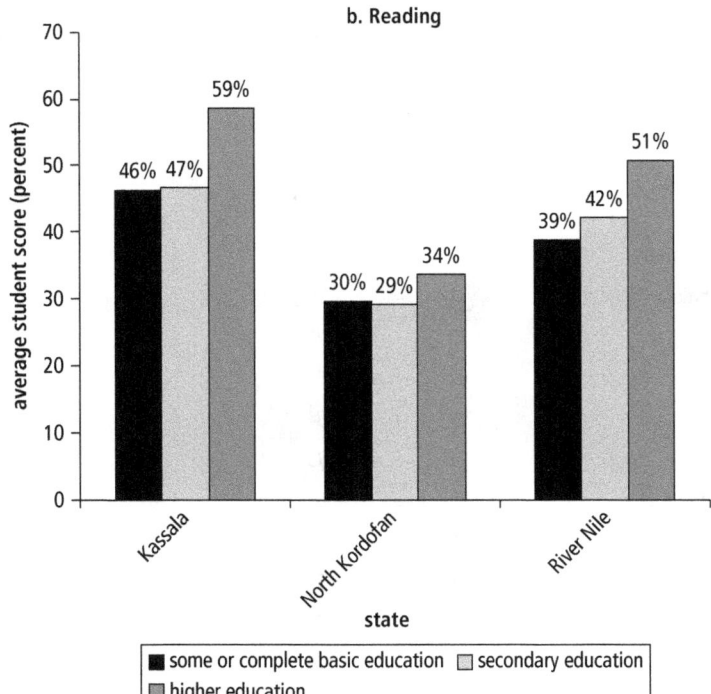

Source: Service delivery survey.

2008, 39 percent of the students came from public schools, 21 percent from private schools, 29 percent from Teachers' Union programs, and 11 percent were "informal" candidates (table 5.15).

On average, girls performed better than boys on the examinations. Close to 74 percent of girls passed, compared with 69 percent of boys (BoSE 2009). The average national pass rate was 74–75 percent for students from public and private schools and for informal candidates, compared with 65 percent for students from Teachers' Union programs, a pattern that has remained stable since 2004 (BoSE 2009). The lower average pass rate for students from Teachers' Union programs is primarily the result of the role served by these schools.[14] They tend to cater to students who want to repeat the final grade of the secondary cycle in order to improve their results on the Secondary School Certificate examination and to students who previously failed the examinations while attending one of the other types of schools.[15]

Table 5.15 Pass Rates for Secondary School Examinations in Northern Sudan, by School Type and State, 2008

State	School type			
	Public	Private	Teachers' Union	Informal
Blue Nile	56	75	59	60
Al Qadarif	73	76	69	78
Al Jazirah	76	80	74	87
Kassala	84	64	52	79
Khartoum	84	75	62	69
Northern Darfur	59	83	63	67
North Kordofan	71	76	49	67
Northern	93	75	66	72
Red Sea	62	81	60	66
River Nile	92	84	63	75
Sinnar	76	73	69	81
Southern Darfur	55	62	67	70
South Kordofan	50	63	57	67
Western Darfur	53	65	60	56
White Nile	74	81	65	76
Average	70	74	62	71
Number of candidates	127,459	70,008	102,578	33,183

Source: BoSE 2009.

Students from Kassala and River Nile who attended public schools have, on average, higher pass rates than the national average, whereas students from public schools in North Kordofan have pass rates below the national average. In particular, in Kassala and River Nile, pass rates for students from public schools were 84 percent and 92 percent, respectively, compared with 64 percent and 84 percent, respectively, for students from private schools. By contrast, in North Kordofan, students from private schools had higher average pass rates than did students from public schools, 76 percent compared with 71 percent, respectively. This finding lends further support to the result from the SDS that students in Kassala and River Nile performed better, on average, than students from North Kordofan on the grade 5 learning assessment.

In most states, when pass rates for students from public schools are low (below average), pass rates for private school students are relatively high, and conversely, when public pass rates are high, private school pass rates tend to be lower. This pattern may be an indication that private schools serve to meet the demand for an education that will enable students to pass the Secondary School Certificate examinations when public schools fail to do so.

SUMMARY

Based on the data collected by the SDS (2009), student learning levels in the sample schools in Kassala, North Kordofan, and River Nile states are generally low. The findings also highlight the lack of resources in many basic schools and room for improvement in how resources are managed. The results also indicate that family background variables, such as wealth and parental education, are related to student learning outcomes in line with existing evidence. The main findings of the SDS are summarized as follows:

- Classroom resources were generally scarce, with shortages of textbooks, desks, and functional chalkboards in many of the sample schools.
- Textbooks are meant to be provided by the government, but a large share of students in the sample schools did not have textbooks even after education councils purchased them to make up for the shortfalls.
- The chalkboard is one of the most important teaching tools, especially given the shortage of textbooks, and most observed classrooms had chalkboards; however, in many cases, they were not in usable condition.

- Many students did not have desks, but instead sat on chairs without desks or on the ground, particularly in rural sample schools.
- Most students in all three states had learning materials, such as notebooks and pens/pencils. In many of the sample schools, education councils provided support for these learning materials.
- Syllabus coverage was low in many of the sample schools, which tends to have adverse consequences for student learning.
- Despite the relatively low average student-teacher ratios in the three states, a substantial share of sample schools had large class sizes, which can also affect student-teacher contact time.
- Student learning outcomes as measured by the learning assessment for mathematics and reading were generally poor in the sample schools in all three states.
- Girls performed significantly better on both the mathematics and reading learning assessments than did boys, and both boys and girls tended to do better on reading.
- Students from richer households and whose fathers had completed tertiary education relative to basic or secondary education performed better on the learning assessments, which indicates the importance of household and family background for student performance, in addition to school and classroom environment.

ANNEX: PROBABILITY OF STILL BEING IN SCHOOL BY GRADE 8

Table 5A.1 Logistic Regression Results: Probability of Still Being in School by Grade 8, by Location, Income, and Gender, circa 2005

Dependent variable	Probability of still being in school by grade 8 (retention)
Constant	−0.2299
Boy	0.0313***
Urban	0.786***
Wealth quintile 2 and 3 (second-poorest and middle quintile)	−0.1469***
Wealth quintile 4 and 5 (richest two quintiles)	0.00328***
Memo items:	
Age group	Ages 15–19
Number of observations	6,950
"R^2" (Sommer'D statistic)	0.20

Source: Authors' analysis of the 2006 Sudan Household Health Survey (GoNU and GoSS 2006).
Note: These data apply to those students who have attended grade 1.
***Statistically significant at the 1% level.

NOTES

1. The SDS collected a large amount of data. This chapter presents a subset of these data, which are considered highly relevant for student learning outcomes and service delivery in basic education schools in the three states.
2. The 2008 baseline survey on basic education in the northern states of Sudan (FMoGE 2008) surveyed all 15 states, and the main findings of that survey are corroborated and complemented by the findings of the SDS (2009).
3. A total of 3,900 students were interviewed and tested, but 7 were removed because of incorrect student identifiers.
4. Peri-urban and rural schools are similarly resource constrained, but peri-urban schools tend to be larger than rural schools. The number of peri-urban schools in the sample is too small for these to be analyzed separately in a meaningful way.
5. This chapter does not deal with the quality of instruction time.
6. This is the case unless schools compensate for lost time.
7. This finding is not affected by taking into account schools that report that they are closed two months or more per year because of inaccessibility.
8. The SDS (2009) did not assess whether the records shown were up-to-date or complete.
9. The same test was used to assess learning achievements of grade 5 students in Benin.
10. On the mathematics component, 25 of 30 questions had four answer options and the rest of the questions had five answer options. On the reading component, all questions had four answer options.
11. For the construction of the asset index, each of the nine assets was assigned a weight equal to the fraction of students who owned the asset. If a student's home had none of the nine assets, then the asset index was zero.
12. Of the 3,893 students, 66 percent responded to the questions on their father's education level; therefore, the results should be interpreted with some caution. A larger share of students responded to the question in North Kordofan (77 percent) than in Kassala (62 percent) and River Nile (57 percent).
13. Fewer students answered the question on their mother's education level than on their father's education level; therefore, the results on father's education are presented.
14. Six percent of all students in secondary education are enrolled in Teachers' Union programs (see chapter 2, on enrollment).
15. It is estimated that about 40 percent of all repeaters in the secondary cycle attend Teachers' Union programs (see chapter 3, on student flow).

REFERENCES

BoSE (Board of Sudan Examinations). 2009. "General Results for 2008 Secondary School Examinations." Khartoum: Republic of Sudan Board of Sudan Examinations.

Case, Anne, and Angus Deaton. 1999. "School Inputs and Educational Outcomes in South Africa." *Quarterly Journal of Economics* 114 (3): F1047–84.

Das, Jishnu, Stefan Dercon, James Habyarimana, and Pramila Krishnan. 2007. "Teacher Shocks and Student Learning: Evidence from Zambia." *Journal of Human Resources* 42: 820–62.

EFA (Education for All). 2006. *EFA Global Monitoring Report 2006. Literacy for Life.* Paris: United Nations Educational, Scientific, and Cultural Organization. Available at http://unesdoc.unesco.org/images/0014/001416/141639e.pdf

EU (European Union). 2008. Cost and Financing Study. European Union.

FMoGE (Federal Ministry of General Education). 2008. "Baseline Survey on Basic Education in the Northern States of Sudan: Final Report June 2008." Khartoum.

———. Various years. "Statistical Yearbooks." Khartoum

Glewwe, Paul, and Hanan Jacoby. 1994. "Student Achievement and Schooling Choice in Low-Income Countries: Evidence from Ghana." *The Journal of Human Resources* 29(3): 843–64.

GoNU (Government of National Unity) and GoSS (Government of Southern Sudan). 2006. *Sudan Household Health Survey (SHHS) 2006.* Khartoum/Juba: Central Bureau of Statistics and Southern Sudan Center for Census, Statistics, and Evaluation.

IAEEA (International Association for the Evaluation of Educational Attainment). 2008. "Report from Test Administration in Benin." IAEEA, Hamburg, Germany.

Mingat, A., and K. Majgaard. 2010. *Education in Sub-Saharan Africa: A Comparative Analysis.* Washington, DC: World Bank.

UNESCO (United Nations Educational, Scientific, and Cultural Organization). 2007. *Education Counts: Benchmarking Progress in 19 WEI Countries: World Education Indicators.* Paris: UNESCO.

CHAPTER 6

Teachers

This chapter provides an overview of the status of teachers in northern Sudan. The first section profiles teachers and includes total numbers, types of teachers, gender, qualifications, and training. Next is a description of how teachers are recruited, deployed, and utilized. The chapter then examines teacher supervision, including school record keeping of time and attendance. Information is provided on teacher remuneration and incentives before the chapter ends with a summary of the main conclusions. The three sources of data for this chapter are (a) the federal Ministry of General Education (FMoGE) statistical yearbooks for 2000–09; (b) data collected from state visits (excluding the two Darfur states); and (c) the service delivery survey (SDS) conducted in Kassala, North Kordofan, and River Nile states in 2009, which was referred to in chapter 5.

PROFILE OF TEACHERS IN NORTHERN SUDAN

The performance of teachers is one of the most important determinants of student learning outcomes. Evidence shows that students of better teachers consistently achieve better learning outcomes (Hanushek and others 2003; Rivkin, Hanushek, and Kain 2005; Vegas and Umansky 2005). Given this fact, the effective functioning of the system for managing teachers in terms of recruitment, deployment, utilization, remuneration, and supervision is critical to the efficiency and performance of the education sector.

NUMBERS OF TEACHERS

A total of 94 percent of public education sector staff in 13 states of northern Sudan are school based. Teachers constitute the main staff category across all levels of education, but there are also nonteaching staff, such as administrators and inspectors, as well as drivers, guards, and janitors. To provide a complete picture, table 6.1 includes the numbers for all staff categories in the public education system in the 13 states. In total, there are 216,824 education staff on the government's payroll and 17,458 national service, or volunteer, teachers.[1]

The composition of education staff differs across education levels. At the preschool level, government teachers account for 62 percent of total staff, and national service and volunteer teachers account for 33 percent (figure 6.1). Literacy programs have an ever-larger share of national service and volunteer teachers (64 percent), with government teachers accounting for only 27 percent of total staff.

In basic education, by contrast, government teachers account for 80 percent of all staff. Government nonteaching staff constitute 12 percent of all staff, whereas non-school-based staff and national service and volunteer teachers compose 4 percent each. Similarly, at the secondary level, 4 percent of staff are national service and volunteer teachers, and 6 percent are non–school-based staff. Government teachers are the largest group (63 percent), followed by government nonteaching staff (27 percent).

GENDER

The teaching profession for basic education in northern Sudan comprises mainly female teachers, who account for roughly two-thirds of

Table 6.1 Numbers of Education Staff in Northern Sudan, by Education Level, 2009

			School based			
Education level	Total education staff on government payroll (a)+(b)+(c)	(a) Central and decentralized education staff	(b) Government nonteaching staff	(c) Government teachers	(d) National service and volunteer teachers	Total teachers (c) + (d)
Preschool	9,592	444	327	8,821	4,196	13,017
Basic	153,010	8,415	18,486	126,109	5,388	131,497
Secondary	50,857	3,790	13,515	33,552	1,964	35,516
Literacy programs	3,365	756	110	2,499	5,910	8,409
Total	216,824	13,405	32,438	170,981	17,458	188,439

Source: FMoGE 2008–09 statistical yearbook; state visits.
Note: Southern Darfur and Western Darfur are not included.

Figure 6.1 Types of Staff in Northern Sudan, by Education Level, 2009

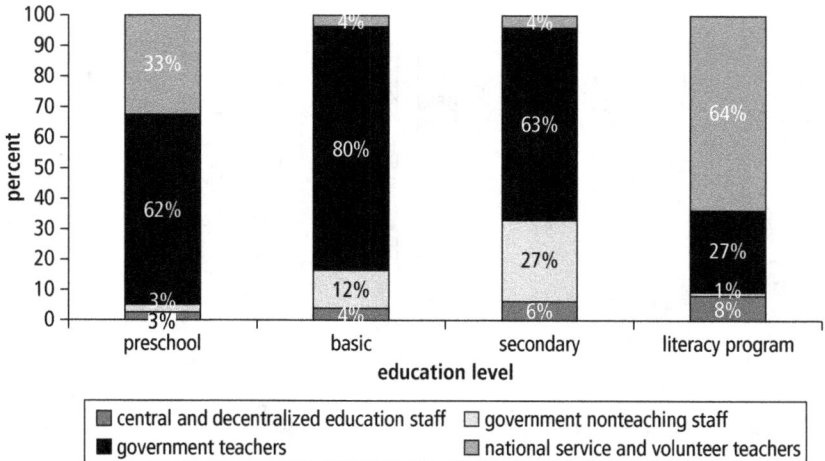

Source: Staff estimates based on state data.

the workforce (67 percent), as shown in figure 6.2. Female teachers constitute more than 60 percent of teachers in most states. The exceptions are South Kordofan, which has an equal number of male and female teachers, and Western Darfur and Northern Darfur, which have 54 percent and 57 percent female teachers, respectively. This finding could indicate that the teaching profession, at least with regard to basic education, is not as attractive to men as to women; men may find better earning opportunities in other professions. For women, however, the teaching profession seems to be quite attractive. Research shows that the presence of more female teachers in schools has a positive influence on attracting girls to schools.

In secondary education, female teachers constitute 56 percent of the teaching workforce in northern Sudan, as shown in figure 6.3. Some potential reasons why secondary education, compared with basic education, is able to attract more male teachers are the following: (a) average salaries for government secondary education teachers are higher than those for basic education and are possibly more competitive with other professions; and (b) fewer female teachers may be qualified to teach secondary education.[2] Interestingly, all three Darfur states have fewer female than male secondary education teachers (40 percent female secondary teachers in Northern Darfur, 33 percent female in Southern Darfur, and 22 percent female in Western Darfur). Al Qadarif and South Kordofan also have fewer female than male secondary education teachers, with 48 percent and 42 percent female teachers, respectively.

Figure 6.2 Percentage of Female and Male Teachers in Basic Education in Northern Sudan, by State, 2009

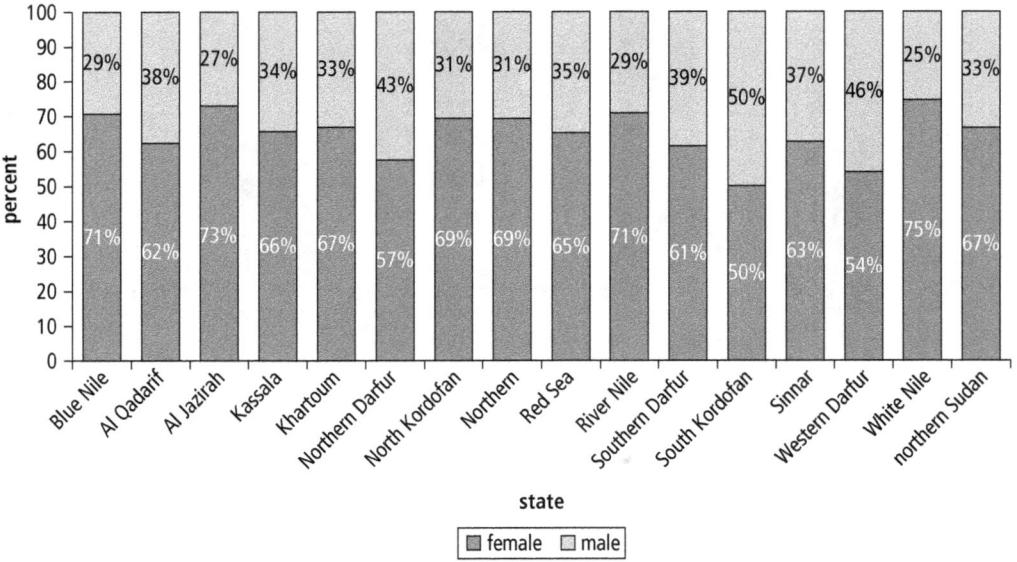

Source: FMoGE 2008–09 statistical yearbook.

Figure 6.3 Percentage of Female and Male Teachers in Secondary Education in Northern Sudan, by State, 2009

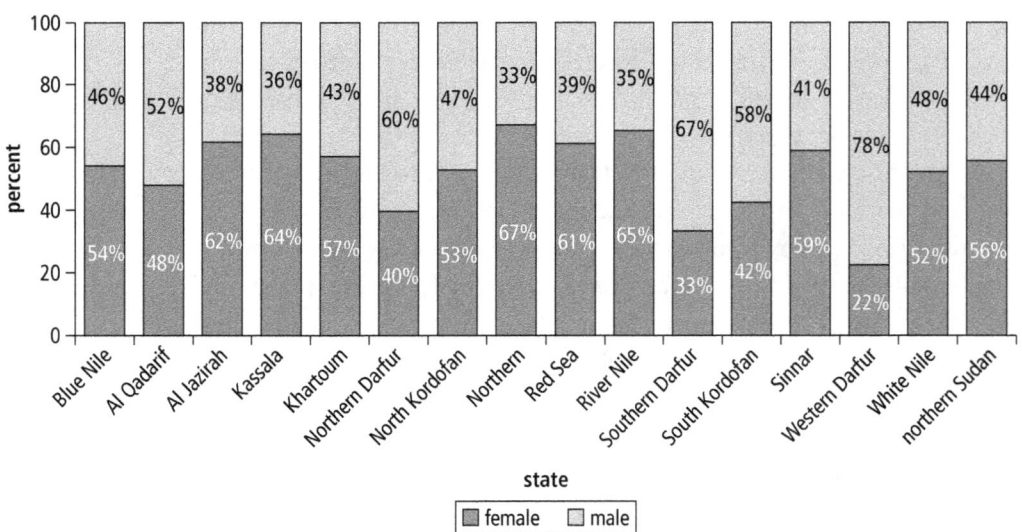

Source: FMoGE 2008–09 statistical yearbook.

TEACHER QUALIFICATIONS AND TRAINING

In 1993, the preservice qualification for basic education teachers was revised from a two-year teaching diploma to a four-year bachelor of education (B.Ed.) degree. The two-year diploma course was offered by a network of 73 in-service education training institutes (ISETI) across northern Sudan. Teachers attended the institutes one day per week and taught in the schools for the remainder of the work week. Funding for the ISETI diploma ceased in 1993, and the staff of the larger training institutes were absorbed into the universities as faculties of education, which would ultimately be responsible for qualifying basic education teachers through the B.Ed. degree.

The preservice qualification for a secondary school teacher in northern Sudan is a four-year bachelor of education (B.Ed.) degree offered by faculties of education in universities. These faculties are responsible for developing both the content of the training and the accreditation process for teachers in secondary schools.

As part the education sector reform in 1993, responsibility for preservice teacher training was transferred from the Ministry of General Education (MoGE) to the Ministry of Higher Education and Scientific Research (MoHESR). At the time, few students were enrolling in the B.Ed. degree program, and even fewer were successfully graduating and eventually teaching. This situation may have occurred because teachers were still being hired regardless of whether they had a B.Ed. In addition, the relatively high cost to students (both fees and opportunity costs) resulted in low numbers enrolling and eventually teaching (UNICEF 2008). In 2003, the Sudan Open University (SOU) introduced a partial B.Ed. degree course for teachers who were in service and had no B.Ed. The SOU also introduced a one-year diploma in education for graduates of other disciplines. By 2004, the MoGE stopped funding teachers through faculties of education and funded them solely through the SOU.

In 2008, it was estimated that only 10 percent of basic education teachers were officially qualified, though these numbers have presumably increased since the graduation of three years of B.Ed. students, from 2008 through 2010 (UNICEF 2008). Assuming that 75 percent of the teachers admitted completed the course, the estimated number who would have graduated with a B.Ed. from the SOU by the end of 2010 is a little over 56,000 (see table 6.2), which is about 31 percent of the total number of teachers in northern Sudan and does not include those who already had a B.Ed. from the faculties of education.

Table 6.2 Sudan Open University Bachelor of Education Degree Output, 2008–12

Year of intake	Number admitted	Number or estimated number due to graduate (year of graduation)
2003	6,006	4,547 (2008)
2004	14,645	10,984 (2009)
2005	53,983	40,487 (2010)
2006	15,560	11,670 (2011)
2007	8,379	6,284 (2012)

Source: FMoGE 2008.

The 2008–09 FMoGE statistical yearbook does not capture the number of teachers who are qualified according to the B.Ed. requirement, though it does disaggregate teachers by those who received education training (through the ISETI diploma, Sudan Open Learning Organization Teacher Assistance Course, or the B.Ed.), who are considered *trained,* and those who did not receive any teacher training, who are considered *untrained*.[3] It should be noted that *untrained* teachers could include individuals who have a university degree that is not focused on education, for example, a bachelor or master of science.

As figure 6.4 illustrates, 38 percent of the teachers in northern Sudan had not received any formal education training in 2009. Only a subset of those classified as trained had earned the prerequisite B.Ed. degree. Notably, 82 percent of the teachers in Western Darfur were considered trained, though it is not known what percentage of these teachers had the minimum requirement of the B.Ed. degree. Blue Nile had the highest percentage of untrained teachers (73 percent), while Al Qadarif, Kassala, and Southern Darfur had approximately 50 percent untrained teachers.

Figure 6.5 shows the academic qualifications and preservice training of the 819 full-time government teachers in service delivery survey. Across the three states studied (Kassala, North Kordofan, and River Nile), the most common qualifications and training were the following: completion of secondary school only, 7–38 percent; attainment of a bachelor of arts (B.A.) or bachelor of science degree (B.Sc.), 11–26 percent; and attainment of a B.A. or B.Sc. degree and a B.Ed. degree, 9–37 percent. There were some differences across regular teachers in rural and urban schools. Two general observations are worth noting. First, there is an age effect: older teachers, who were trained before the new B.Ed. policy was introduced, did not have a B.Ed. (unless they had gone back to a university). Second, in the sample, it was primarily regular teachers with a B.A. or B.Sc. who also had a B.Ed.

Figure 6.4 Percentage of Trained and Untrained Teachers in Northern Sudan, by State, 2009

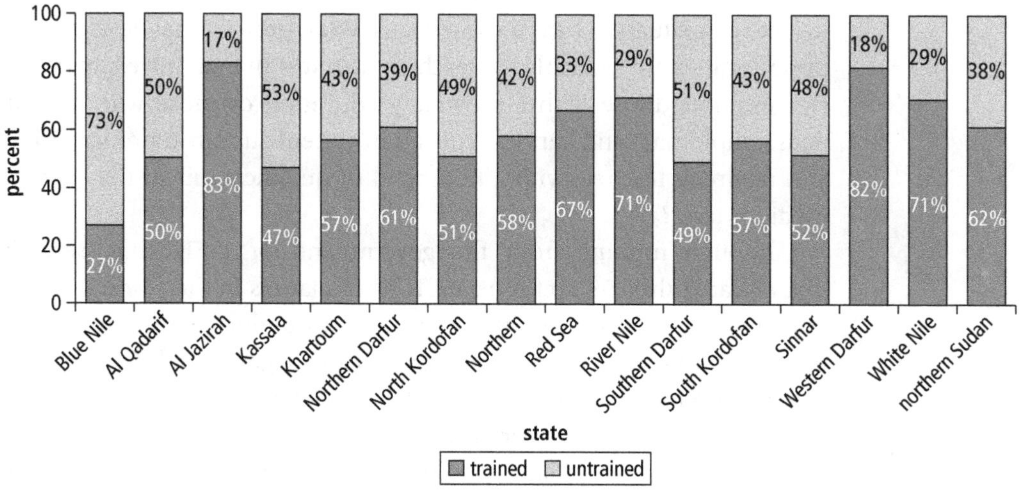

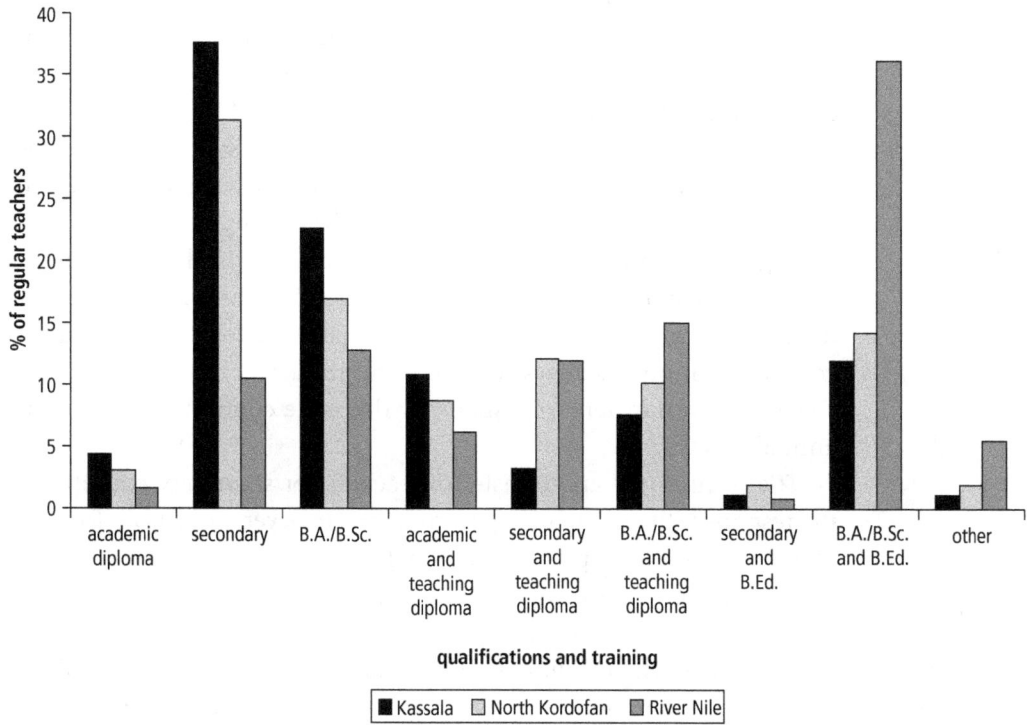

Source: FMoGE 2008–09 statistical yearbook.

Figure 6.5 Full-Time Government Teachers' Academic Qualifications and Preservice Training in Kassala, North Kordofan, and River Nile States, 2009

Source: Service delivery survey.
Note: The number of regular teachers in the service delivery survey was 819.

It appears that the opportunities for additional qualifications had primarily been provided to teachers who had already earned a university degree. This situation begs the questions, What professional development opportunities are available for teachers with less than a university degree (for example, those with a secondary education or those with an academic diploma), and can the education system sustain training, hiring, and retaining teachers with a high level of qualifications in the short to medium term?

Although funding from the government for ISETIs was severely reduced after the 1993 reforms, ISETI headquarters in the FMoGE and its state branches continue to organize in-service training courses. Apart from the 36-day certificate course, training courses are generally between 3 and 14 days and focus on informing teachers about curricula changes, as well as specific subjects. The responsibility for funding in-service training is decentralized to the states, but the United Nations Children's Fund (UNICEF) and the multidonor-financed Basic Education Project make significant contributions in this regard.

TEACHER RECRUITMENT, DEPLOYMENT, AND TRANSFER

In northern Sudan, the process of forecasting teacher requirements (regular, full-time, government school teachers) is based on assessments of the situation in each school and the level of financing available. The service delivery survey in Kassala, North Kordofan, and River Nile found that head teachers were requested to assess the need for additional teachers in their own schools and to submit a request to the local government for basic education schools and to the state government for secondary schools. Based on these requests and the availability of funding, a committee comprising state and local representatives conducted annual reviews to determine the number of new recruits. Decisions on transfers were made by the same committees during the annual meeting.

The recruitment and transfer of teachers for secondary education is the responsibility of the state government. However, these tasks for basic education are the responsibility of either the state or the local government, and the decision as to which one depends on the capacity of the local government as well the state's willingness to devolve responsibility to the locality. The recruitment of volunteer teachers is the responsibility of the education council because the council covers the costs for these teachers. Although information on the number of volunteer teachers is captured within the FMoGE statistical yearbooks, it is unclear whether this information is complete.

The link between the number of students and the number of teachers in schools is weak, which indicates that factors other than student enrollment influence teacher deployment. One would expect that as the number of students in a school increases, so too would the number of teachers. However, this is not always the case in northern Sudan. For example, looking at line A in figure 6.6, the number of teachers at schools with about 450 students ranges from 5 to 33. Line B indicates that the number of students enrolled in schools that employ 10 teachers ranges from less than 100 to more than 1,200.

Khartoum State has the greatest variation in the deployment of teachers, which means that there is a very weak correlation between the number of teachers deployed in the schools and the number of students enrolled. This is often the case in capital cities, where there is generally an oversupply of teachers because of their preference to work in urban areas. The scatterplot in figure 6.7 shows the relationship between number of teachers and student enrollments for Red Sea State. In Red Sea State, the number of teachers is more closely correlated to the number of students enrolled.

Figure 6.6 Number of Teachers in Relation to Student Enrollment in Basic Education Schools in Northern Sudan, 2008–09

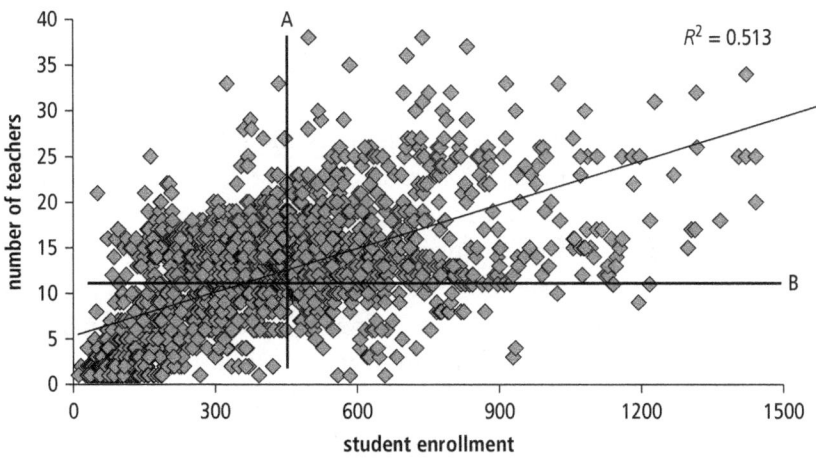

Source: The data are based on the FMoGE 2008–09 statistical yearbook and state visits.
Note: R^2 measures the extent to which the number of teachers in a school is proportionate to the size of its enrollment. If the number of teachers deployed to a school is perfectly proportionate to the size of enrollment, then R^2 will be equal to one. Conversely, an R^2 of zero would indicate that there is no relationship between the number of teachers deployed to a school and the number of students enrolled in that school.

Figure 6.7 Number of Teachers in Relation to Student Enrollment in Basic Education Schools, Red Sea State, 2008–09

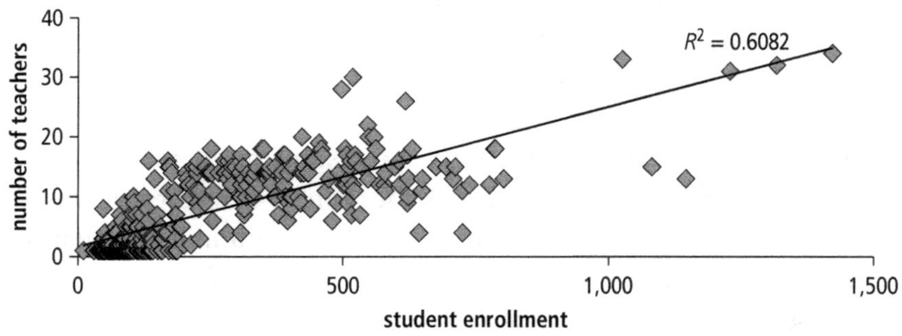

[Scatter plot: x-axis "student enrollment" (0 to 1,500), y-axis "number of teachers" (0 to 40), with trend line and $R^2 = 0.6082$]

Source: The data are based on the FMoGE 2008–09 statistical yearbook and state visits.
Note: The number of schools in Red Sea State is 369.

Figure 6.8 shows that northern Sudan is among the weakest compared with other countries in the region with regard to effectively deploying teachers according to student enrollment. Whereas 49 percent of northern Sudan's teachers are deployed based on factors other than student enrollment, countries such as Mozambique, Senegal, and Zambia are doing much better, with less than 20 percent of teachers so deployed. The only countries faring worse than northern Sudan in this instance are Burundi and Liberia.

In northern Sudan, structural factors influence the deployment of teachers. These factors include the following:

- *Subject specialization.* Teachers are required to specialize in a particular subject from grade 3 onward. This specialization means that instead of having one teacher who covers all subjects, the students have different teachers for each subject. Teachers are therefore deployed partly based on the needs of a school for subject specialists.
- *Family status and living conditions.* Female teachers are required to be posted close to their spouses; therefore, their deployment is based on where their spouse lives. Further, women will be posted to rural areas only if there are adequate accommodations. Given that 67 percent of teachers in basic education schools are women, these two criteria create a significant bottleneck in deploying teachers to the rural areas.
- *Health status.* Teachers can request to be posted near a functioning health facility if they suffer from hypertension or diabetes, or if they are pregnant. Depending on the severity of the condition, this criterion may also favor deployment of teachers to urban areas, where health services are more readily available or of higher perceived quality.

Figure 6.8 International Comparisons: Randomness in Teacher Allocations in Basic Education, by Country

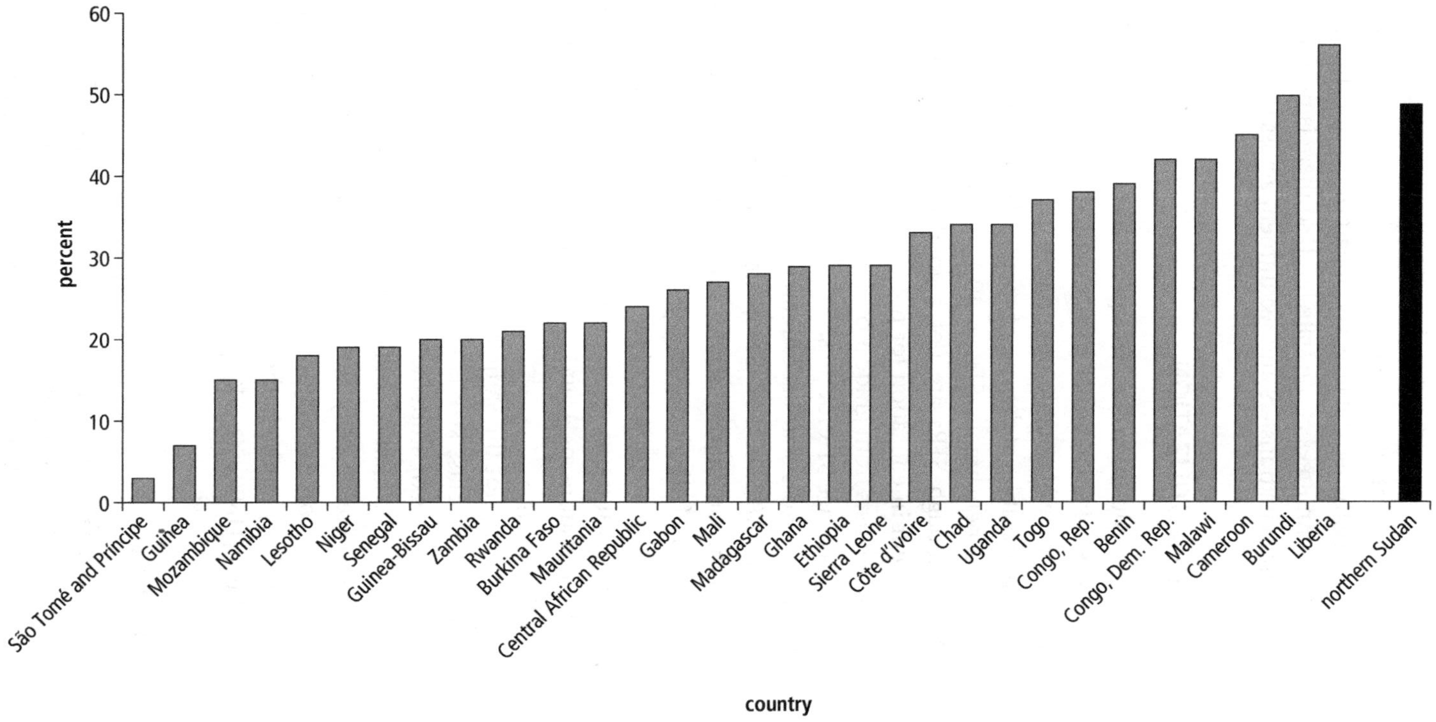

Source: The data are compiled from various World Bank country status reports.

- *Decentralization of deployment decisions.* The decentralization of recruitment and transfer decisions to the state and local levels makes the deployment of teachers across states difficult to implement. This is because the federal level is not part of the informal review meetings of the committees at the state level, so there is no formal mechanism to coordinate transfers and recruitment across states.

TEACHER UTILIZATION

For basic education, the average student-teacher ratio (STR) in northern Sudan is 34:1 (national service and volunteer teachers not included), though there is notable variation in STRs at the state level (see table 6.3 and annex tables at the end of chapter 7). The Education for All Fast-Track Initiative benchmark STR is 40:1 for basic education in Sub-Saharan Africa, though STRs are not a good measure of the human resources investment in education for northern Sudan given that teachers are subject specialists from grade 3 onward.

The average STR for preschool is 85:1 for northern Sudan, though the variation across states is extremely large, ranging from 18:1 in Northern State to 198:1 in Red Sea State. High STRs explain the reliance of preschools on national service and volunteer staff, both of which account for a third of all education staff within this subsector. For secondary education, the average student-teacher ratio is 16:1 for both the academic and the technical tracks, with a small degree of variation across states (standard deviations of 4 and 5 for the academic and the technical tracks, respectively).

STRs are not the same as class size. The relationship between STRs and average class size is affected by many factors including the number of classes or students for whom a teacher is responsible, the number of hours that a student attends class each day, the length of a teacher's working day, the division of a teacher's time between instruction and noninstructional activities (that is, planning or preparing instruction), and whether a school runs multiple shifts with the same teachers (UNESCO 2007).

CLASS SIZE

The average class size for basic education in northern Sudan is approximately 48 students per class, according to the FMoGE 2008–09 statistical yearbooks. Available empirical studies show that class sizes within the range of 30–60 students per teacher have a relatively equal level of

Table 6.3 Student-Teacher Ratios in Northern Sudan, by State, 2009

	Student-teacher ratios			
			Secondary	
State	Preschool	Basic	Academic	Technical
Northern	18	17	10	11
River Nile	175	22	13	10
Khartoum	15	30	16	21
Al Jazirah	25	30	17	16
Blue Nile	71	24	7	8
Sinnar	31	33	13	13
White Nile	75	30	17	18
North Kordofan	76	42	16	12
South Kordofan	153	39	22	26
Northern Darfur	60	47	18	14
Southern Darfur	64	44	20	15
Western Darfur	195	64	23	21
Red Sea	198	27	18	14
Kassala	76	31	14	23
Al Qadarif	47	38	16	14
Average	85	34	16	16
Standard deviation	63	12	4	5

Source: FMoGE 2008–09 statistical yearbook.

student learning (Behaghel and Coustère 1999; Bernard 2003). Classes with fewer than 30 students do tend to produce better learning outcomes, but such small class sizes are uncommon and financially unsustainable in most countries in Sub-Saharan Africa (World Bank forthcoming). Class sizes above 60 students, however, tend to have a negative impact on student learning.

Class sizes for basic education vary according to school type and grade. Schools for internally displaced persons (IDPs) have an average of 92 students per class, whereas village schools have an average of 30 students, and nomadic schools 33 students, per class (see table 6.4). The average class size also decreases in the higher grades, except in IDP and village schools. Within small schools, such as village and nomadic schools, which have correspondingly small class sizes, the practice of subject specialization by teachers is inefficient, and in many cases, it may not be possible given the potentially insufficient numbers of teachers in those schools. In order to deal with this issue, village and nomadic schools are multigrade, which means that teachers require special skill sets and different teaching materials. It is not clear whether there is additional or differentiated training for teachers who work within nomadic and village schools in northern Sudan.

INSTRUCTIONAL TIME

The official instructional time for basic and secondary students is 25 hours per week. Given that the official number of school days in the academic year is 210 in northern Sudan, this information can be translated into approximately 1,050 hours of intended instructional time for basic and secondary education students per year.

However, actual instructional time is significantly less than the official number of hours. The average weekly number of instructional hours by teachers is 17 for northern Sudan, which translates into about 714 actual instructional hours annually.[4] This figure means that students receive an average of 336 hours less instructional time annually than what is officially sanctioned. There may be several reasons for this loss in actual

Table 6.4 Average Class Size in Northern Sudan, by School Type and Grade, 2008–09

Grade	Average class size (number of students per form)					
	Boys	Girls	Co-ed	Village[a]	IDP[b]	Nomadic[c]
1	53	52	45	32	86	37
2	52	52	44	32	90	32
3	52	52	45	28	88	29
4	53	51	44	26	91	29
5	52	50	45	43	93	36
6	50	48	44	n.a.	94	31
7	50	47	42	n.a.	114	26
8	47	45	40	n.a.	87	26
Average grades 1–8	51	50	44	30	92	33

Source: FMoGE 2008–09 statistical yearbook; authors' calculations.
Note: IDP = internally displaced person; n.a. = not applicable.
a. Village schools are only for grades 1–5 and are only in North Kordofan and South Kordofan states, according to the FMoGE statistical yearbooks.
b. IDP schools are only in Northern, Northern Darfur, Southern Darfur, and Western Darfur states. The three IDP schools located in Northern State are excluded here because they have notably smaller class sizes than do the IDP schools in the three Darfur states.
c. There are nomadic schools in all but Khartoum and Al Jazirah states. In some states, nomadic schools do not cover all grades.

Table 6.5 Number of Hours Taught by Teachers in Different Salary Scales

Teacher salary scale	Hours to be taught per week
2 and 3	5
4 and 5	7.5
8	10
9	15
10, 12, and 14	25

Source: State visits.

instructional time, such as school closures because of weather conditions, which is common during the rainy and extremely hot seasons in parts of Sudan, as well as teacher absenteeism, in-service teacher training, strikes, conflict, or the use of schools as polling stations.

In addition, senior teachers spend less time teaching compared with junior teachers. Table 6.5 shows the salary scales of teachers and the numbers of hours they are expected to teach per week. Teachers in the highest salary scales (2 and 3) are expected to teach about 5 hours per week, whereas teachers in the lowest salary scales (10, 12, and 14) are expected to teach about 25 hours per week. Senior teachers are expected to do administrative and managerial work with the balance their time. Given that teachers on higher salary scales are presumably more experienced and that more experienced teachers teach fewer hours, it follows that less-experienced teachers would be teaching the lower basic education grades (grades 1–2) because there is one teacher per class for the entire day.

SCHOOL RECORD KEEPING: TEACHER LEAVE AND TIME/ATTENDANCE

The options for leave for teachers in northern Sudan are extensive. Teachers follow the civil service leave guidelines, which specify the following entitlements:

- Special leave without pay: 1 month
- Feeding leave: 1 hour leave per day for 2 years
- Sick leave: 3–7 days
- Social leave: 15 days
- Funeral leave: 3 days
- Local leave: not to exceed 7 days during the year
- Leave for religious purposes (Haj or Omra): 1 month once during his or her life in service

- Leave to represent northern Sudan in international conferences and delegations: not to exceed the period stated
- Leave for union members for union activities: not to exceed 30 days
- Maternity leave:
  1. 8 weeks with full pay at delivery
  2. 1 year with basic salary
  3. 2 years without pay, and it can be divided
- Widow leave:
  1. 4 months and 10 days if not pregnant with full pay
  2. If pregnant, will be given the 4 months and 10 days, and if she delivers a baby before the end of the period, the leave will end and she will be entitled to maternity leave
- Sick leave up to
  1. First 6 months with full pay
  2. Next 6 months with half pay (terms and conditions apply)
- Sick leave outside the country: case-by-case basis
- Leave to accompany sick member of employee's family: up to 90 days with full pay; after which the employee can take leave without pay (terms and conditions apply)
- Work injury leave (terms and conditions apply): case-by-case basis

According to the service delivery survey, the average number of days taken for personal leave (all types) by school for the six months prior to the survey was 30 in Kassala, 17 in North Kordofan, and 18 in River Nile (figure 6.9). Within the personal leave category, the largest number of days were taken for sick leave in all three states. Other reasons for personal leave included family illness, emergencies, and social events. The reported average official leave during six months in 2009 was lower: 15 days in Kassala, 13 days in North Kordofan, and 6 days in River Nile. For official leave, the most common reasons were the following: training in Kassala and River Nile, and to collect salary in North Kordofan.

Many schools do not maintain adequate leave records, or any other records, for teachers. Given the large number of leave days teachers are taking, it is important that leave records are properly maintained to ensure accountability. However the service delivery survey shows that only 37 percent of rural schools and 76 percent of urban schools in Kassala kept leave records. In North Kordofan, 79 percent of rural and 70 percent of urban schools were able to show their records on teacher leave, and in River Nile, the corresponding shares were 70 percent for rural schools and 68 percent for urban schools.

Figure 6.9 Average Number of Leave Days by Purpose over Six Months in Kassala, North Kordofan, and River Nile States, 2009

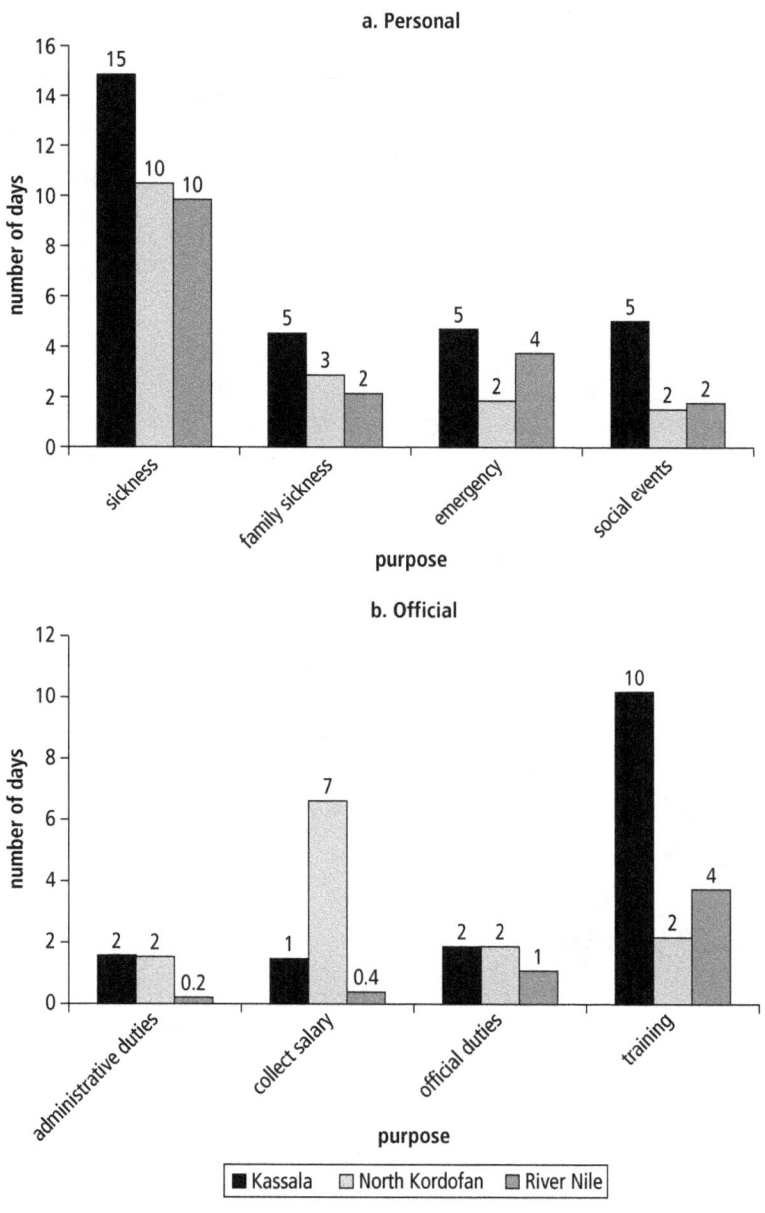

Source: Service delivery survey.
Note: These data are based on the responses by the head teachers interviewed in each school.

However, most rural and urban schools in Kassala and North Kordofan recorded when teachers arrived and departed, whereas less than half of the rural schools in River Nile kept similar records (table 6.6). In River Nile, a much smaller share of schools was required to keep such time and

Table 6.6 School Record Keeping in Kassala, North Kordofan, and River Nile States State Averages, 2009
percent

Country/location	Schools able to show records of		Schools where teachers must report	
	Teacher leave	Teacher arrivals/ departures	When arriving at school	When departing school
Kassala				
Urban	76	88	96	92
Rural	37	84	89	89
North Kordofan				
Urban	70	96	98	98
Rural	79	95	100	98
River Nile				
Urban	68	44	48	44
Rural	70	67	74	74

Source: Service delivery survey.
Note: These data are based on the head teacher in each school showing the relevant records to the enumerator.

attendance records: 44–48 percent of urban schools and 74 percent of rural schools required teachers to report their arrival and departure times. In line with this reporting requirement, 44 percent of urban schools and 67 percent of rural schools in River Nile were able to present their teacher arrival/departure records.

TEACHER SUPERVISION

Management control and oversight are necessary to establish accountability by teachers and thereby improve their performance. Real accountability hinges on having well-defined standards and adequate information about performance in education provision to enable policy makers and program administrators to improve service delivery (Lewis and Pettersson 2009). In northern Sudan, the ratio of regular teachers to inspectors is 36:1 for basic education and 41:1 for secondary education (see data in table 6.7).

In northern Sudan, teachers are supervised by head teachers, education councils, and local or state (depending on the available capacity) inspectors. However, supervision by the local or state inspectors is the main avenue for promoting or disciplining teachers, though the inspectors seek

Table 6.7 Number of Teachers, Inspectors, Volunteers, and National Service Staff in Basic and Secondary Education, by State, 2009

State	Basic education			Secondary education (academic and technical)		
	Teachers	Inspectors	Volunteers and national service	Teachers	Inspectors	Volunteers and national service
River Nile	8,128	211	177	2,565	50	77
Sinnar	6,778	162	0	1,971	50	0
Kassala	5,367	120	536	1,191	29	0
White Nile	10,239	247	1430	2,326	79	620
Al Jazirah	22,309	538	1430	7,810	84	620
Al Qadarif	5,708	102	226	1,444	30	110
Blue Nile	5,203	92	650	1,340	30	350
Red Sea	3,677	116	226	717	10	110
Khartoum	25,188	886	536	7,027	308	0
North Kordofan	12,360	326	177	2,453	64	77
South Kordofan	6,846	211	0	1,205	32	0
Northern	6,741	194	0	1,808	17	0
Northern Darfur	7,565	330		1,695	0	
Southern Darfur	8,679	235		1,755		
Western Darfur	4,315	117		613		
Total	139,103	3,887	5,388	35,920	783	1,964

Source: FMoGE 2008–09 statistical yearbook.

input from head teachers in their reports. The inspectors are former teachers, often approaching retirement age, and are attached to state or local education units; where administration units exist, some inspectors are organizationally located at that level. Across states in both basic and secondary education, teachers are supposed to be monitored two to four times per year by the state or inspector. Inspectors supervise the performance only of regular teachers, whereas volunteer or national service and part-time teachers are generally supervised by the education councils, which use different standards. This divide is of particular concern in preschool, where more than a third of teachers are volunteers or national service staff.

The majority of teachers in the service delivery survey were regularly monitored by inspectors during the course of the year. The study indicates that 90 percent of regular teachers in basic schools in River

Nile, 89 percent in North Kordofan, and 71 percent in Kassala were visited by state or local inspectors within the last three months during 2009 (see figure 6.10). However, the study did not reach many remote rural schools. Evidence from other countries shows that costs related to time and transport restrict regular supervision of teachers in remote schools.

Inspectors use supervision instruments to rate teachers on a scale based on technical aspects, as well as other facets that can influence teaching and learning in the classroom. The ratings are based on inspector observation of teachers. In some states, however, the supervision is more participatory because it includes a self-evaluation by the teacher. In River Nile State, 60 percent of the supervision instrument is completed by the inspector, and the balance is completed by the head teacher.

Depending on the state, 68–80 percent of teachers surveyed in the service delivery survey were also visited by head teachers within the month prior. As for education council supervision, 38–58 percent of the regular teachers had received a visit within the last month. However, it is not clear what role education council supervision plays in terms of teacher promotions, transfers, and training.

Figure 6.10 Local Supervision: Visits to the Teachers in Kassala, North Kordofan, and River Nile States, 2009
percent

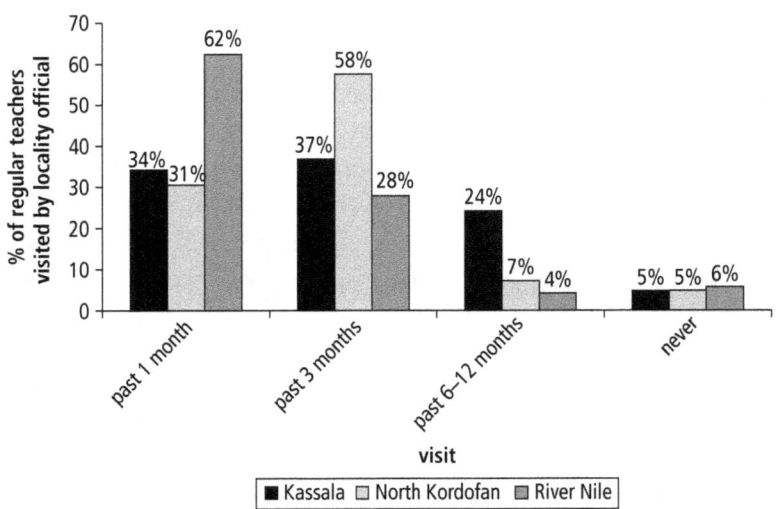

Source: Service delivery survey.

TEACHER SALARIES AND MOTIVATION

The average annual salary for government teachers in 2009 was 5,300 Sudanese pounds (SDG) for preschool, SDG 6,700 for basic education, SDG 8,200 for secondary school, and SDG 5,150 for literacy programs, as indicated in chapter 7, on education finance. Because there are no data on the salary levels of other civil servant professionals, it is not possible to assess teachers' incomes relative to similarly qualified civil servants.

The service delivery survey found that most regular teachers were paid their full salaries in the month preceding the survey. Figure 6.11 shows that 94 percent and 96 percent of regular teachers in Kassala and River Nile, respectively, received their full salaries. However, only 47 percent of regular teachers in North Kordofan received their full salaries in the month preceding the survey.[5] Payments for part-time and volunteer teachers did not seem to be as consistent as payments for regular teachers, with volunteers having it the worst. This could be because part-time and volunteer teachers generally rely on communities for their payments, whereas regular teacher salaries are funded by the government.

Figure 6.11 Payment of Teacher Salaries in Kassala, North Kordofan, and River Nile States, by Teacher Type, 2009
percent

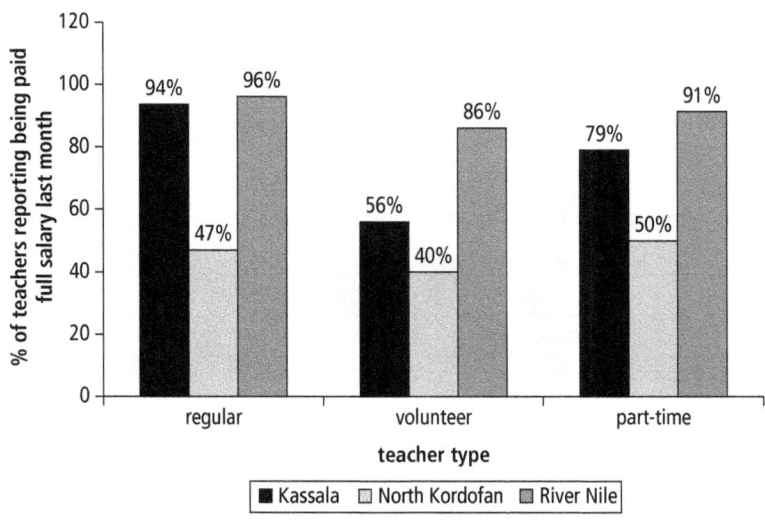

Source: Service delivery survey.
Note: These data are based on the responses by the sample of teachers interviewed in each school.

Data from the service delivery survey also show that depending on the state, between 6 and 20 percent of regular teachers had outside jobs or provided private tutoring to students, indicating a need for supplementary income (table 6.8). In North Kordofan, 6 percent of regular teachers had outside jobs, whereas in Kassala and River Nile, 11 percent and 13 percent, respectively, had outside jobs. Those regular teachers who provided tutoring were as follows: 13 percent in Kassala, 17 percent in North Kordofan, and 21 percent in River Nile. As expected, compared with regular teachers a greater number of volunteer and part-time teachers had outside jobs to supplement their incomes. Although the study did not ascertain the types of jobs teachers were undertaking outside of school or the amount of income earned through these sources, the data suggest that some teachers are seeking to supplement their salaries.

Teachers working in rural, IDP, and nomadic schools do not receive any additional benefits from the government. Communities in some rural schools provide additional incentives (either in cash or in kind) for teachers to attract them to those areas. This means that the poorest rural communities cannot compete with other, more wealthy rural communities that offer a better standard of living. In some states (such as South Kordofan), teachers in nomadic schools receive additional remuneration from UNICEF. Evidence from the baseline survey (FMoGE 2008) show that there were more untrained teachers in nomadic (63.9 percent) and IDP (62.1 percent) schools than in any other type of school.

Although financial incentives may influence teacher performance and thus student learning, there are other, nonfinancial incentives that can be used to attract experienced and qualified teachers. For example, teachers may exert more effort if doing so improves their standing in the local community. A good work environment also tends to improve

Table 6.8 Outside Jobs and Private Tutoring in Kassala, North Kordofan, and River Nile States, by Teacher Type, 2009

	Percentage of teachers who report					
	Having outside job			Providing private tutoring		
State	Regular	Volunteer	Part-time	Regular	Volunteer	Part-time
Kassala	11	0.3	12	13	0.2	0.0
North Kordofan	6	18	14	17	14	26
River Nile	13	14	22	21	0	9
Total number of teachers	833	65	114	833	65	114

Source: Service delivery survey.
Note: These data are based on the responses by the sample of teachers interviewed in each school.

Table 6.9 Teacher Incentives to Perform, or Not

Nonfinancial incentives	Financial incentives
Career development prospects	Employer power to fire
Good work environment	Job security
Intrinsic motivation	Pay level
Prestige in local community	Performance pay
Professional recognition	
Student/parent appreciation	

Source: Lewis and Pettersson 2009, adapted from Vegas and Umansky 2005.
Note: The ordering of incentives does not indicate relative importance. Work environment includes things such as number of hours worked per week, class size, availability of teaching materials, and the physical condition of classrooms and schools.

teacher performance. The list in table 6.9 is not exhaustive but indicative of the wide range of factors that influence teacher performance.

In all focus group discussions among teachers in five states, mention was made of improving their salaries, gaining access to better training, and providing suitable accommodations to make the profession more attractive (UNICEF 2008). Experience from other countries shows that a comprehensive benefits package (housing, insurance, hardship allowances, family relocation, and opportunities for continuing education and training) and rotations with defined service periods can serve to make remote and rural areas more attractive (or at least more acceptable) to qualified teachers. Another, potentially complementary, strategy is to hire local teachers under the presumption that people with roots in the area will be more willing to return to and remain in the area (Lewis and Pettersson 2009).

SUMMARY

- In northern Sudan, basic education teachers are not deployed based on the size of the schools, and as a result, teachers are concentrated in or close to urban areas. The main constraints to the effective deployment of teachers are threefold: (a) a large proportion of basic education teachers are female (67 percent) and are hence deployed close to their spouses; (b) there are no financial incentives (cash or housing) provided by the government to work in remote schools—financial incentives are provided by communities, which in turn means that the poorest and most remote communities cannot attract teachers; and (c) there are no career incentives (for example, faster promotion) for working in remote areas.

- The average size of a class in basic education is 48 students, but class size varies significantly by the type of school and by grade level. Of particular concern are IDP schools, which have an average of 92 students per class and thus have the potential for poor learning outcomes.
- On average, students receive 336 fewer hours of annual instructional time than the government-mandated number. This deficit results in insufficient time for learning.
- There is not sufficient evidence yet to ascertain whether the new prequalification requirements yield better performance by teachers. More research is needed to determine the cost-effectiveness of the new program compared to the old program.

NOTES

1. Government teachers, administrators, inspectors, and other nonteaching staff are on the government payroll, whereas national service and volunteer teachers are not.

2. The average annual salary at the secondary level is 8,184 Sudanese pounds (SDG), as opposed to SDG 6,708 at the basic level (per chapter 7, on education finance).

3. The Teacher Assistance Course is a nine-month open learning course developed and delivered by the Sudan Open Learning Organization, a national nongovernmental organization.

4. The average actual instructional time is calculated by dividing the intended number of instructional hours by the number of teachers and multiplying this ratio by the total number of classes.

5. The survey was conducted one month after a teacher's strike, which was initiated because of a lack of salary payments to teachers in October 2009.

REFERENCES

Behaghel, L., and P. Coustère. 1999. *Les facteurs d'efficacité de l'apprentissage dans l'enseignement primaire: les résultats du programme PASEC sur huit pays d'Afrique.* Dakar, Senegal: PASEC (Programme d'analyse des systèmes éducatifs de la CONFEMEN [Conférence des ministres de l'éducation des pays ayant le français en partage]).

Bernard, Jean-Marc. 2003. "Elements to Assess the Quality of Primary Education in French-Speaking Africa: Programme for the Analysis of Educational Systems of the CONFEMEN countries (PASEC)." ADEA (Association for the Development of Education in Africa) biennial meeting, Grand Baie, Mauritius, December 3–6, 2003.

FMoGE (Federal Ministry of General Education). 2008. "Baseline Survey on Basic Education in the Northern States of Sudan: Final Report June 2008." Online document available at http://planipolis.iiep.unesco.org/epiweb/E029336e.pdf.

———. Various years. "Statistical Yearbooks." Khartoum.

Hanushek, Eric A., John F. Kain, Jacob M. Markman, and Steven G. Rivkin. 2003. "Does Peer Ability Affect Student Achievement?" *Journal of Applied Econometrics* 18: 527–44.

Lewis, Maureen, and Gunilla Pettersson. 2009. "Governance in Education: Raising Performance in the Sector." Draft. Development Economics Vice Presidency and Human Development Network, World Bank, Washington, DC. Available at http://siteresources.worldbank.org/EXTHDOFFICE/Resources/5485726-1239047988859/Governance-in-education-master-22Dec09-GP.pdf.

Rivkin, Steven G., Eric A. Hanushek, and John F. Kain. 2005. "Teachers, Schools, and Academic Achievement." *Econometrica* 73 (2): 417–58.

UNESCO (United Nations Educational, Scientific, and Cultural Organization). 2007. *Education Counts: Benchmarking Progress in 19 WEI Countries: World Education Indicators.* Paris: UNESCO.

UNICEF (United Nations Children's Fund). 2008. "Teacher Training Assessment for Northern States of Sudan." Khartoum.

Vegas, Emiliana, and Ilana Umansky. 2005. *Improving Teaching and Learning through Effective Incentives: What Can We Learn from Education Reforms in Latin America?* Washington, DC: World Bank.

World Bank. Forthcoming. "Education in Sub-Saharan Africa: A Comparative Analysis." Africa Region Technical Department, Education, World Bank, Washington, DC.

CHAPTER 7

Education Finance

This chapter provides an overview and analysis of public education spending in northern Sudan, with the objective of guiding future spending and informing resource allocation to promote progress in achieving the education Millennium Development Goals and Education for All targets.[1] This examination is particularly important in the context of northern Sudan because the education system is decentralized, with varying capacities to deliver education services across states, and because there are significant state differences in education inputs, outputs, and outcomes.

After a brief introduction, the chapter examines trends in public education spending, spending on education by administrative level and education level (preschool, basic, secondary, and tertiary), and the composition of recurrent education spending.[2] It then analyzes the composition of public per-student spending and spending on education staff. A brief discussion of household out-of-pocket, per-student spending is also provided. This discussion is followed by an analysis at the state level of the share of education spending in total public spending, of per-student spending, and of the composition of recurrent education spending. Federal transfers and the size of transfers received by each state are also examined. The chapter concludes with a summary of the main findings. For the analysis in this chapter, it was necessary to collect primary data; see box 7.1.[3] Regional comparisons are provided throughout the chapter whenever possible.

BACKGROUND

There are three administrative levels in the education system in northern Sudan: federal, state, and local government (localities). The provision of

> **BOX 7.1 STATE VISITS TO COLLECT INFORMATION ON EDUCATION SPENDING**
>
> Between December 2009 and February 2010, a team composed of federal Ministry of General Education (FMoGE) and World Bank staff visited 10 of the 15 states of northern Sudan to collect data for this chapter. Prior to the visits, the team designed a template to collect the financial data. The team visited Al Qadarif, Al Jazirah, Blue Nile, Kassala, Khartoum, North Kordofan, Red Sea, River Nile, South Kordofan, and White Nile states. Of the five remaining states, three—Northern, Northern Darfur, and Sinnar—sent the requested information to the team. For the other two, Southern Darfur and Western Darfur, the team made multiple efforts to obtain data, but these states were unable to provide the information.
>
> During each visit, the team met with the state ministry of education, the state ministry of finance, and in some cases, the state ministry of local government. Financial information was generally collected for the two years 2008 and 2009, and more-detailed payroll data were collected for one month of 2009. The team also visited two to three localities in each state to verify the consistency across state-level and local-level information, and to collect information about community spending on schools. Data from the different state ministries and localities were cross-checked for consistency, and were found to be of generally good quality. In some states, donors helped to finance the education system, but data on these contributions were not available at the time of the completion of this report.

- preschool, basic education, and secondary education is decentralized to the states, whereas the federal government is responsible for higher education (World Bank 2003). States receive transfers from the federal government that are intended to match resources to education needs across states. The federal transfers consist of block transfers (part of which the states allocate to education) and earmarked transfers (for specific purposes including higher education and graduate salaries).

As a result of the government's decentralization policy, the responsibilities of the states have increased significantly since the 2005 Comprehensive Peace Agreement, together with education spending at the state level. However, in practice, the fiscal autonomy of the states is still limited because they continue to rely heavily on federal transfers, and

ANALYSIS OF PUBLIC EDUCATION SPENDING

The following section shows trends in public education spending over the period 2000–09, and places education spending in northern Sudan in a regional context. It also provides a breakdown of total education spending by development and recurrent spending, and by administrative and education levels.

TRENDS IN SPENDING

There has been a substantial increase in public education spending in northern Sudan since 2000, which signals the government's commitment to expand and improve education opportunities. Table 7.1 shows total public education spending at the federal and state levels. In nominal terms, total education spending for the public school system increased from 319 million Sudanese pounds (SDG) in 2000 to SDG 2.7 billion in 2009. In real terms (adjusting for inflation by expressing all spending in 2008 SDG), total education spending nearly quadrupled, from SDG 660 million to SDG 2.4 billion between 2000 and 2009, equivalent to 15.5 percent average annual real growth.

Table 7.1 Estimated Total Public Education Spending, 2000–09

Indicator	2000	2002	2004	2005	2006	2007	2008	2009
Nominal education spending (current SDG millions)	319	556	902	1,010	1,527	1,966	2,509	2,714
Recurrent	317	466	846	941	1,446	1,845	2,288	2,469
Development	2	90	56	69	80	121	221	245
Real education spending (constant 2008 SDG millions)	660	1,037	1,335	1,332	1,892	2,276	2,509	2,404
Recurrent	656	869	1,252	1,241	1,792	2,136	2,288	2,187
Development	4	168	83	91	100	140	221	217
Education spending as a percentage of total public spending	8.1	9.2	7.1	7.3	10.2	11.2	13.2	12.0
Education spending as a percentage of GDP	1.3	1.8	2.0	1.9	2.4	2.7	2.7	2.7

Source: World Bank staff estimates (see box 7.1).
Note: The data include both federal and state spending. GDP = gross domestic product; SDG = Sudanese pounds.

The shares of gross domestic product (GDP) and total public spending allocated to education have also risen, further indicating the importance the government attaches to the education sector. Since 2000, the share of education in total public spending has increased by close to 4 percentage points to 12 percent, and as a share of GDP, it has more than doubled to 2.7 percent (table 7.1).

The government's efforts to expand public education are also shown by the increase in total (federal and state) recurrent education spending per school-age child since 2000 (figure 7.1).[4] In real terms, spending per school-age child (6–16 years old) has grown by approximately 13 percent per year since 2000 to SDG 265 in 2009. The number of school-age children grew by roughly 1.7 percent annually between 2000 and 2009, but enrollment grew even faster (at 3.7 percent) as a result of the sustained increase in education spending over this period. However, between 2008 and 2009, there was a slight decline in public per-student spending, arguably the result of the downward pressure on overall public spending applied by the financial crisis.

The continuous increase in education spending may not be sustainable, however, if economic growth slows down. GDP has grown rapidly since 2000, mainly because of growth in oil revenues, which has enabled a substantial expansion of the public sector (see chapter 1, on setting the scene).

Figure 7.1 Recurrent Public Education Spending per School-Age Child, 2000–09
constant 2008 Sudanese pounds

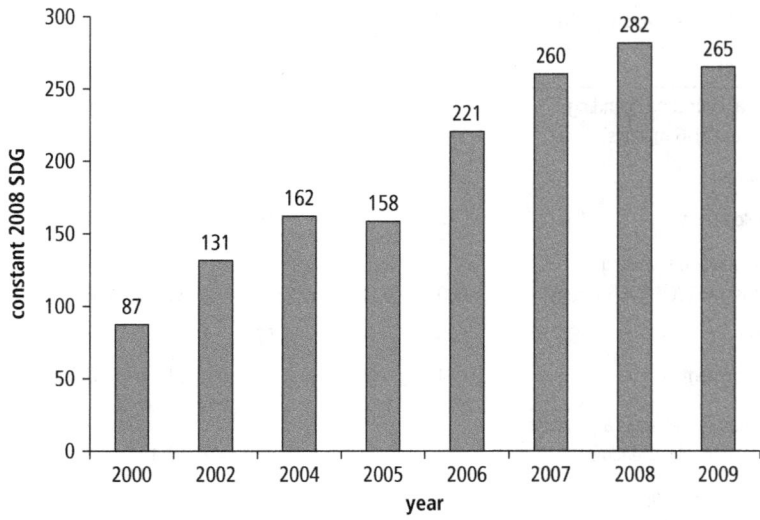

Source: World Bank staff estimates (see box 7.1).

But available estimates suggest that oil production will peak in 2012 (World Bank 2010a), and if oil production or oil prices decline, lower government revenues may put downward pressure on education spending.

Despite the increase in education spending since 2000, northern Sudan spends less as a share of total public spending and of GDP than do countries with similar incomes and other countries in the region with comparable dependency ratios (see annex table 7A.1).[5] In 2008, education spending as a share of total public spending was roughly 13 percent (figure 7.2). By comparison, other countries spent more—including neighboring Chad, Ethiopia, and Kenya; other lower-middle-income countries in the Sub-Saharan African region; and Morocco and Tunisia.

Northern Sudan also spent relatively less on education as a share of GDP: 2.7 percent compared with 3–7 percent of GDP for neighboring countries Chad, Ethiopia, and Kenya (figure 7.2). Other lower-middle-income countries also spent more by this measure: Cape Verde, Côte d'Ivoire, and Lesotho in Sub-Saharan Africa, and the Arab Republic of Egypt, Morocco, and Tunisia in North Africa.

Recurrent spending accounts for the vast majority of total education spending (figure 7.3 and annex table 7A.2).[6] In 2000, real recurrent edu-

Figure 7.2 Comparison of Public Education Spending, by Country, 2005–08

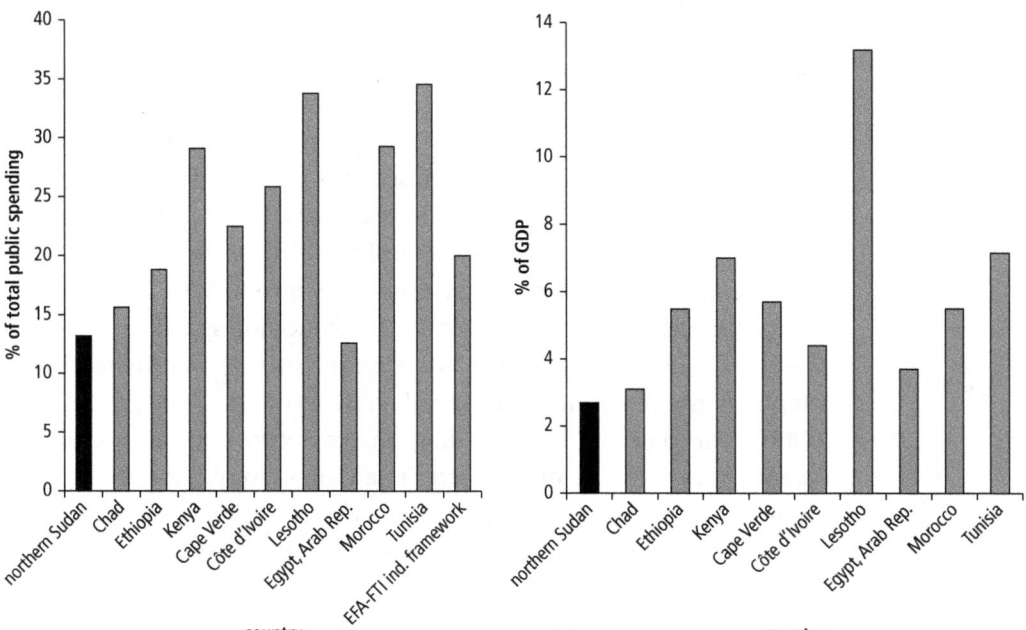

Sources: World Bank staff estimates (see box 7.1); Pôle de Dakar database 2010; World Bank 2010b; HNP Database 2010.
Note: The data are for the latest year available for 2005–08.

Figure 7.3 Development and Recurrent Public Education Spending Shares, 2000–09
percent

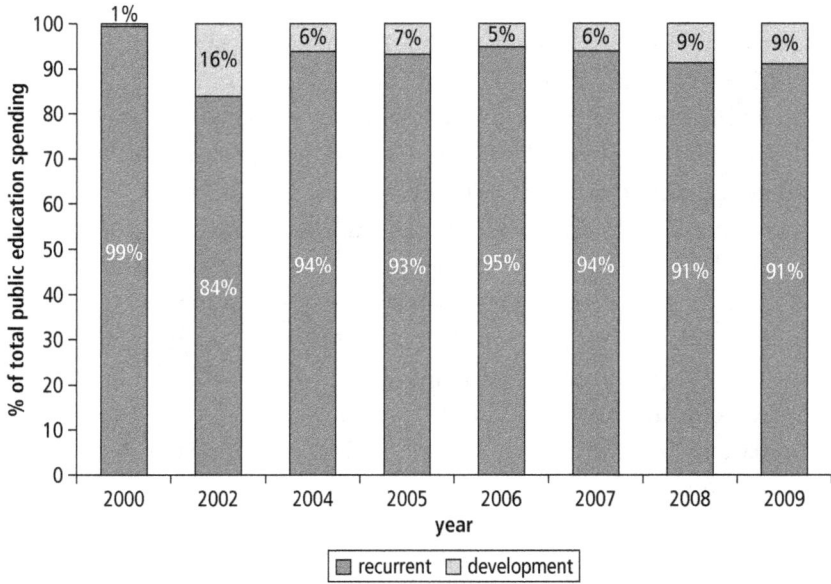

Source: World Bank staff estimates (see box 7.1).

cation spending was SDG 656 million and accounted for more than 99 percent of total education spending. By 2009, its share had declined to 91 percent of total education spending, but in absolute terms, it had risen to SDG 2.2 billion because of the overall expansion of education spending.

Development spending has increased over the period but remains low (figure 7.3 and annex table 7A.3).[7] In real terms, it was SDG 4 million in 2000, constituting less than 1 percent of total education spending. However, development spending has increased over time to SDG 217 million in 2009, equivalent to 9 percent of total public education spending. The larger share of development spending in 2002 (16 percent) was the result of a temporary rise in development spending in Khartoum State (World Bank 2010b). The generally low spending on development poses a challenge because many schools in northern Sudan are of very poor quality.[8] For instance, in 2007, 42 percent of classrooms in basic schools were in need of repairs, and 9 percent required complete replacement (FMOGE 2008).

Education spending at the state level has increased since 2000, and 83 percent of total public education spending took place at the state level in 2009 (figure 7.4 and annex table 7A.2). In 2000, state-level education spending in real terms was SDG 380 million, which by 2009, had risen to

Figure 7.4 Public Education Spending, by Administrative Level, 2000–09

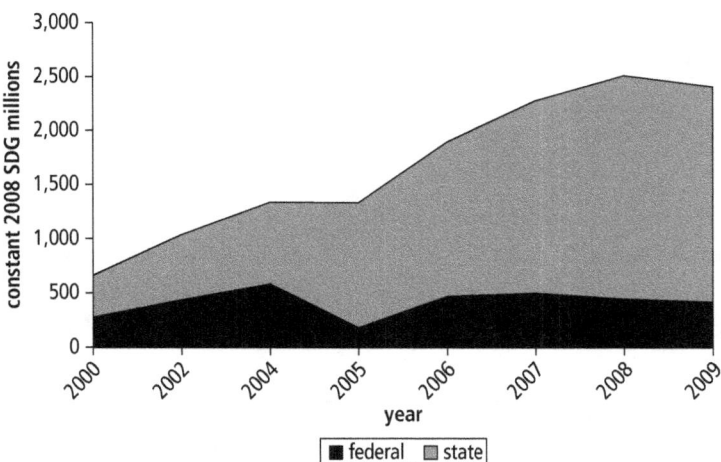

Source: World Bank staff estimates (see box 7.1).

almost SDG 2 billion. Spending at the federal level also increased over the period, from SDG 280 million in 2000 to SDG 420 million in 2009. But there was a decline in education spending at both the federal and the state levels between 2008 and 2009, which was likely the result of a tightening of overall public spending, including that for education, caused by the financial crisis.[9]

The share of recurrent education spending assigned to each education level provides an indication of government education priorities, with basic education accounting for the largest share at 49 percent in 2009 (table 7.2). Because basic education in northern Sudan is eight years long rather than six years, after adjusting for length, the share of basic education in total education spending was even lower at 37 percent. Technical secondary education constituted only 1 percent of recurrent education spending, whereas academic secondary accounted for 16 percent. Given the increase in enrollment in basic education, demand for secondary education is likely to rise, thereby requiring more spending at this level to accommodate a larger number of students while also maintaining the quality of education. The share of total recurrent education spending allocated to higher education was 30 percent in 2009. By contrast, preschool spending accounted for just 2 percent, and literacy programs for 1 percent, of total recurrent education spending. The relatively small spending share for literacy programs contrasts with the large share of children who have never attended school (see chapter 4, on disparities).

Table 7.2 Recurrent Public Education Spending, by Education Level, 2009

Education level	Recurrent education spending (constant 2008 SDG millions)	Share of total recurrent education spending (percent)	Share of total public enrollment (percent)
Preschool	54	2	7
Basic	1,068	49	74
Secondary			
Academic	359	16	9
Technical	20	1	0.4
Literacy program	22	1	3
Higher[a]	663	30	7
Total	2,187	100	100

Source: World Bank staff estimates (see box 7.1).
Note: The data include both federal and state spending. SDG = Sudanese pounds.
a. The 2009 budget allocation with the 2008 percentage execution rate; excludes Juba University.

The share of basic education in total education spending in northern Sudan was lower than that in most countries in Sub-Saharan Africa and North Africa, as shown in table 7.3.[10] For instance, Egypt, Kenya, and Morocco spent 40 percent, 55 percent, and 46 percent, respectively, of total public education spending on primary education, compared with 37 percent in northern Sudan (after adjusting for eight years, rather than six, of basic education).

On academic secondary education, northern Sudan spent a smaller share of total recurrent education spending (16 percent) than did the lower-middle-income countries of Morocco (19 percent) and Tunisia (22 percent). The spending share for higher education in northern Sudan was 30 percent, compared with 39 percent in Egypt, 22 percent in Tunisia, and 16 percent in Morocco.

COMPOSITION OF RECURRENT EDUCATION SPENDING

Teacher salaries accounted for the largest share of total recurrent education spending at an average of 75 percent, excluding higher education (table 7.4 and figure 7.5).[11] In 2009, teacher salary spending ranged from 62 percent for literacy programs to 81 percent for preschool. Nonteaching staff salaries and spending on goods and services each accounted for an average of 11 percent of recurrent education spending. In higher education, teacher and nonteaching staff salaries jointly accounted for 69 percent of recurrent spending. The share of nonteaching staff salaries

Table 7.3 Comparison of Public Education Spending, by Region/Country and Education Level, 2005–08
percent

Subsector	Primary	Upper secondary	Higher
Northern Sudan	37 *(49)*[a]	16	30
Neighboring countries			
Chad	48	12	23
Ethiopia	51	8	20
Kenya	55	12	16
Lower-middle-income countries in Sub-Saharan Africa			
Cape Verde	39	16	12
Côte d'Ivoire	43	10	21
Lesotho	36	11	37
Lower-middle-income countries in North Africa			
Egypt, Arab Rep.	40	—	39
Morocco	46	19	16
Tunisia	35	22	22

Sources: World Bank staff estimates (see box 7.1); Pôle de Dakar database 2010; World Bank 2010b; HNP Database 2010.
Note: The data are for the latest year available for 2005–08; — = not available.
a. The share of primary education in total public education spending is adjusted to six years for northern Sudan, and the data are for six years of primary education for all other countries shown. The 49 percent in parentheses is for eight years of basic education.

Table 7.4 Composition of Recurrent Public Education Spending, by Education Level, 2009
constant 2008 SDG millions

Subsector	Teacher salaries	Nonteaching staff salaries	Goods and services	Student subsidy	Total
Preschool	44	6	4	n.a.	54
Basic	827	192	50	n.a.	1,068
Academic secondary	247	83	29	n.a.	359
Technical secondary	14	5	2	n.a.	20
Literacy program	13	5	4	n.a.	22
Higher	460		108	96	663
Total					2,187

Source: World Bank staff estimates (see box 7.1).
Note: The data include both federal and state spending; n.a. = not applicable.

Figure 7.5 Composition of Recurrent Public Education Spending, by Education Level, 2009
percent

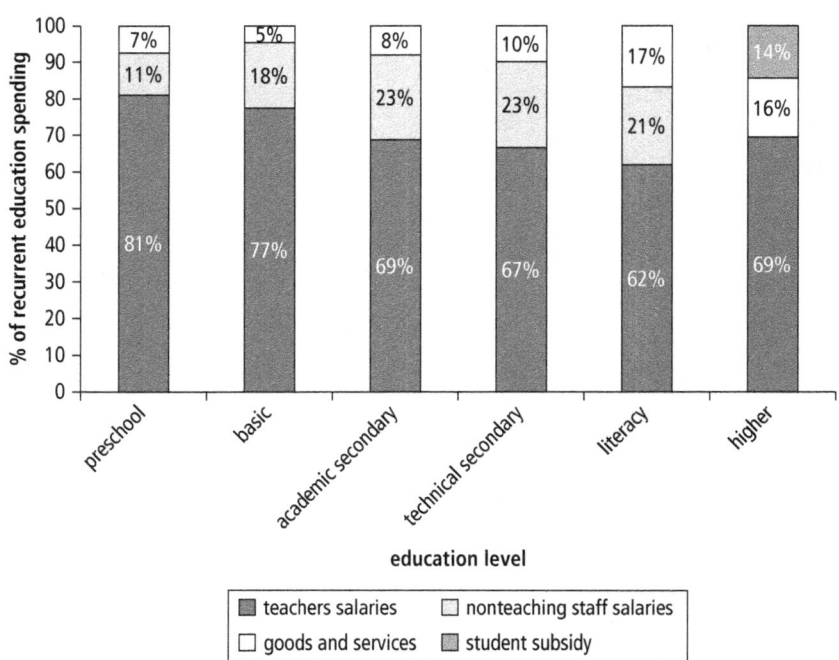

Source: World Bank staff estimates (see box 7.1).
Note: The data include both federal and state spending. Teacher salaries for higher education include nonteaching staff salaries.

was smallest for preschool (11 percent) and largest for academic secondary and technical secondary education (each 23 percent). For higher education, student subsidies made up 14 percent of total spending.

Spending on goods and services is generally low, and particularly so for basic education. Goods and services accounted for only 5 percent of recurrent spending for basic education, 16 percent for higher education, and up to 17 percent for literacy programs. The relatively small share of goods and services in basic education is frequently supplemented by household spending for school running costs (see annex table 7A.1; EU 2008; and chapter 5, on service delivery).

PUBLIC PER-STUDENT SPENDING

The next section examines per-student spending to provide insights into the allocation of resources across different education levels and into the composition of spending for the average student at each education level. Per-student spending in northern Sudan in 2009 was computed as recurrent public education spending per student enrolled at each education level for 13 of the 15 states (Southern Darfur and Western Darfur were excluded because of data limitations).

COMPOSITION OF PER-STUDENT SPENDING

The more advanced the education level, the higher the per-student spending. As shown in table 7.5, average per-student spending was lowest for preschool (SDG 119) and basic education (SDG 231) and highest for higher education (SDG 1,532), with academic secondary and technical secondary education falling in between (SDG 664 and SDG 709, respectively).

For basic education, average per-student spending in northern Sudan in 2009 equaled just over 8 percent of GDP per capita compared with the Sub-Saharan African regional average of 12 percent (table 7.6). Public per-student spending as a share of GDP per capita in northern Sudan was also lower than that share in all other regions, including the Middle East and North Africa, which spent a much higher share (17 percent of GDP per capita) on basic education.

Average spending per student in secondary education in northern Sudan (25 percent) was roughly in line with that of other regions (table 7.6). For instance, the Middle East and North Africa spent, on average, 20 percent of GDP per capita for each student in secondary education, and South Asia spent 19 percent. Average per-student

Table 7.5 Composition of Per-Student Spending, by Education Level, 2009

Education level	Percentage of GDP per capita	Teachers	Nonteaching staff[a]	Goods and services	Student subsidy	Total spending (constant 2008 SDG)
Preschool	4.3	96	14	9	n.a	119
Basic	8.4	179	42	11	n.a	231
Secondary						
Academic	24.1	456	154	54	n.a	664
Technical	25.7	471	166	71	n.a	709
Higher	55.6	1,062		249	221	1,532

Source: World Bank staff estimates (see box 7.1).
Note: Per-student spending excludes development spending and the states of Southern Darfur and Western Darfur; n.a. = not applicable.
a. Nonteaching staff includes, for example, administrators, inspectors, cleaners, and guards.

Table 7.6 Comparison of Public Per-Student Spending, by Region and Education Level, 2002–08

	Percentage of GDP per capita			
Country/region	Basic	Secondary	Higher	Higher (2005 US$, current prices)
Northern Sudan	8	25	56	950
Sub-Saharan Africa	12	30	322	1,780
Low-income countries	12	33	359	1,460
Lower-middle-income countries	12	18	97	3,700
East Asia and Pacific	13	14	59	1,530
Eastern Europe and Central Asia	15	18	23	1,040
Middle East and North Africa	17	20	40	1,240
South Asia	14	19	61	285

Sources: World Bank staff estimates (see box 7.1); Mingat and Majgaard 2010; World Bank 2010b.

spending in Sub-Saharan Africa for both low-income and lower-middle-income countries was higher at 30 percent and 33 percent, respectively.

Northern Sudan spent roughly 56 percent of GDP per capita for each student in higher education, which placed it between the average of 40 percent of GDP per capita for the Middle East and North Africa region and 97 percent for middle-income countries in Sub-Saharan Africa. Per-student spending as a share of GDP per capita in other regions ranged from 23 percent in Eastern Europe and Central Asia to 359 percent in low-income Sub-Saharan African countries. In absolute terms, per-student spending in northern Sudan (US$950) was higher than such spending in South Asia (US$285), similar to it in the Eastern Europe and Central Asia region (US$1,040), but lower than per-student spending in the Middle East and North Africa region (US$1,240).

ANALYSIS OF SPENDING ON EDUCATION STAFF

The public education system has non–school-based and school-based staff. Non–school-based staff includes administrators and inspectors at the central and decentralized levels. The school-based staff consists of government teachers, national service and volunteer teachers, and nonteaching staff.[12] Of the school-based staff, government teachers, administrators, inspectors, and other nonteaching staff are on the government payroll, whereas national service and volunteer teachers are not.[13] In 2009, there was a total of approximately 217,000 education staff on the government payroll in 13 of the 15 states in northern Sudan (table 7.7).[14] In terms of school-based staff, the majority were government teachers

Table 7.7 Composition of Education Staff, by Education Level, 2009

Education level	(a) + (b) + (c) Total education staff on government payroll	(a) Central and decentralized education staff	School based			(c) + (d) Total teachers
			(b) Government nonteaching staff	(c) Government teachers	(d) National service and volunteer teachers[a]	
Preschool	9,592	444	327	8,821	4,196	13,017
Basic	153,010	8,415	18,486	126,109	5,388	131,497
Secondary	50,857	3,790	13,515	33,552	1,964	35,516
Literacy program	3,365	756	110	2,499	5,910	8,409
Total	216,824	13,405	32,438	170,981	17,458	188,439

Source: World Bank staff estimates (see box 7.1).
Note: The data exclude Southern Darfur and Western Darfur.
a. These teachers are not on the government payroll.

(170,981) followed by government nonteaching staff (32,438), and national service and volunteer teachers (17,458). There were also about 13,405 non–school-based education staff at the central and decentralized levels.

An oversupply of teachers is costly because salaries constitute by far the largest spending component; however, an insufficient number of teachers can affect the quality of education services. According to the Education for All Fast-Track Initiative (EFA-FTI), the recommended student-teacher ratio (STR) for primary education in Sub-Saharan Africa is 40:1. The average STR for basic education in northern Sudan is 34:1 (excluding national service and volunteer teachers), which is below the EFA-FTI recommendation. However, there is notable variation in STRs at the state level (see Analysis of State-Level Education Spending later in this chapter), and given teacher subject specialization, class sizes are sometimes large (see chapter 6, on teachers).

In 2009, the average salary for school-based education staff was approximately SDG 6,400 per year, the equivalent of 2.1 times GDP per capita (table 7.8).[15,16] Examining average annual salaries by staff type shows that administrators had the highest salaries, at about SDG 8,800 (2.6 times GDP per capita), followed by inspectors, at SDG 7,600 (2.4 times GDP per capita). By comparison, government teachers earned an average of SDG 6,900 (2 times GDP per capita), and other nonteaching staff (that is, cleaners, drivers, and guards) earned SDG 3,200 (1.1 times per capita income). The relatively high salaries of administrators and inspectors were mainly the result of higher qualifications and greater

Table 7.8 Average Salaries of School-Based Staff in Northern Sudan, by Education Level, 2009

		Nonteaching staff			
Education level	Government teachers	Administrators	Inspectors	Other nonteaching staff[a]	Total
Average salary (current SDG)	**6,892**	**8,828**	**7,621**	**3,173**	**6,385**
Preschool	5,160	6,790	6,271	3,750	5,162
Basic	6,708	8,320	7,298	3,238	6,325
Secondary	8,184	9,691	9,390	3,062	6,885
Literacy program	5,091	7,665	7,240	3,424	5,143
Average salary (multiple of GDP per capita)	**2.0**	**2.6**	**2.4**	**1.1**	**2.1**
Preschool	1.7	2.2	2.0	1.2	1.7
Basic	2.2	2.7	2.3	1.0	2.0
Secondary	2.6	3.1	3.0	1.0	2.2
Literacy program	1.6	2.5	2.3	1.1	1.7

Source: World Bank staff estimates (see box 7.1).
Note: The table excludes Southern Darfur and Western Darfur and national service and volunteer teachers because of data limitations.
a. Other nonteaching staff includes, for example, cleaners, drivers, gardeners, guards, and janitors.

experience than teachers (EU 2008). To assess whether teacher salaries are comparable to those of other professionals with similar educational attainment requires labor market data on earnings, which were not available at the time of the preparation of this report.

For administrators, inspectors, and teachers, average salaries rose with the education level at which they worked (table 7.8). This suggests that teachers with more training were paid more, as would be expected. Other nonteaching staff, which exclude administrators and inspectors, earned roughly the same salaries at each education level because they performed similar tasks and had similar training regardless of the education level at which they worked.

Average salaries for primary teachers in northern Sudan measured as a multiple of GDP per capita were lower than those in neighboring countries and lower-middle-income countries in Sub-Saharan Africa (table 7.9). In neighbors Chad, Ethiopia, and Kenya, primary school teachers earned about 5–7 times GDP per capita compared with 2 times GDP per capita in northern Sudan in 2009. In the lower-middle-income countries of Côte d'Ivoire and Lesotho, teacher salaries were roughly 5 times GDP per capita, and in Morocco, they were 3.4 times larger. By

Table 7.9 Comparison of Average Primary Teacher Salaries, by Region/Country, 2002–08

Region/country	Average primary teacher salary (multiple of GDP per capita)
Northern Sudan	2.2
Neighboring countries	
Chad	5.4
Ethiopia	7.3
Kenya	5.3
Lower-middle-income countries in Sub-Saharan Africa	
Cape Verde	—
Côte d'Ivoire	4.9
Lesotho	5.0
Lower-middle-income countries in North Africa	
Egypt, Arab Rep.	0.5
Morocco	3.4
Tunisia	1.8

Sources: World Bank staff estimates (see box 7.1); Pôle de Dakar database 2010; UNESCO Institute for Statistics 2006.
Note: The data are for the latest year available for 2002–08; — = not available.

contrast, primary teacher salaries in Egypt and Tunisia were 0.5 and 1.8 times GDP per capita, respectively.

HOUSEHOLD OUT-OF-POCKET EDUCATION SPENDING

Basic education in northern Sudan is supposed to be provided for free, but when public education spending is insufficient, households pay out-of-pocket to make up for shortfalls. The data presented in this section are drawn from several small-scale surveys because data on household education spending are not collected on a regular basis in northern Sudan. Table 7.10 presents some of the data available for students enrolled in public schools. These household out-of-pocket payments are only for school running costs, including school maintenance, water and electricity, and supplementary teacher salary payments. Other school costs incurred by households—for uniforms, transport, and textbooks, for example—are excluded.

In North Kordofan State, household out-of-pocket spending per student was SDG 13 for preschool, SDG 19 for basic education, and SDG 20

Table 7.10 Average Annual Household Out-of-Pocket Spending per Student, Selected States, 2008–09
current SDG

Source (year)	Preschool	Basic education	Secondary education
State visits (2009)[a]	—	15	46
Service delivery study (2008–09)[b]	—	13	—
North Kordofan data (2008–09)	13	19	20

Note: The data exclude household spending on uniforms, transport, textbooks, and the like; — = not available.
a. These are the averages for Al Qadarif, Kassala, South Kordofan, and White Nile states.
b. This is the average for Kassala, North Kordofan, and River Nile, states.

for academic secondary education in 2008–09. In Al Qadarif, Kassala, South Kordofan, and White Nile states, average household out-of-pocket spending was SDG 15 per student for basic education; and in Kassala, North Kordofan, and River Nile, the average was SDG 13 per student.

The average SDG 15 per student spent by households on basic school running costs in 2009 was higher than the government spending per student for school running costs, which was SDG 12.[17] This means that in many schools, household out-of-pocket payments provided the main source of financing for everyday school running costs. The household spending in table 7.10 was only for school operating costs, but households incur additional costs for uniforms, textbooks, meals, and so on.

In 2009, urban households reported spending an average of SDG 84, and rural households SDG 24, per person on education per year (Castro 2010). Although rural households notably spent less, on average, than urban households in absolute terms, education accounted for 2 percent of consumption for rural households compared with 3 percent for urban households.

Education accounted for a larger share of consumption for poor rural households (2 percent) than for nonpoor rural households (1 percent) (Castro 2010). For urban households, both poor and nonpoor, education spending accounted for 3 percent of consumption. Thus, for the poorest households, out-of-pocket costs pose a barrier to education, and even more so when a family has many children, with implications for student attendance and dropout (EU 2008).

ANALYSIS OF STATE-LEVEL EDUCATION SPENDING

The education system in northern Sudan is decentralized, with large differences in education spending and capacities to deliver education services across the 15 states. This section provides an overview of these differences.

STATE EDUCATION SPENDING

Most states allocated a large share of their total public spending to education, 31 percent, on average, in 2009 (figure 7.6).[18] Dividing states into groups based on gross enrollment rates (GERs)—high (Al Jazirah, Khartoum, Northern, River Nile, and White Nile), intermediate (Al Qadarif, North Kordofan, Sinnar, South Kordofan, and Western Darfur), and low (Blue Nile, Kassala, Northern Darfur, Red Sea, and Southern Darfur)—as in chapter 4 on disparities, shows that some states spent a larger share of their total public spending on education.

In the high-GER group, the education share in total state public spending ranged from 22 to 48 percent compared with 14–37 percent for the intermediate-GER group and 12–47 percent for the low-GER group. These data suggest that some states, given their available resources, prioritize education more highly. However, certain states arguably have to spend more on other sectors, such as security, leaving fewer resources for education.

PER-STUDENT SPENDING BY STATE

Public per-student spending also varied widely across states. Again, grouping them into high-, intermediate-, and low-GER states illustrates the big differences in average per-student spending across education levels for the three groups (figure 7.7). The high-GER group, on average, spent more per student at each education level than did the intermediate- and low-GER groups.[19]

In individual states, there is no clear pattern in per-student spending by education level (figure 7.8). Some states had relatively low per-student spending across the three education levels, whereas others had relatively high per-student spending for one education level and low spending for another. For instance, both Al Qadarif and South Kordofan spent about SDG 200 per student in basic education, yet Al Qadarif spent much more than South Kordofan in secondary education, about SDG 741 per student compared with SDG 416.

At the preschool level, average per-student spending was SDG 121 and ranged from a low of SDG 31 in Western Darfur to a high of SDG 329 in Khartoum State (see annex table 7A.3). The education systems in the three Darfur states were also supported by the donor community, and nongovernmental organizations (NGOs) played a substantial role, which

Figure 7.6 State Education Spending as a Share of State Total Public Spending, 2009
percent

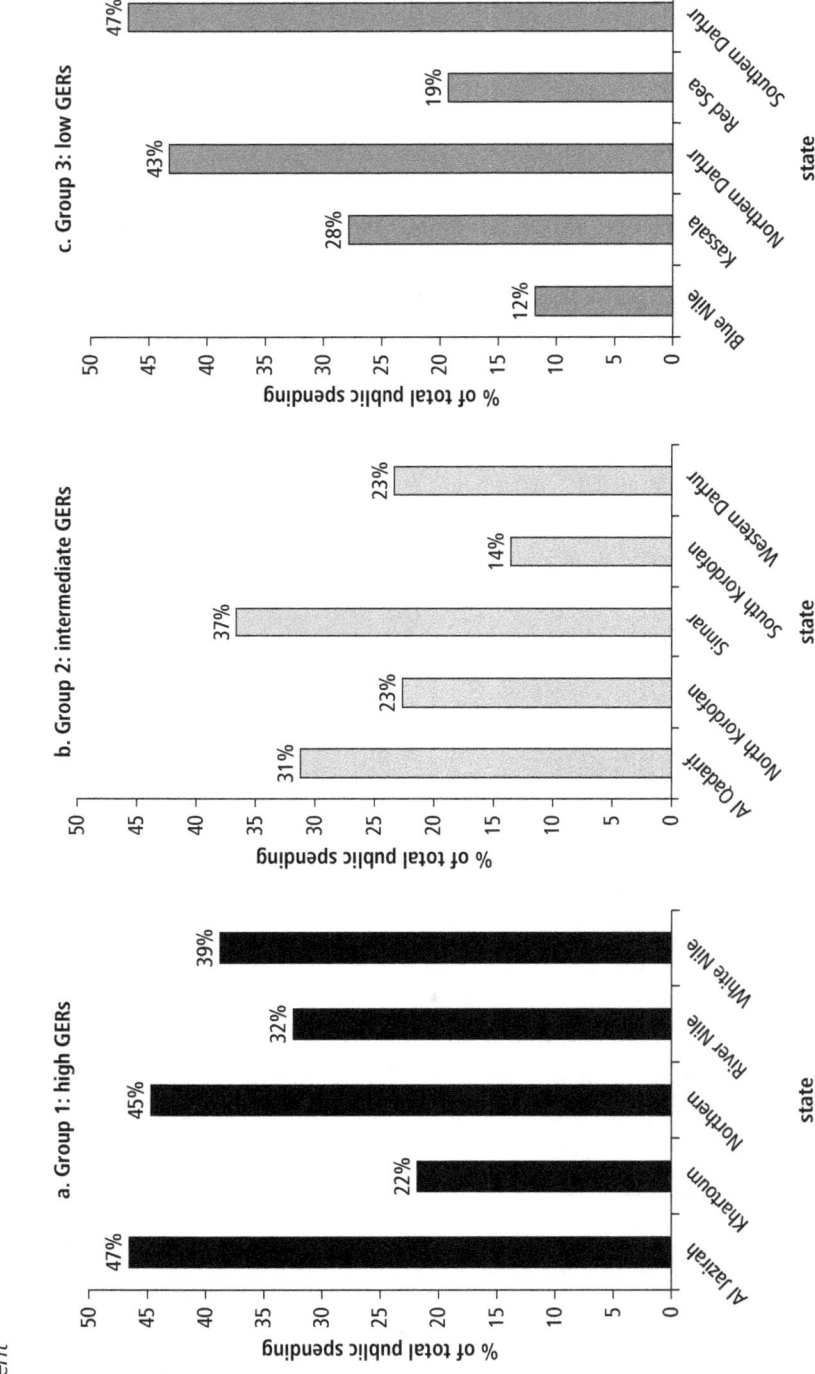

Source: World Bank staff estimates (see box 7.1).

Figure 7.7 Average Public Per-Student Spending, by GER Group, 2009

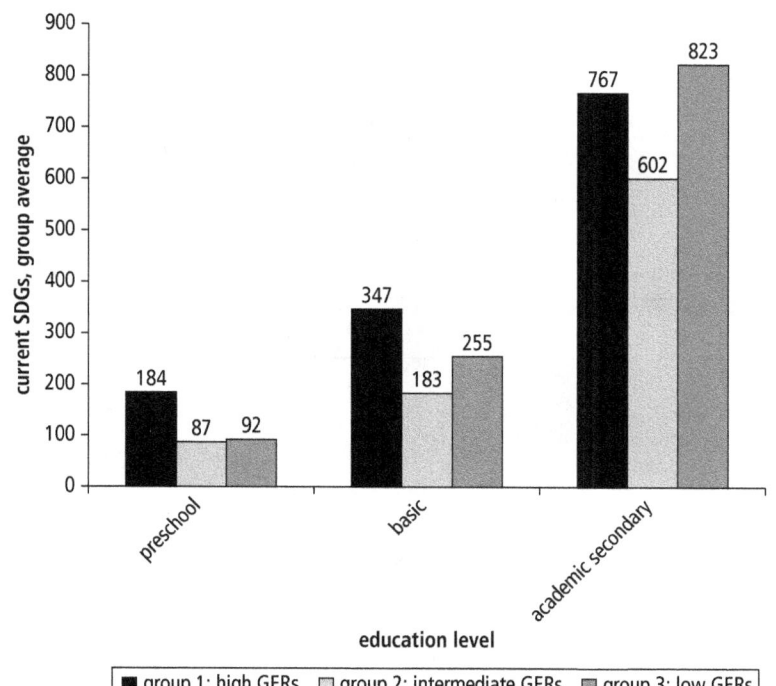

Source: World Bank staff estimates (see box 7.1).

potentially compensated for the relatively low public per-student spending at the state level. However, data on donor and NGO financing for education were not available during the preparation of this report.

An example of the variation in preschool spending per student was provided by Northern and Red Sea states. They had quite similar numbers of students, but per-student spending was four times higher in Northern State, and teacher salaries as a multiple of GDP per capita were lower (1.2 times GDP per capita in Northern compared with 2.2 times GDP per capita in Red Sea). This information may partly explain the large difference in average student-teacher ratios (STRs), which were 18:1 in Northern State and 198:1 in Red Sea State. Another reason for the big variation in STRs is that in some states, teachers not on the government payroll—for instance, volunteer teachers paid by the community—constituted a large share of preschool teachers. When these teachers were included, the STRs across states were more similar. That certain states relied to a large extent on communities to finance preschool teachers raises questions about their training and utilization as compared with government teachers.

Figure 7.8 Public Per-Student Spending, by Education Level and State, 2009

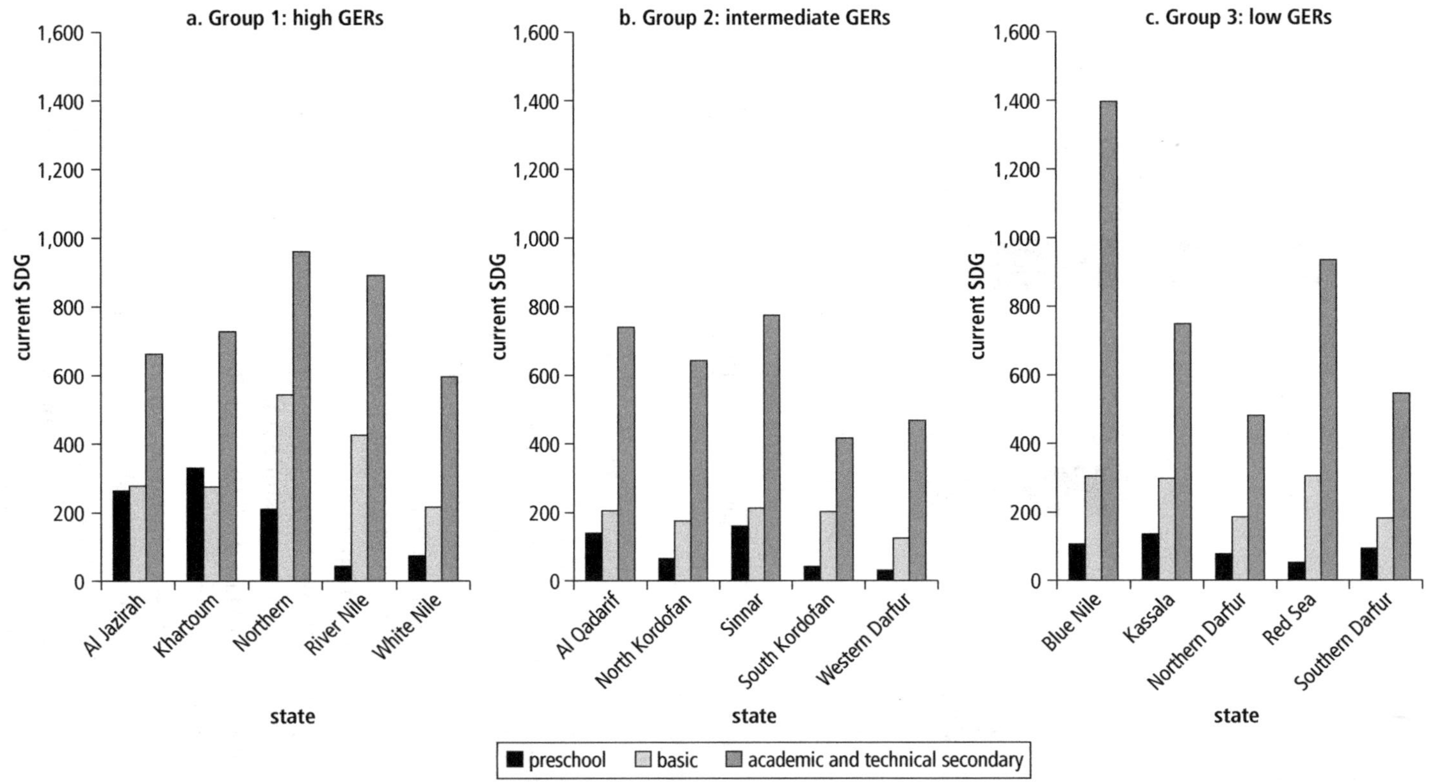

Source: World Bank staff estimates (see box 7.1).
Note: The data exclude national service and volunteer teachers and federal spending.

For basic education, average per-student spending across states was SDG 262, but varied from SDG 124 in Western Darfur to SDG 542 in Northern State (see annex table 7A.4). Teacher salaries were fairly similar across states because they are centrally determined, which implies that the variation in spending per student was largely driven by differences in spending on nonteaching staff and goods and services, and in the number of teachers. There was also less variation in average STRs in basic education than in preschool, with STRs ranging from 17:1 in Northern State to 64:1 in Western Darfur.

Per-student spending for academic secondary education started at SDG 417 in South Kordofan and rose to SDG 1,416 in Blue Nile State (see annex table 7A.5). For technical secondary education, spending per student was generally somewhat higher than for the academic track. It ranged from SDG 354 in South Kordofan to SDG 1,194 in Red Sea (see annex table 7A.6). Secondary education STRs varied less across states than did those for either preschool or basic education.

FEDERAL TRANSFERS TO STATES

Since 2005, northern Sudan has undergone a process of fiscal decentralization, which is seen as key to addressing regional inequalities in the postconflict environment. The 15 states receive transfers from the federal government, and the states in turn transfer resources to local governments (localities). The federal transfers consist primarily of nonsector-specific block transfers, and the states determine how much of these to allocate to education; but some transfers are also earmarked for specific items.

Federal transfers constitute a substantial share of state and local revenues in most states. In 2009, the share of federal transfers in total revenues by state ranged from a high of 91 percent in Blue Nile State to 51 percent in Kassala and Red Sea states and a low of 27 percent in Khartoum State (figure 7.9).

Given the importance of federal transfers in state budgets, the unpredictability of transfers (in terms of discrepancies between budgeted and realized transfers and delays in disbursements) makes it difficult for states to plan their education spending. There are notable differences in transfer realization rates across items. For instance, the budget execution rate for earmarked transfers for higher education goods and services spending ranged from a low of 6 percent to a high of 92 percent, and for salaries, from 93 percent to 118 percent during the period 2005 to 2008 (World Bank 2007).

Figure 7.9   Federal Transfers and State Own Revenues as a Share of Total Revenues, 2008
percent

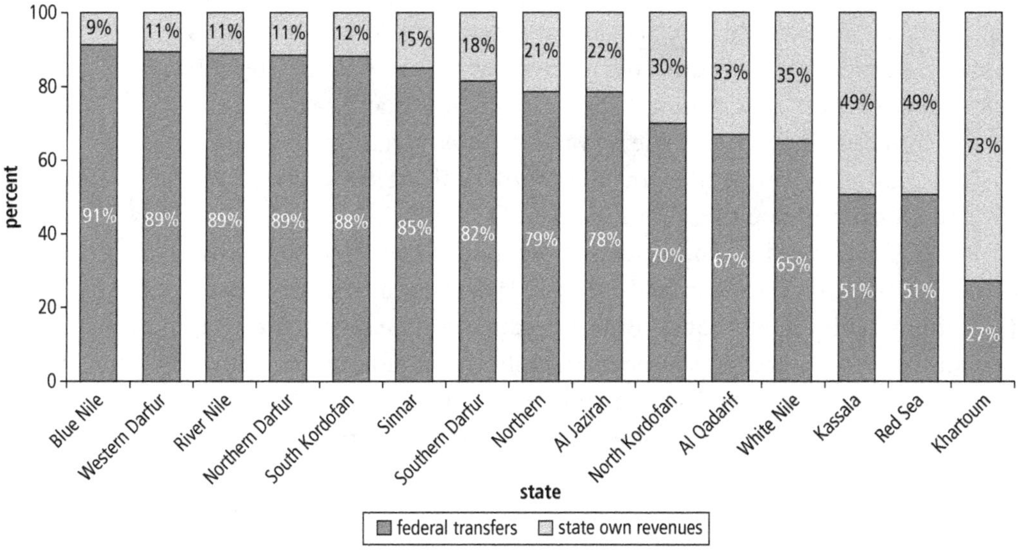

State	federal transfers	state own revenues
Blue Nile	91%	9%
Western Darfur	89%	11%
River Nile	89%	11%
Northern Darfur	89%	11%
South Kordofan	88%	12%
Sinnar	85%	15%
Southern Darfur	82%	18%
Northern	79%	21%
Al Jazirah	78%	22%
North Kordofan	70%	30%
Al Qadarif	67%	33%
White Nile	65%	35%
Kassala	51%	49%
Red Sea	51%	49%
Khartoum	27%	73%

Source: World Bank Poverty Reduction and Economic Management, Africa Region, preliminary estimates.

The intention behind federal transfers is to redistribute resources so that all states are given equal opportunity to provide public services, including education, to their citizens.[20] The federal transfers are meant to be determined according to a formula based on a state's financial performance, population size, natural resources, human resources, infrastructure, education status, security status, and per capita income, where each component is assigned a weight that indicates the importance given to it by the government (EU 2008).

However, in practice, the basis on which federal transfers are allocated is not clear. Although the formula is known, the computations used to determine the size of actual federal transfers to each state are not available, which makes it impossible to assess whether the intent of providing larger transfers to states with larger needs occurs in practice. Rather, discussions with the states indicate that transfers for education are primarily based on a state's existing payroll and obligations (last year's budget plus a negotiated increment) (also see EU 2008). Although this system helps states honor their payroll obligations and keep existing education services running, it also tends to perpetuate existing inequalities and reduce states' spending autonomy. For example, states need approval from the federal level before they can hire more teachers, or they risk not being able to honor their payroll, particularly if their own revenues are small. Thus, although the provision of public education is decentralized, the federal government agencies that negotiate the recurrent transfers with states largely determine the pace of growth in the provision of services in states with fewer own resources.

States with higher average GERs received, on average, larger federal transfers per capita, which suggests that the states with greater education needs may not be receiving the larger federal transfers (figure 7.10).[21,22] Some high-GER states (group 1)—for instance, River Nile and Northern states—with relatively high per-student spending and GERs, received relatively large transfers. At the same time, some low-GER states (group 3) with relatively low per-student spending—such as Southern Darfur, Northern Darfur, and Kassala—received smaller per capita transfers.

Figure 7.10 Federal Transfers per Capita and Average GER, by State, 2008–09

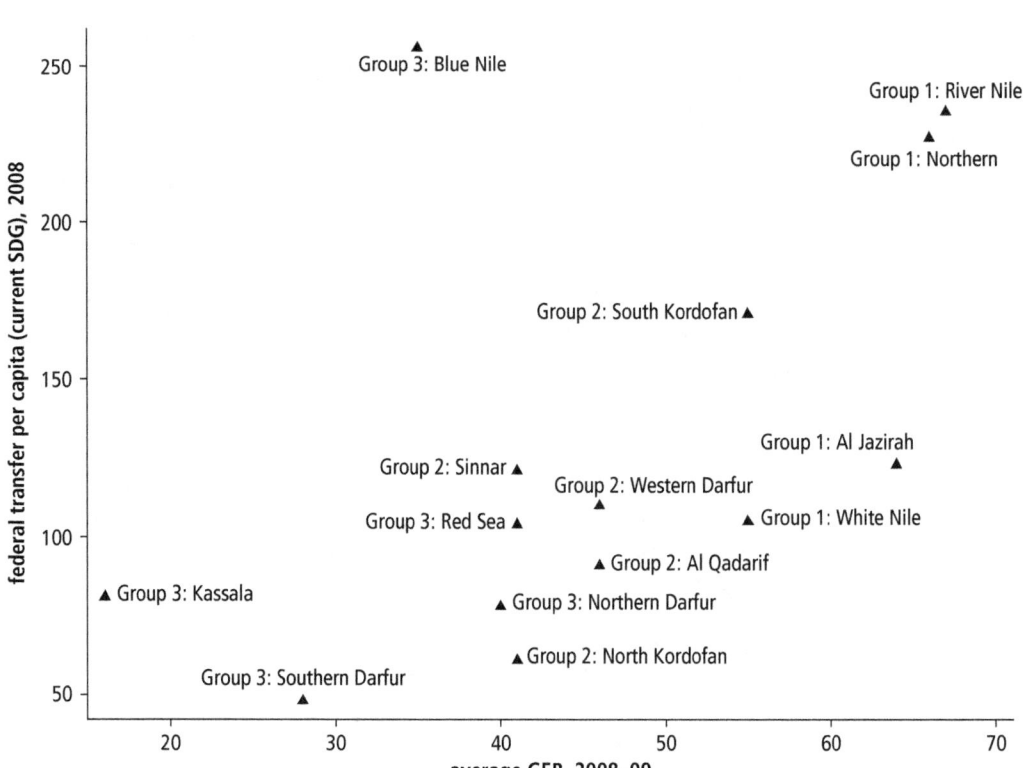

Source: World Bank Poverty Reduction and Economic Management, Africa Region, preliminary estimates.
Note: The federal transfers refer to all sectors. The average GER (gross enrollment rate) applies to preschool, basic school, and secondary school.

SUMMARY

- Total public education spending in northern Sudan has increased substantially over time and so has public spending per student, which indicates the commitment and effort of the government to expand educational opportunities. But total public education spending was relatively low from a regional perspective, both as a share of GDP and as a share of total public spending. Public per-student spending was also generally low compared with that in other countries in the region for each education level.
- The share of public spending on basic education in northern Sudan was smaller than the share in neighboring countries and lower-middle-income countries in both Sub-Saharan and North Africa. It was also smaller than the EFA-FTI benchmark. The steady rise in enrollment in basic education will also put pressure on secondary education spending to accommodate rising demand for secondary education over the next few years.
- Teacher salaries constituted the largest spending component, on average 76 percent of total recurrent spending (excluding higher education). The 24 percent spent on goods and services and the non-teaching staff is notably less than the 33 percent EFA-FTI benchmark. In basic education, in particular, public spending on goods and services was low and accounted for only 5 percent of total recurrent spending.
- Household out-of-pocket payments covered a large share of school running costs, especially for basic education, implying that basic education is not always free in practice. Moreover, education accounted for a larger share of consumption for poor rural households than for non-poor rural households, which has implications for equity in access to education.
- Most states allocated a large share of their total public spending to education, on average, 31 percent. However, there were notable differences in public per-student spending across the 15 states. Federal transfers constitute the bulk of state revenues, and are intended to assist lagging states to catch up in terms of public service provision, including education. But in practice, federal transfers seem to be determined largely by a state's payroll obligations plus an increment, and therefore tend to perpetuate existing disparities.

ANNEX: SPENDING ON EDUCATION

Table 7A.1 Comparison of Public Education Spending, by Region/Country, 2005–08

Region/country	Public education spending		School-age population over total population (percent)	GDP per capita (PPP US$)
	Percentage of total public spending	Percentage of GDP		
Northern Sudan	13.2	2.7	26	1,990
Neighboring countries				
Chad	15.6	3.1	29	1,342
Ethiopia	18.8	5.5	28	740
Kenya	29.1	7.0	25	1,432
Lower-middle-income countries in Sub-Saharan Africa				
Cape Verde	22.5	5.7	23	2,957
Côte d'Ivoire	25.8	4.4	26	1,526
Lesotho	33.8	13.2	22	1,444
Lower-middle-income countries in North Africa				
Egypt, Arab Rep.	12.6	3.7	20	4,212
Morocco	29.3	5.5	19	3,722
Tunisia	34.6	7.1	15	6,743

Sources: World Bank staff estimates (see box 7.1); Pôle de Dakar database 2010; World Bank 2010b; HNP Database (2010).
Note: The data for the latest year available for 2005–08. GDP = gross domestic product; PPP US$ = purchasing power parity in U.S. dollars.

Table 7A.2 Total, Recurrent, and Development Education Spending, by Administrative Level, 2000–09

Administrative level/type of spending	2000	2002	2004	2005	2006	2007	2008	2009
Federal								
Total	280	438	584	183	468	498	447	420
Recurrent	280	438	529	135	433	451	400	374
Development	0	0	55	48	36	47	47	46
State								
Total	380	599	752	1,149	1,423	1,778	2,062	1,984
Recurrent	376	431	723	1,105	1,359	1,685	1,889	1,813
Development	4	168	28	44	64	93	174	171

(continued next page)

Table 7A.2 *(continued)*

Administrative level/type of spending	2000	2002	2004	2005	2006	2007	2008	2009
Federal and state combined								
Total	660	1,037	1,335	1,332	1,892	2,276	2,509	2,404
Recurrent	656	869	1,252	1,241	1,792	2,136	2,288	2,187
Development	4	168	83	91	100	140	221	217

Source: World Bank staff estimates (see box 7.1).

Table 7A.3   Preschool: Overview of State Education Spending and STRs, by Group and State, 2009

Group/state	Per-student spending (current SDG)	Teacher salaries as a multiple of GDP per capita	Student-teacher ratio	Number of students
Group 1: high GERs	184	1.6	62	
Al Jazirah	264	2.0	25	83,263
Khartoum	329	1.3	15	12,362
Northern	210	1.2	18	19,910
River Nile	44	2.1	175	37,012
White Nile	73	1.6	75	43,936
Group 2: intermediate GERs	87	1.6	100	
Al Qadarif	138	1.9	47	28,182
North Kordofan	65	1.3	76	42,347
Sinnar	160	1.3	31	7,355
South Kordofan	41	1.9	153	29,450
Western Darfur	31	1.7	195	24,571
Group 3: low GERs	92	1.7	94	
Blue Nile	106	1.9	71	9,497
Kassala	136	1.5	76	13,841
Northern Darfur	77	1.3	59	45,498
Red Sea	52	2.2	198	17,777
Southern Darfur	93	1.7	64	36,946
Total				451,947

Source: Staff estimates.
Note: The table excludes national service and volunteer teachers and federal spending.

Table 7A.4 Basic Education: Overview of State Education Spending and STRs, by Group and State, 2009

Group/state	Per-student spending (current SDG)	Teacher salaries as a multiple of GDP per capita	Student-teacher ratio	Number of students
Group 1: high GERs	347	2.3	26	
Al Jazirah	278	2.3	30	660,747
Khartoum	274	2.2	30	751,053
Northern	542	2.3	17	111,528
River Nile	425	2.6	22	181,569
White Nile	216	1.9	30	306,663
Group 2: intermediate GERs	183	2.1	43	
Al Qadarif	204	2.1	38	216,709
North Kordofan	174	2.0	42	515,927
Sinnar	212	2.1	33	226,895
South Kordofan	202	2.0	39	265,455
Western Darfur	124	2.2	64	277,882
Group 3: low GERs	255	2.1	34	
Blue Nile	305	1.9	24	122,409
Kassala	297	2.3	31	167,951
Northern Darfur	185	2.1	44	335,905
Red Sea	305	2.2	27	100,062
Southern Darfur	182	2.2	44	381,098
Total				4,621,853

Source: Staff estimates.
Note: The table excludes national service and volunteer teachers and federal spending.

Table 7A.5 Academic Secondary Education: Overview of State Education Spending and STRs, by Group and State, 2009

Group/state	Per-student spending (current SDG)	Teacher salaries as a multiple of GDP per capita	Student-teacher ratio	Number of students
Group 1: high GERs	767	2.6	15	
Al Jazirah	662	2.9	17	126,513
Khartoum	739	2.5	16	107,422

(continued next page)

Table 7A.5 *(continued)*

Group/state	Per-student spending (current SDG)	Teacher salaries as a multiple of GDP per capita	Student-teacher ratio	Number of students
Northern	965	2.4	10	17,634
River Nile	872	2.7	13	30,183
White Nile	598	2.6	17	36,429
Group 2: intermediate GERs	602	2.7	18	
Al Qadarif	724	2.8	17	21,086
North Kordofan	630	2.6	16	37,361
Sinnar	774	3.0	13	25,158
South Kordofan	417	2.4	22	26,357
Western Darfur	463	2.6	23	13,684
Group 3: low GERs	823	2.5	16	
Blue Nile	1,416	2.2	7	8,435
Kassala	773	2.4	14	15,801
Northern Darfur	480	2.3	18	28,745
Red Sea	910	3.1	19	12,051
Southern Darfur	537	2.6	20	33,839
Total				**540,698**

Source: Staff estimates.
Note: The table excludes national service and volunteer teachers and federal spending.

Table 7A.6 Technical Secondary Education: Overview of State Education Spending and STRs, by Group and State, 2009

Group/state	Per-student spending (current SDG)	Teacher salaries as a multiple of GDP per capita	Student-teacher ratio	Number of students
Group 1: high GERs	777	2.6	15	
Al Jazirah	669	2.9	16	3,302
Khartoum	567	2.5	21	7,336
Northern	911	2.4	11	1,256
River Nile	1,174	2.7	10	1,968
White Nile	564	2.6	18	2,507
Group 2: intermediate GERs	681	2.7	17	
Al Qadarif	881	2.8	14	2,409
North Kordofan	848	2.6	12	2,211

(continued next page)

Table 7A.6 *(continued)*

Group/state	Per-student spending (current SDG)	Teacher salaries as a multiple of GDP per capita	Student-teacher ratio	Number of students
Sinnar	778	3.0	13	706
South Kordofan	354	2.4	26	309
Western Darfur	542	2.6	21	620
Group 3: low GERs	838	2.5	15	
Blue Nile	1,137	2.2	8	614
Kassala	478	2.4	23	1,414
Northern Darfur	608	2.3	14	1,696
Red Sea	1,194	3.1	14	1,074
Southern Darfur	773	2.6	15	1,233
Total				28,655

Source: Staff estimates.
Note: The table excludes national service and volunteer teachers and federal spending.

NOTES

1. The analysis of education spending in northern Sudan is hampered by the lack of a consolidated budget for the three levels of government (federal, state, and local); spending not being classified by function and purpose; data typically being for budget allocations rather than executed amounts; and weak financial management capacities at the state and local levels, resulting in incomplete reporting of spending at these levels (World Bank 2007).

2. *Spending* refers to public education spending unless stated otherwise. In addition to the public school system, there are private schools (not discussed here), which help alleviate pressure on the public education system.

3. The "Northern States Budget Review Notes" also contain data on education spending, but these data are less comprehensive than those compiled for the ESR: the state public education spending data reported are lower than those in the ESR because they exclude teacher wages for preschool, basic school, and secondary education (World Bank 2010a).

4. Because of data limitations, this measure is computed as recurrent spending for all subsectors (not just basic and secondary education) divided by the number of children 6–16 years old.

5. The *dependency ratio* is defined as the school-age population as a share of the total population.

6. *Recurrent spending* is purchases of assets or services to be consumed within one year.

7. *Development spending* is for physical assets with benefits extending into the future.

8. Moreover, in some schools, teaching takes place only in the nonrainy season because schools are built of tree branches and get destroyed during the rainy season (World Bank forthcoming).

9. Total recurrent public spending for all sectors declined between 2008 and 2009.

10. This observation is for the spending share of 37 percent adjusted to six years rather than eight years of basic education.

11. Spending on teaching and nonteaching staff salaries cannot be separated for higher education; therefore, these salaries are excluded when computing the average 75 percent salary share in recurrent education spending. When salaries are included, the share remains very similar.

12. The term *nonteaching staff* includes administrators, inspectors, cleaners, drivers, guards, and janitors.

13. The limited information available suggests that in several cases, volunteer teachers are paid by communities, but also in some cases, work for free.

14. The two states excluded were Southern Darfur and Western Darfur.

15. This figure excludes national service and volunteer teachers.

16. Average salaries were computed as total salary spending for each staff type divided by the total number of such staff.

17. For the purposes of this comparison, public per-student spending on school running costs is defined as spending on goods and services.

18. This figure is for 13 states, excluding Southern Darfur and Western Darfur because of data limitations.

19. The high average spending for academic secondary education for the low-GER group was driven by Blue Nile State; when excluding this state, we see that the high-GER group spends more.

20. The rules governing fiscal transfers are scattered throughout many documents, including the Comprehensive Peace Agreement of 2005, the Darfur Peace Agreement of 2006, and the Eastern Sudan Peace Agreement of 2006.

21. Whether Blue Nile State was included did not affect this relationship, because it is not an influential observation. For the 14 states, excluding Khartoum, having a higher average GER was significantly associated with higher federal transfers.

22. The data are for one year only, and it could be that states with relatively high GERs achieved these rates because of receiving large federal transfers in previous years. Also, states with more of their own revenues may have been using these revenues in the education sector in addition to federal transfers. However, social sector outputs tend to be correlated; thus, states that perform relatively well in the education sector may also be more likely to perform better in the other sectors.

REFERENCES

Castro, Martín, Cumpa. 2010. "Poverty in Northern Sudan. Estimates from the NBHS 2009." Draft. World Bank, Washington, DC.

EU (European Union). 2008. Cost and Financing Study. European Union.

FMoGE (Federal Ministry of General Education). 2008. "Baseline Survey on Basic Education in the Northern States of Sudan: Final Report June 2008." Khartoum. Online document available at http://planipolis.iiep.unesco.org/epiweb/E029336e.pdf.

HNP Stats. 2010. Health, Nutrition and Population Unit, World Bank, Washington, DC. Available at http://databank.worldbank.org/ddp/home.do?Step=12&id=4&CNO=311.

Mingat, A., and K. Majgaard. 2010. *Education in Sub-Saharan Africa: A Comparative Analysis*. Washington, DC: World Bank.

UNESCO Institute for Statistics. 2006. "Teachers and Educational Quality: Monitoring Global Needs for 2015." UNESCO Institute for Statistics report, Montreal.

World Bank. 2003. "Sudan. Stabilization and Reconstruction." Country Economic Memorandum, Volume 1: Main text. Report 24620-SU. Poverty Reduction and Economic Management 2, Africa Region, World Bank, Washington, DC.

———. 2007. "Sudan. Public Expenditure Review. Synthesis Report." Report 41840-SD. Poverty Reduction and Economic Management Unit, Africa Region, World Bank, Washington, DC.

———. 2010a. "Northern States Budget Review Notes." Draft. Poverty Reduction and Economic Management Unit, Africa Region, World Bank, Washington, DC.

———. 2010b. *World Development Indicators*. World Bank, Washington, DC. Available at http://data.worldbank.org/data-catalog/world-development-indicators.

———. Forthcoming. "Service Delivery in Basic Schools in Four States in Northern Sudan: Findings from the 2010/11 Service Delivery Survey." Draft. Education, Africa Region, World Bank, Washington, DC.

State: Northern   Year: 2008–09

Indicator	State	Northern Sudan	State–northern Sudan ratio
Demographic pressure (population ages 5–16 as a percentage of total population)	28	32	0.88
School life expectancy (SLE), excluding higher education (years)	7.1	6.3	1.12
Effort: spending per school-age population (Sudanese pounds [SDG])	429	165	2.59
Efficiency of education spending: spending per child (in population) per year of SLE produced (SDG)	60	26	2.31

Student Flow and Socioeconomic Disparities

Education level	Enrollments	Gross enrollment rate (percent)		Share of girls in total enrollments (percent)		Share of private school enrollments (percent)	
		State	Northern Sudan	State	Northern Sudan	State	Northern Sudan
Preschool	21,786	64	37	51	47	—	—
Basic	112,254	85	72	49	46	1	5
Secondary	23,158	50	29	52	48	18	23
Academic	21,902	47	28	54	49	19	24
Technical	1,256	3	1	9	25	0	0
Literacy program	12,340	n.a.	n.a.	n.a.	n.a.	n.a.	n.a.

Note: — = not available; n.a. = not applicable.

Student Annual Growth Rate 2005–09
percent

Education level	State	Northern Sudan
Preschool	6	15
Basic	−3	5
Secondary	5	7

Share of Enrollment in Basic Education
percent

Schools	State	Northern Sudan
Nomadic	3	3
Internally displaced person (IDP)	1	4

KEY POINTS

General
- Lower demographic pressure than northern Sudan average
- Relatively high school life expectancy
- Very low efficiency in use of resources

Preschool
- Relatively low increase in enrollment
- High gross enrollment rate (GER), 70 percent higher than the average

Basic education
- Better coverage (GER 13 percentage points higher than the average)
- But no increase in GER (no improvement process)
- Share of nomadic schools at the average

Secondary education
- Better coverage (GER 19 percentage points higher than the average)
- Relatively low increase in enrollment

Educational Pyramid for Northern State (Basic and Secondary Only)

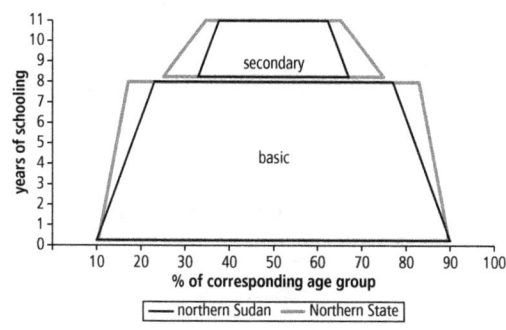

Internal Efficiency
percent

	Gross intake rate		Completion rate		Retention rate		Share of repeaters	
Education level	State	Northern Sudan	State	Northern Sudan	State	Northern Sudan	State	Northern Sudan
Basic	79	80	66	54	83	68	13	4
Secondary	50	34	30	25	61	72	—	14

Note: — = not available.

KEY POINTS

Basic education
- Intake rate at the average
- Better retention and completion
- High repetition (three times the average)
- High transition between basic education and secondary cycle

Secondary education
- Low retention
- High dropout

Government School: Teachers

	Student-teacher ratio		Voluntary and national service (percent)		Teacher-nonteacher ratio	
Education level	State	Northern Sudan	State	Northern Sudan	State	Northern Sudan
Preschool	18	48	0	33	87	18
Basic	17	33	0	3	3	5
Secondary	10	16	0	8	1	1

Government School: Facilities

	Students per school		Students per form	
Education level	State	Northern Sudan	State	Northern Sudan
Preschool	—	—	—	—
Basic	240	332	32	48
Secondary	190	238	39	45

Note: — = not available.

Education Expenditures
percent

Indicator	State	Northern Sudan
Education as a percentage of all expenditures	45	27
Salaries as a percentage of education expenditures	83	85

Per-Student Spending at the State Level
Sudanese pounds

Indicator	State			Relative to northern Sudan		
	Preschool	Basic	Secondary	Preschool	Basic	Secondary
Total	210.2	542.2	961.1	1.7	2.3	1.4
Teachers	207.0	433.1	712.9	1.9	2.1	1.4
Nonteachers	1.6	102.3	204.4	0.2	3.5	1.6
Goods and services	1.7	6.8	43.7	0.2	0.8	1.0

KEY POINTS

General
- High share of education budget
- High per-student spending
- Very low spending on goods and services

Preschool
- Low student-teacher ratio (STR) and class size
- Very few nonteaching staff (high number of teachers per nonteaching staff)
- High per-student spending

Basic education
- Low STR and class size
- No volunteer teachers
- High share of nonteaching staff
- High per-student spending
- Smaller school size

Secondary education
- Very low STR
- Low STR and class size
- High per-student spending
- Smaller school size

Degree of Randomness in Teacher Allocations, Primary School

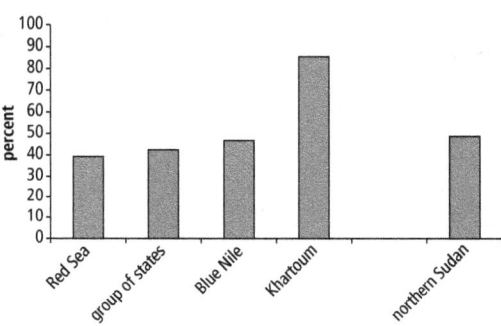

Note: Group of states is the average for all states in northern Sudan except for Red Sea, Blue Nile, and Khartoum. Disaggregated data were unavailable for the other states, so just the average is included.

KEY POINTS

- Two main challenges regarding student flow: improving access to basic education and retention in secondary education
- Larger amount spent per-student in Northern State than the northern Sudan average in general but very small amount per-student on goods and services

Literacy Rates for Adults 20–30 Years Old, by Number of Years of School

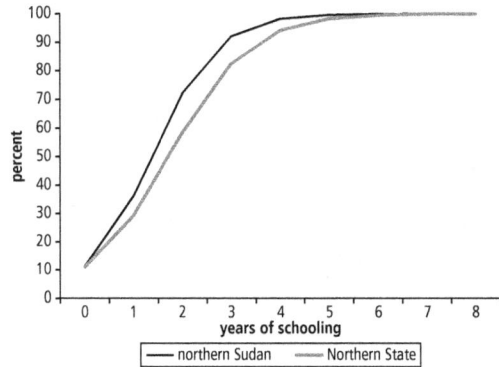

194 • Appendix: State-Level Data Sheets—Red Sea

State: Red Sea   Year: 2008–09

Indicator	State	Northern Sudan	State–northern Sudan ratio
Demographic pressure (population ages 5–16 as a percentage of total population)	35	32	1.09
School life expectancy, excluding higher education	3.1	6.3	0.49
Effort: spending per school-age population (SDG)	102	165	0.62
Efficiency of education spending: spending per child (in population) per year of SLE produced (SDG)	33	26	1.27

Student Flow and Socioeconomic Disparities

Education level	Enrollments	Gross enrollment rate (percent)		Share of girls in total enrollments (percent)		Share of private school enrollments (percent)	
		State	Northern Sudan	State	Northern Sudan	State	Northern Sudan
Preschool	48,827	64	37	40	47	—	—
Basic	110,707	37	72	44	46	10	5
Secondary	16,759	17	29	47	48	22	23
Academic	15,685	16	28	48	49	23	24
Technical	1,074	1	1	26	25	0	0
Literacy program	36,189	n.a.	n.a.	n.a.	n.a.	n.a.	n.a.

Note: — = not available; n.a. = not applicable.

Student Annual Growth Rate 2005–09
percent

Education level	State	Northern Sudan
Preschool	72	15
Basic	2	5
Secondary	–1	7

Share of Enrollment in Basic Education
percent

Schools	State	Northern Sudan
Nomadic	5	3
IDP	0	4

KEY POINTS

General
- Demographic data problem
- Very low school life expectancy (less than half of northern Sudan SLE average)
- Relatively less effort for education
- Relatively low efficiency in use of resources

Preschool
- Huge increase in preschool enrollment
- GER 70 percent (highest coverage)

Basic education
- Low coverage (GER almost half the average)
- Low increase in enrollment (no catchup process)

Secondary education
- Low coverage (GER)
- Low increase in enrollment

Educational Pyramid for Red Sea (Basic and Secondary Only)

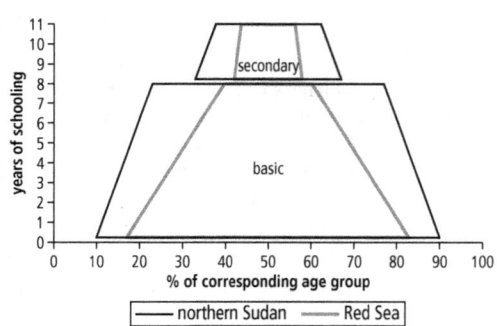

Internal Efficiency
percent

	Gross intake rate		Completion rate		Retention rate		Share of repeaters	
Education level	State	Northern Sudan	State	Northern Sudan	State	Northern Sudan	State	Northern Sudan
Basic	66	80	20	54	31	68	9	4
Secondary	16	34	13	25	79	72	—	14

Note: — = not available.

KEY POINTS

Basic education
- Low intake
- Very low retention, low completion
- High dropout (occurring mainly within the cycle)
- High transition between basic education and secondary cycle

Secondary education
- High retention

Government School: Teachers

	Student-teacher ratio		Voluntary and national service (percent)		Teacher-nonteacher ratio	
Education level	State	Northern Sudan	State	Northern Sudan	State	Northern Sudan
Preschool	198	48	87	33	6	18
Basic	27	33	6	3	5	5
Secondary	18	16	32	8	1	1

Government School: Facilities

	Students per school		Students per form	
Education level	State	Northern Sudan	State	Northern Sudan
Preschool	—	—	—	—
Basic	240	332	41	48
Secondary	274	238	41	45

Note: — = not available.

Education Expenditures
percent

Indicator	State	Northern Sudan
Education as a percentage of all expenditures	19	27
Salaries as a percentage of education expenditures	59	85

Per-Student Spending at the State Level
Sudanese pounds

Indicator	State			Relative to northern Sudan		
	Preschool	Basic	Secondary	Preschool	Basic	Secondary
Total	51.7	304.5	933.4	0.4	1.3	1.3
Teachers	33.9	248.6	529.9	0.3	1.2	1.0
Nonteachers	14.5	30.3	163.6	2.2	1.0	1.2
Goods and services	3.3	25.6	239.8	0.4	2.9	5.4

KEY POINTS

General
- Low share of education budget
- Intensive use of volunteer teachers
- High share of goods and services spending

Preschool
- Very high STR

Basic education
- Smaller STR
- Smaller school size

Secondary education
- Slightly high STR
- Bigger school size

Degree of Randomness in Teacher Allocations, Primary School

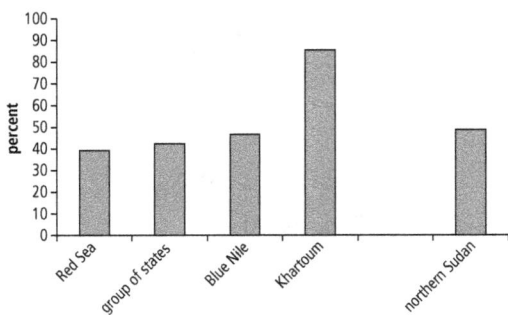

Note: *Group of states* is the average for all states in northern Sudan except for Red Sea, Blue Nile, and Khartoum. Disaggregated data were unavailable for the other states, so just the average is included.

KEY POINTS

- Very low on both access and retention
- Very small secondary education coverage
- Low effort on education
- Intensive use of volunteers teachers

Literacy Rates for Adults 20–30 Years Old, by Number of Years of School

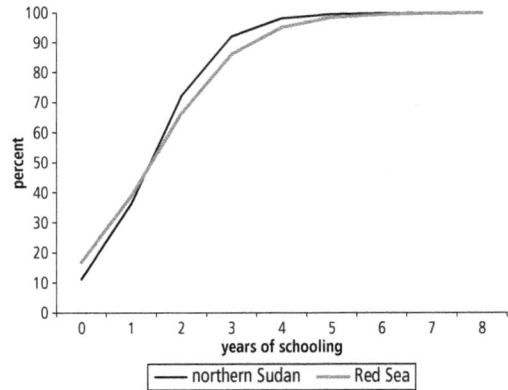

State: River Nile   Year: 2008–09

Indicator	State	Northern Sudan	State–northern Sudan ratio
Demographic pressure (population ages 5–16 as a percentage of total population)	28	32	0.86
School life expectancy, excluding higher education	7.8	6.3	1.24
Effort: spending per school-age population (SDG)	360	165	2.18
Efficiency of education spending: spending per child (in population) per year of SLE produced (SDG)	46	26	1.76

Student Flow and Socioeconomic Disparities

Education level	Enrollments	Gross enrollment rate (percent)		Share of girls in total enrollments (percent)		Share of private school enrollments (percent)	
		State	Northern Sudan	State	Northern Sudan	State	Northern Sudan
Preschool	37,878	65	37	51	47	—	—
Basic	183,605	89	72	47	46	1	5
Secondary	33,875	47	29	53	48	5	23
Academic	31,907	44	28	55	49	5	24
Technical	1,968	3	1	20	25	0	0
Literacy program	5,335	n.a.	n.a.	n.a.	n.a.	n.a.	n.a.

Note: — = not available; n.a. = not applicable.

Student Annual Growth Rate 2005–09
percent

Education level	State	Northern Sudan
Preschool	14	15
Basic	0	5
Secondary	4	7

Share of Enrollment in Basic Education
percent

Schools	State	Northern Sudan
Nomadic	4	3
IDP	0	4

KEY POINTS

General
- Relatively low demographic pressure
- Relatively high school life expectancy
- High level of spending per school-age population
- Less efficient use of resources
- Very low share of private schools

Preschool
- High GER
- More girls than boys enrolled

Basic education
- Better coverage (GER 12 percentage points higher than the average)
- But no increase in GER (no improvement process)
- Higher share of nomadic schools than the average

Secondary education
- Better coverage (GER 16 percentage points higher than the average)
- Relatively low increase in enrollment

Educational Pyramid for River Nile (Basic and Secondary Only)

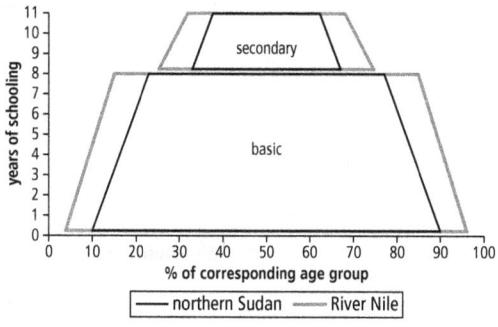

Internal Efficiency
percent

	Gross intake rate		Completion rate		Retention rate		Share of repeaters	
Education level	State	Northern Sudan	State	Northern Sudan	State	Northern Sudan	State	Northern Sudan
Basic	92	80	70	54	76	68	7	4
Secondary	49	34	36	25	73	72	—	14

Note: — = not available.

KEY POINTS

Basic education
- High intake rate
- Low retention
- High dropout
- Relatively high completion rate
- High transition between basic education and secondary cycle

Secondary education
- Low retention
- High dropout

Government School: Teachers

	Student-teacher ratio		Voluntary and national service (percent)		Teacher-nonteacher ratio	
Education level	State	Northern Sudan	State	Northern Sudan	State	Northern Sudan
Preschool	175	48	86	33	24	18
Basic	22	33	0	3	5	5
Secondary	13	16	0	8	0	1

Government School: Facilities

	Students per school		Students per form	
Education level	State	Northern Sudan	State	Northern Sudan
Preschool	—	—	—	—
Basic	241	332	37	48
Secondary	199	238	41	45

Note: — = not available.

Education Expenditures
percent

Indicator	State	Northern Sudan
Education as a percentage of all expenditures	32	27
Salaries as a percentage of education expenditures	96	85

Per-Student Spending at the State Level
Sudanese pounds

Indicator	State			Relative to northern Sudan		
	Preschool	Basic	Secondary	Preschool	Basic	Secondary
Total	43.9	425.5	890.5	0.4	1.8	1.3
Teachers	36.8	359.6	661.0	0.3	1.8	1.3
Nonteachers	5.9	57.3	211.6	0.9	2.0	1.6
Goods and services	1.3	8.5	17.8	0.2	1.0	0.4

KEY POINTS

General
- High share of education budget
- Very high share of wages and salaries

Preschool
- Very high STR
- Intensive use of volunteer teachers
- Low per-student spending

Basic education
- Low STR
- No volunteer teachers
- High per-student spending
- Smaller school size

Secondary education
- Low STR
- High per-student spending
- Smaller school size

Degree of Randomness in Teacher Allocations, Primary School

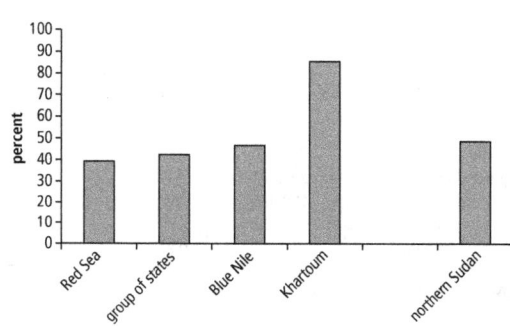

Note: Group of states is the average for all states in northern Sudan except for Red Sea, Blue Nile, and Khartoum. Disaggregated data were unavailable for the other states, so just the average is included.

KEY POINTS

- Great effort and high per-student spending.
- High dropout in both basic and secondary education

Literacy Rates for Adults 20–30 Years Old, by Number of Years of School

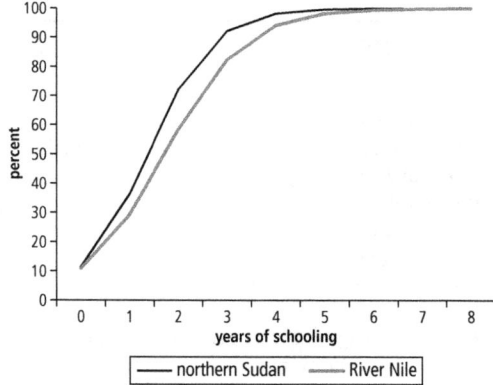

State: Khartoum Year: 2008–09

Indicator	State	Northern Sudan	State–northern Sudan ratio
Demographic pressure (population ages 5–16 as a percentage of total population)	32	32	0.99
School life expectancy, excluding higher education	8.8	6.3	1.40
Effort: spending per school-age population (SDG)	216	165	1.31
Efficiency of education spending: spending per child (in population) per year of SLE produced (SDG)	24	26	0.94

Student Flow and Socioeconomic Disparities

		Gross enrollment rate (percent)		Share of girls in total enrollments (percent)		Share of private school enrollments (percent)	
Education level	Enrollments	State	Northern Sudan	State	Northern Sudan	State	Northern Sudan
Preschool	111,497	43	37	49	47	—	—
Basic	862,170	94	72	50	46	13	5
Secondary	205,801	61	29	51	48	44	23
Academic	198,465	59	28	52	49	46	24
Technical	7,336	2	1	22	25	0	0
Literacy program	0	n.a.	n.a.	n.a.	n.a.	n.a.	n.a.

Note: — = not available; n.a. = not applicable.

Student Annual Growth Rate 2005–09
percent

Education level	State	Northern Sudan
Preschool	4	15
Basic	6	5
Secondary	14	7

Share of Enrollment in Basic Education
percent

Schools	State	Northern Sudan
Nomadic	0	3
IDP	0	4

KEY POINTS

General
- Relatively high school life expectancy
- High level of spending per school-age population
- Very high share of private schools

Preschool
- High GER
- Very small increase over the past 5 years
- More girls than boys enrolled

Basic education
- Better coverage (GER 22 percentage points higher than the average)
- Steady increase in GER

Secondary education
- Better coverage (more than two times higher than the average)
- Rapid and sharp increase in enrollment and GER

Educational Pyramid for Khartoum (Basic and Secondary Only)

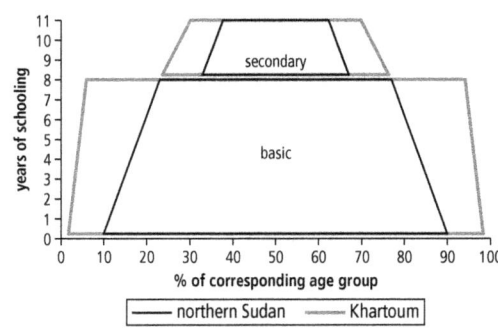

Internal Efficiency
percent

	Gross intake rate		Completion rate		Retention rate		Share of repeaters	
Education level	State	Northern Sudan	State	Northern Sudan	State	Northern Sudan	State	Northern Sudan
Basic	97	80	88	54	91	68	1	4
Secondary	53	34	40	25	75	72	—	14

Note: — = not available.

KEY POINTS

Basic education
- High intake rate
- High retention
- Relatively high completion rate
- Limited transition between basic education and secondary cycle

Secondary education
- Low retention
- High dropout

Government School: Teachers

	Student-teacher ratio		Voluntary and national service (percent)		Teacher-nonteacher ratio	
Education level	State	Northern Sudan	State	Northern Sudan	State	Northern Sudan
Preschool	15	48	0	33	50	18
Basic	30	33	0	3	5	5
Secondary	16	16	0	8	0	1

Government School: Facilities

	Students per school		Students per form	
Education level	State	Northern Sudan	State	Northern Sudan
Preschool	—	—	—	—
Basic	474	332	51	48
Secondary	313	238	47	45

Note: — = not available.

Education Expenditures
percent

Indicator	State	Northern Sudan
Education as a percentage of all expenditures	23	27
Salaries as a percentage of education expenditures	80	85

Per-Student Spending at the State Level
Sudanese pounds

Indicator	State			Relative to northern Sudan		
	Preschool	Basic	Secondary	Preschool	Basic	Secondary
Total	329.2	274.4	727.9	2.6	1.1	1.0
Teachers	261.8	233.4	467.3	2.4	1.2	0.9
Nonteachers	4.5	25.9	198.0	0.7	0.9	1.5
Goods and services	62.9	15.1	62.5	8.5	1.7	1.4

KEY POINTS

General
- Low STR for all levels of education
- No volunteers teachers
- Smaller share of resources allocated to education

Preschool
- Large number of teachers per nonteaching staff (2.5 times larger than the average)
- High per-student spending (2.6 times higher than the average)
- More spending on goods and services (8.5 times larger than the average)

Basic education
- No volunteer teachers
- Bigger school size
- Larger class size
- High per-student spending (2.4 times higher than the average)
- More spending on goods and services

Secondary education
- Bigger school size
- More spending on goods and services

Degree of Randomness in Teacher Allocations, Primary School

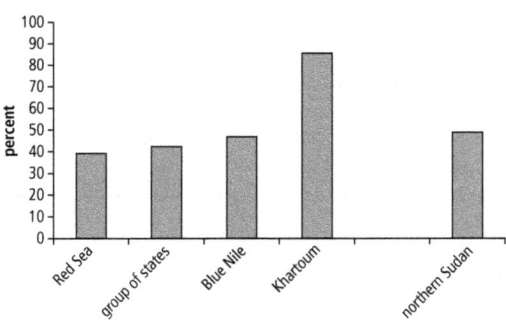

Note: Group of states is the average for all states in northern Sudan except for Red Sea, Blue Nile, and Khartoum. Disaggregated data were unavailable for the other states, so just the average is included.

KEY POINTS

Basic education
- Very weak relationship between number of teachers and number of students

Literacy Rates for Adults 20–30 Years Old, by Number of Years of School

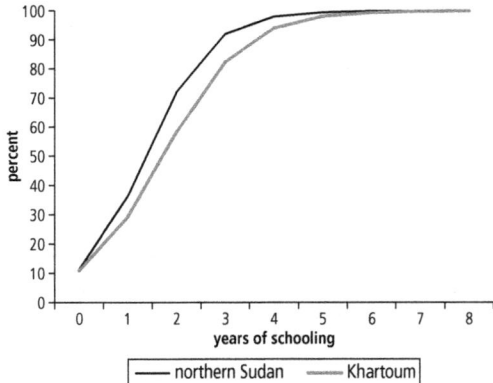

State: Al Jazirah   Year: 2008–09

Indicator	State	Northern Sudan	State–northern Sudan ratio
Demographic pressure (population ages 5–16 as a percentage of total population)	33	32	1.03
School life expectancy, excluding higher education	8.6	6.3	1.35
Effort: spending per school-age population (SDG)	272	165	1.65
Efficiency of education spending: spending per child (in population) per year of SLE produced (SDG)	32	26	1.22

Student Flow and Socioeconomic Disparities

Education level	Enrollments	Gross enrollment rate (percent)		Share of girls in total enrollments (percent)		Share of private school enrollments (percent)	
		State	Northern Sudan	State	Northern Sudan	State	Northern Sudan
Preschool	92,878	44	37	51	47	—	—
Basic	667,422	90	72	47	46	1	5
Secondary	144,578	57	29	52	48	10	23
Academic	141,276	56	28	53	49	10	24
Technical	3,302	1	1	15	25	0	0
Literacy program	13,354	n.a.	n.a.	n.a.	n.a.	n.a.	n.a.

Note: — = not available; n.a. = not applicable.

Student Annual Growth Rate 2005–09
percent

Education level	State	Northern Sudan
Preschool	11	15
Basic	0	5
Secondary	6	7

Share of Enrollment in Basic Education
percent

Schools	State	Northern Sudan
Nomadic	0	3
IDP	0	4

KEY POINTS

General
- Relatively low demographic pressure
- Relatively high school life expectancy
- High level of spending per school-age population
- Less efficient use of resources
- Low share of private schools

Preschool
- High GER
- More girls than boys enrolled

Basic education
- High GER (18 percentage points higher than the average)
- No increase in GER

Secondary education
- High GER (two times the average)
- No enrollment increase

Educational Pyramid for Al Jazirah (Basic and Secondary Only)

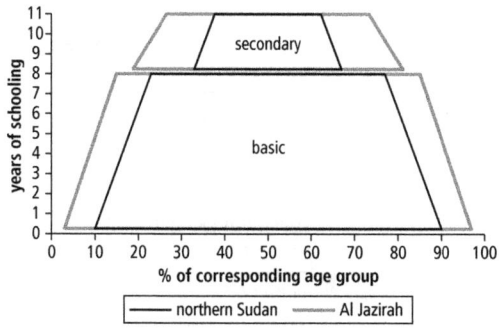

Internal Efficiency
percent

	Gross intake rate		Completion rate		Retention rate		Share of repeaters	
Education level	State	Northern Sudan	State	Northern Sudan	State	Northern Sudan	State	Northern Sudan
Basic	94	80	70	54	75	68	2	4
Secondary	62	34	47	25	75	72	—	14

Note: — = not available.

KEY POINTS

Basic education
- High intake rate
- High retention
- Relatively high completion rate
- Limited transition between basic education and secondary cycle

Secondary education
- Low retention
- High dropout

Government School: Teachers

	Student-teacher ratio		Voluntary and national service (percent)		Teacher-nonteacher ratio	
Education level	State	Northern Sudan	State	Northern Sudan	State	Northern Sudan
Preschool	15	48	0	33	50	18
Basic	30	33	0	3	5	5
Secondary	16	16	0	8	0	1

Government School: Facilities

	Students per school		Students per form	
Education level	State	Northern Sudan	State	Northern Sudan
Preschool	—	—	—	—
Basic	474	332	51	48
Secondary	313	238	47	45

Note: — = not available.

Education Expenditures
percent

Indicator	State	Northern Sudan
Education as a percentage of all expenditures	47	27
Salaries as a percentage of education expenditures	92	85

Per-Student Spending at the State Level
Sudanese pounds

Indicator	State			Relative to northern Sudan		
	Preschool	Basic	Secondary	Preschool	Basic	Secondary
Total	264.0	277.7	662.1	2.1	1.2	1.0
Teachers	250.2	238.3	545.4	2.3	1.2	1.1
Nonteachers	10.5	35.2	99.8	1.6	1.2	0.8
Goods and services	3.3	4.1	16.9	0.4	0.5	0.4

KEY POINTS

Preschool
- Low STR
- Low share of volunteers
- Large number of teachers per nonteaching staff

Basic education
- Large share of volunteer teachers (two times the average)
- Relatively high per-student spending (1.2 times higher than the average)
- Very low spending on goods and services

Secondary education
- Smaller school size
- Smaller class size
- Very low spending on goods and services

Degree of Randomness in Teacher Allocations, Primary School

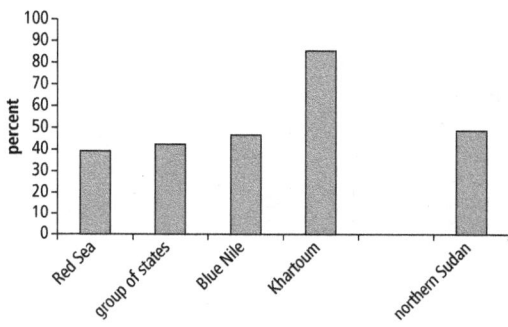

Note: Group of states is the average for all states in northern Sudan except for Red Sea, Blue Nile, and Khartoum. Disaggregated data were unavailable for the other states, so just the average is included.

Literacy Rates for Adults 20–30 Years Old, by Number of Years of School

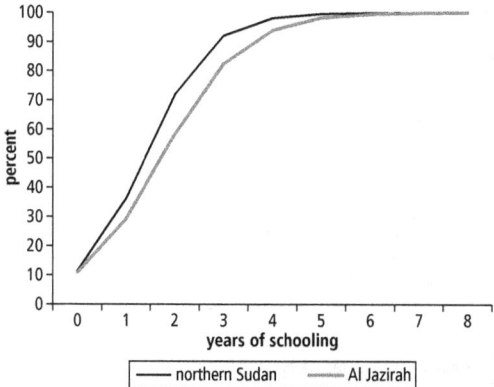

State: Blue Nile   Year: 2008–09

Indicator	State	Northern Sudan	State–northern Sudan ratio
Demographic pressure (population ages 5–16 as a percentage of total population)	34	32	1.06
School life expectancy, excluding higher education	5.6	6.3	0.88
Effort: spending per school-age population (SDG)	201	165	1.22
Efficiency of education spending: spending per child (in population) per year of SLE produced (SDG)	36	26	1.39

Student Flow and Socioeconomic Disparities

Education level	Enrollments	Gross enrollment rate (percent)		Share of girls in total enrollments (percent)		Share of private school enrollments (percent)	
		State	Northern Sudan	State	Northern Sudan	State	Northern Sudan
Preschool	12,248	20	37	50	47	—	—
Basic	122,786	65	72	44	46	0	5
Secondary	10,835	20	29	37	48	16	23
Academic	10,221	19	28	37	49	17	24
Technical	614	1	1	34	25	0	0
Literacy program	0	n.a.	n.a.	n.a.	n.a.	n.a.	n.a.

Note: — = not available; n.a. = not applicable.

Student Annual Growth Rate 2005–09
percent

Education level	State	Northern Sudan
Preschool	26	15
Basic	7	5
Secondary	8	7

Share of Enrollment in Basic Education
percent

Schools	State	Northern Sudan
Nomadic	2	3
IDP	0	4

KEY POINTS

General
- Relatively low school life expectancy
- High level of spending per school-age population
- Less efficient use of resources
- Low share of private schools

Preschool
- Low GER
- No increase in GER over the past 5 years
- More girls than boys enrolled

Basic education
- Lower GER (7 percentage points lower than the average)
- Rapid increase in GER

Secondary education
- Very low GER
- No increase in enrollment

Educational Pyramid for Blue Nile (Basic and Secondary Only)

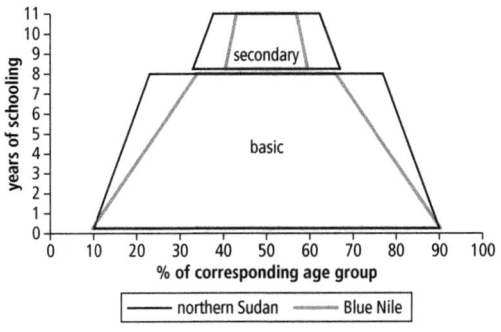

Internal Efficiency

percent

Education level	Gross intake rate		Completion rate		Retention rate		Share of repeaters	
	State	Northern Sudan	State	Northern Sudan	State	Northern Sudan	State	Northern Sudan
Basic	81	80	32	54	40	68	0	4
Secondary	19	34	40	25	73	72	—	14

Note: — = not available.

KEY POINTS

Basic education
- Intake at the average level
- Very low retention
- Low completion
- High dropout (occurring mainly within the cycle)
- Relatively limited transition between basic education and secondary cycle

Secondary education
- Low intake rate
- High retention

Government School: Teachers

Education level	Student-teacher ratio		Voluntary and national service (percent)		Teacher-nonteacher ratio	
	State	Northern Sudan	State	Northern Sudan	State	Northern Sudan
Preschool	71	48	0	33	22	18
Basic	24	33	11	3	5	5
Secondary	7	16	69	8	1	1

Government School: Facilities

Education level	Students per school		Students per form	
	State	Northern Sudan	State	Northern Sudan
Preschool	—	—	—	—
Basic	291	332	49	48
Secondary	201	238	37	45

Note: — = not available.

Education Expenditures

percent

Indicator	State	Northern Sudan
Education as a percentage of all expenditures	19	27
Salaries as a percentage of education expenditures	88	85

Appendix: State-Level Data Sheets—Blue Nile

Per-Student Spending at the State Level
Sudanese pounds

Indicator	State			Relative to northern Sudan		
	Preschool	Basic	Secondary	Preschool	Basic	Secondary
Total	105.5	304.6	1,397.4	0.8	1.3	2.0
Teachers	82.0	255.6	998.9	0.7	1.3	1.9
Nonteachers	2.7	36.0	207.8	0.4	1.2	1.6
Goods and services	20.8	13.0	190.7	2.8	1.5	4.3

KEY POINTS

General
- Smaller school size

Preschool
- High STR
- No volunteer teachers
- Large number of teachers per nonteaching staff
- Low per-student spending
- More spending on goods and services (2.8 times the average)

Basic education
- Low STR
- Relatively high per-student spending (30 percent higher than the average)
- More spending on goods and services

Secondary education
- High per-student spending (2 times the average)
- More spending on goods and services (4.3 times the average)

Degree of Randomness in Teacher Allocations, Primary School

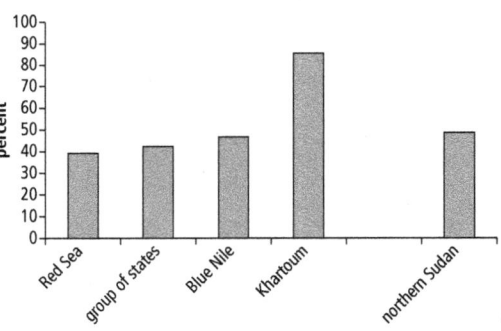

Note: Group of states is the average for all states in northern Sudan except for Red Sea, Blue Nile, and Khartoum. Disaggregated data were unavailable for the other states, so just the average is included.

Literacy Rates for Adults 20–30 Years Old, by Number of Years of School

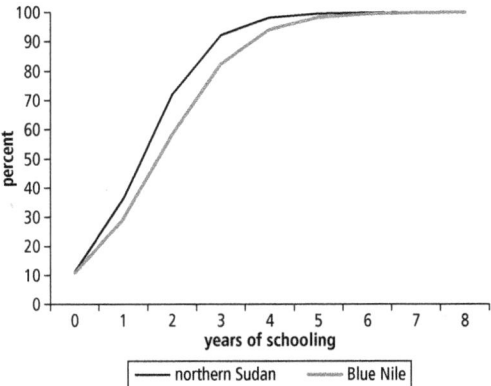

State: Sinnar Year: 2008–09

Indicator	State	Northern Sudan	State–northern Sudan ratio
Demographic pressure (population ages 5–16 as a percentage of total population)	26	32	0.82
School life expectancy, excluding higher education	6.8	6.3	1.08
Effort: spending per school-age population (SDG)	175	165	1.06
Efficiency of education spending: spending per child (in population) per year of SLE produced (SDG)	26	26	0.98

Student Flow and Socioeconomic Disparities

Education level	Enrollments	Gross enrollment rate (percent)		Share of girls in total enrollments (percent)		Share of private school enrollments (percent)	
		State	Northern Sudan	State	Northern Sudan	State	Northern Sudan
Preschool	11,260	13	37	41	47	—	—
Basic	228,286	80	72	46	46	1	5
Secondary	27,940	31	29	48	48	7	23
Academic	27,234	30	28	49	49	8	24
Technical	706	1	1	37	25	0	0
Literacy program	9,946	n.a.	n.a.	n.a.	n.a.	n.a.	n.a.

Note: — = not available; n.a. = not applicable.

Student Annual Growth Rate 2005–09
percent

Education level	State	Northern Sudan
Preschool	5	15
Basic	6	5
Secondary	7	7

Share of Enrollment in Basic Education
percent

Schools	State	Northern Sudan
Nomadic	2	3
IDP	0	4

KEY POINTS

General
- Relatively low demographic pressure
- Low share of private schools

Preschool
- Low GER
- Disparity against girls

Basic education
- GER at the average level
- Steady increase in GER

Secondary education
- GER at the average level
- No GER increase

Educational Pyramid for Sinnar (Basic and Secondary Only)

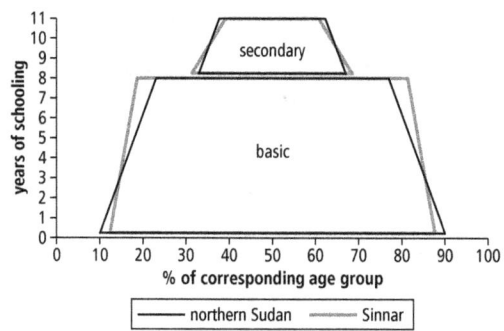

Internal Efficiency

percent

Education level	Gross intake rate		Completion rate		Retention rate		Share of repeaters	
	State	Northern Sudan	State	Northern Sudan	State	Northern Sudan	State	Northern Sudan
Basic	75	80	63	54	83	68	7	4
Secondary	37	34	22	25	58	72	—	14

Note: — = not available.

KEY POINTS

Basic education
- Intake rate lower than the average
- High retention
- Relatively high completion rate
- Limited transition between basic education and secondary cycle

Secondary education
- Low intake rate
- Low retention
- High dropout
- Low completion

Government School: Teachers

Education level	Student-teacher ratio		Voluntary and national service (percent)		Teacher-nonteacher ratio	
	State	Northern Sudan	State	Northern Sudan	State	Northern Sudan
Preschool	31	48	0	33	4	18
Basic	33	33	0	3	8	5
Secondary	13	16	0	8	5	1

Government School: Facilities

Education level	Students per school		Students per form	
	State	Northern Sudan	State	Northern Sudan
Preschool	—	—	—	—
Basic	335	332	50	48
Secondary	149	238	53	45

Note: — = not available.

Education Expenditures

percent

Indicator	State	Northern Sudan
Education as a percentage of all expenditures	37	27
Salaries as a percentage of education expenditures	92	85

Per-Student Spending at the State Level
Sudanese pounds

Indicator	State			Relative to northern Sudan		
	Preschool	Basic	Secondary	Preschool	Basic	Secondary
Total	160.1	211.6	774.1	1.3	0.9	1.1
Teachers	132.3	190.7	708.8	1.2	0.9	1.4
Nonteachers	21.6	17.0	51.2	3.3	0.6	0.4
Goods and services	6.2	3.9	14.2	0.8	0.4	0.3

KEY POINTS

General
- No volunteer teachers
- High share of resources allocated to education
- Very high share of wages and salaries within the education budget

Preschool
- Small number of teacher per nonteaching staff
- High per-student spending (30 percent higher than the average)
- Very small spending on goods and services

Basic education
- Large class size
- STR and per-student spending similar to country average
- Very small spending on goods and services

Secondary education
- Smaller school size
- Smaller STR
- Bigger class size

Degree of Randomness in Teacher Allocations, Primary School

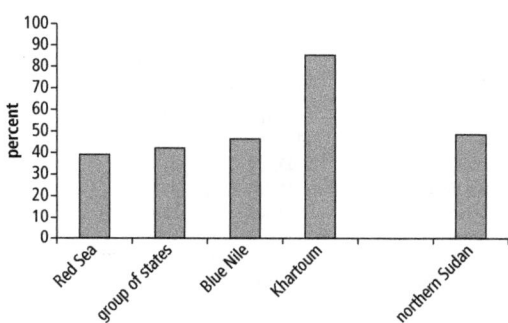

Note: Group of states is the average for all states in northern Sudan except for Red Sea, Blue Nile, and Khartoum. Disaggregated data were unavailable for the other states, so just the average is included.

Literacy Rates for Adults 20–30 Years Old, by Number of Years of School

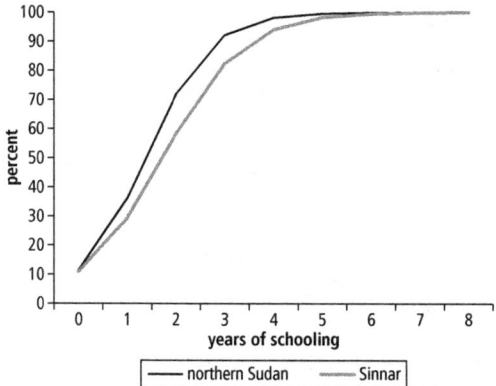

212 • Appendix: State-Level Data Sheets—White Nile

State: White Nile   Year: 2008–09

Indicator	State	Northern Sudan	State–northern Sudan ratio
Demographic pressure (population ages 5–16 as a percentage of total population)	31	32	0.97
School life expectancy, excluding higher education	7.6	6.3	1.20
Effort: spending per school-age population (SDG)	178	165	1.07
Efficiency of education spending: spending per child (in population) per year of SLE produced (SDG)	23	26	0.90

Student Flow and Socioeconomic Disparities

Education level	Enrollments	Gross enrollment rate (percent)		Share of girls in total enrollments (percent)		Share of private school enrollments (percent)	
		State	Northern Sudan	State	Northern Sudan	State	Northern Sudan
Preschool	47,282	43	37	49	47	—	—
Basic	320,967	85	72	46	46	4	5
Secondary	43,772	37	29	48	48	11	23
Academic	41,265	35	28	49	49	12	24
Technical	2,507	2	1	37	25	0	0
Literacy program	0	n.a.	n.a.	n.a.	n.a.	n.a.	n.a.

Note: — = not available; n.a. = not applicable.

Student Annual Growth Rate 2005–09
percent

Education level	State	Northern Sudan
Preschool	17	15
Basic	8	5
Secondary	6	7

Share of Enrollment in Basic Education
percent

Schools	State	Northern Sudan
Nomadic	2	3
IDP	0	4

KEY POINTS

General
- School life expectancy higher than northern Sudan average
- More efficient use of resources
- Low share of private schools

Preschool
- Higher GER
- Relatively high GER increase

Basic education
- Higher GER
- Steady increase in GER

Secondary education
- Higher GER
- Little GER increase

Educational Pyramid for White Nile (Basic and Secondary Only)

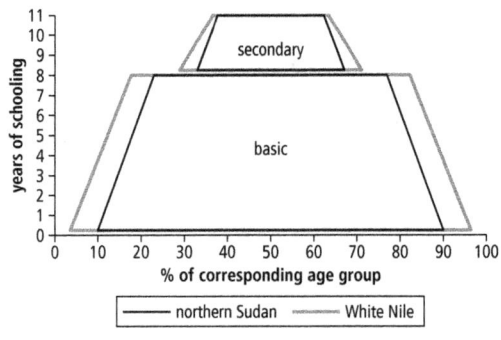

Internal Efficiency

percent

	Gross intake rate		Completion rate		Retention rate		Share of repeaters	
Education level	State	Northern Sudan	State	Northern Sudan	State	Northern Sudan	State	Northern Sudan
Basic	93	80	65	54	70	68	3	4
Secondary	42	34	27	25	64	72	—	14

Note: — = not available.

KEY POINTS

Basic education
- Intake rate larger than the average
- Low retention
- Relatively high completion rate
- Limited transition between basic education and secondary cycle

Secondary education
- Low intake rate
- Very low retention
- High dropout
- Low completion

Government School: Teachers

	Student-teacher ratio		Voluntary and national service (percent)		Teacher-nonteacher ratio	
Education level	State	Northern Sudan	State	Northern Sudan	State	Northern Sudan
Preschool	75	48	66	33	37	18
Basic	30	33	12	3	8	5
Secondary	17	16	33	8	3	1

Government School: Facilities

	Students per school		Students per form	
Education level	State	Northern Sudan	State	Northern Sudan
Preschool	—	—	—	—
Basic	332	332	51	48
Secondary	250	238	41	45

Note: — = not available.

Education Expenditures

percent

Indicator	State	Northern Sudan
Education as a percentage of all expenditures	37	27
Salaries as a percentage of education expenditures	91	85

Per-Student Spending at the State Level
Sudanese pounds

Indicator	State			Relative to northern Sudan		
	Preschool	Basic	Secondary	Preschool	Basic	Secondary
Total	73.2	216.3	596.0	0.6	0.9	0.9
Teachers	65.1	192.5	481.8	0.6	1.0	0.9
Nonteachers	4.8	21.0	76.7	0.7	0.7	0.6
Goods and services	3.4	2.8	37.5	0.5	0.3	0.9

KEY POINTS

General
- Large share of volunteer teachers
- High share of resources allocated to education
- High share of wages and salaries within the education budget

Preschool
- Very high STR
- Large number of teachers per nonteaching staff
- Low per-student spending
- Very small spending on goods and services

Basic education
- STR and per-student spending similar to country average
- Per-student spending similar to country average
- Very small spending on goods and services

Secondary education
- Per-student spending similar to country average

Degree of Randomness in Teacher Allocations, Primary School

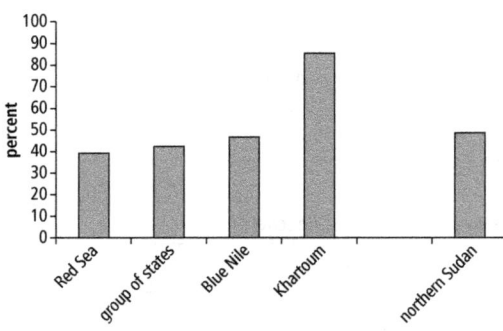

Note: Group of states is the average for all states in northern Sudan except for Red Sea, Blue Nile, and Khartoum. Disaggregated data were unavailable for the other states, so just the average is included.

Literacy Rates for Adults 20–30 Years Old, by Number of Years of School

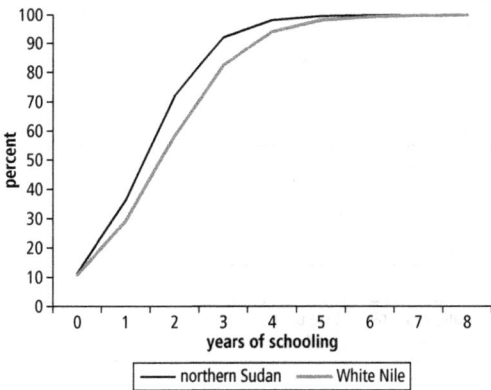

State: North Kordofan   Year: 2008–09

Indicator	State	Northern Sudan	State–northern Sudan ratio
Demographic pressure (population ages 5–16 as a percentage of total population)	32	32	1.01
School life expectancy, excluding higher education	6.2	6.3	0.98
Effort: spending per school-age population (SDG)	130	165	0.79
Efficiency of education spending: spending per child (in population) per year of SLE produced (SDG)	21	26	0.80

Student Flow and Socioeconomic Disparities

Education level	Enrollments	Gross enrollment rate (percent)		Share of girls in total enrollments (percent)		Share of private school enrollments (percent)	
		State	Northern Sudan	State	Northern Sudan	State	Northern Sudan
Preschool	47,875	23	37	51	47	—	—
Basic	529,672	78	72	45	46	3	5
Secondary	43,632	23	29	49	48	9	23
Academic	41,421	22	28	49	49	10	24
Technical	2,211	1	1	30	25	0	0
Literacy program	11,067	n.a.	n.a.	n.a.	n.a.	n.a.	n.a.

Note: — = not available; n.a. = not applicable.

Student Annual Growth Rate 2005–09
percent

Education level	State	Northern Sudan
Preschool	–11	15
Basic	9	5
Secondary	4	7

Share of Enrollment in Basic Education
percent

Schools	State	Northern Sudan
Nomadic	2	3
IDP	0	4

KEY POINTS

General
- School life expectancy same as northern Sudan average
- Low level of spending per school-age population
- More efficient use of resources
- Low share of private schools

Preschool
- Low GER
- Decrease in GER over the past 5 years
- More girls than boys enrolled

Basic education
- Higher GER (6 percentage points higher than the average)
- Rapid increase in GER

Secondary education
- Low GER
- Limited increase in enrollment

Educational Pyramid for North Kordofan (Basic and Secondary Only)

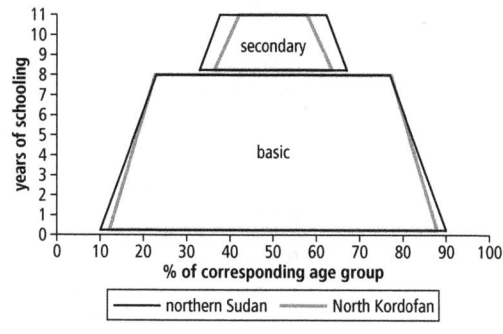

Internal Efficiency
percent

	Gross intake rate		Completion rate		Retention rate		Share of repeaters	
Education level	State	Northern Sudan	State	Northern Sudan	State	Northern Sudan	State	Northern Sudan
Basic	76	80	54	54	72	68	9	4
Secondary	27	34	16	25	58	72	—	14

Note: — = not available.

KEY POINTS

Basic education
- Intake rate a bit lower than the average
- Better retention than the average
- Completion rate at the average level
- Limited transition between basic education and secondary cycle

Secondary education
- Low intake rate
- Low retention
- High dropout
- Low completion

Government School: Teachers

	Student-teacher ratio		Voluntary and national service (percent)		Teacher-nonteacher ratio	
Education level	State	Northern Sudan	State	Northern Sudan	State	Northern Sudan
Preschool	76	48	53	33	15	18
Basic	42	33	1	3	5	5
Secondary	16	16	6	8	1	1

Government School: Facilities

	Students per school		Students per form	
Education level	State	Northern Sudan	State	Northern Sudan
Preschool	—	—	—	—
Basic	277	332	46	48
Secondary	271	238	48	45

Note: — = not available.

Education Expenditures

percent

Indicator	State	Northern Sudan
Education as a percentage of all expenditures	29	27
Salaries as a percentage of education expenditures	86	85

Per-Student Spending at the State Level
Sudanese pounds

Indicator	State			Relative to northern Sudan		
	Preschool	Basic	Secondary	Preschool	Basic	Secondary
Total	64.8	174.3	642.0	0.5	0.7	0.9
Teachers	52.5	146.5	497.5	0.5	0.7	1.0
Nonteachers	7.6	24.2	115.1	1.1	0.8	0.9
Goods and services	4.7	3.7	29.4	0.6	0.4	0.7

KEY POINTS

General
- Close to the northern Sudan average on percentage of education expenditure

Preschool
- Very high student-teacher ratio
- Intensive use of volunteers
- Low per-student spending (half the average)

Basic education
- STR larger than the average but close to benchmark
- Low per-student spending compared to country average
- Very small spending on goods and services

Secondary education
- Bigger school size than the country average
- Per-student spending close to country average

Degree of Randomness in Teacher Allocations, Primary School

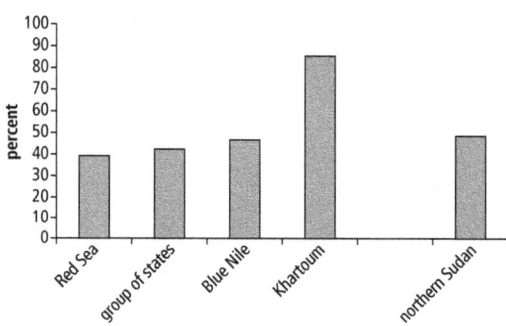

Note: Group of states is the average for all states in northern Sudan except for Red Sea, Blue Nile, and Khartoum. Disaggregated data were unavailable for the other states, so just the average is included.

Literacy Rates for Adults 20–30 Years Old, by Number of Years of School

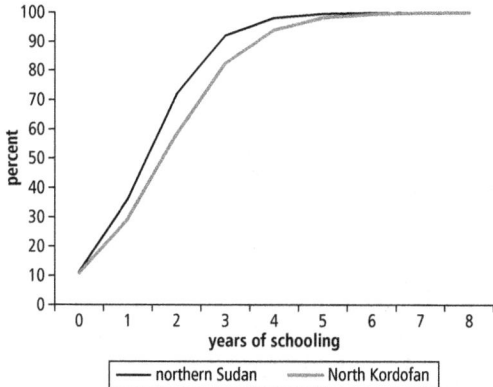

State: South Kordofan   Year: 2008–09

Indicator	State	Northern Sudan	State–northern Sudan ratio
Demographic pressure (population ages 5–16 as a percentage of total population)	33	32	1.02
School life expectancy, excluding higher education	7.2	6.3	1.14
Effort: spending per school-age population (SDG)	148	165	0.90
Efficiency of education spending: spending per child (in population) per year of SLE produced (SDG)	21	26	0.79

Student Flow and Socioeconomic Disparities

Education level	Enrollments	Gross enrollment rate (percent)		Share of girls in total enrollments (percent)		Share of private school enrollments (percent)	
		State	Northern Sudan	State	Northern Sudan	State	Northern Sudan
Preschool	55,728	52	37	45	47	—	—
Basic	273,102	82	72	45	46	3	5
Secondary	29,542	32	29	41	48	10	23
Academic	29,233	32	28	42	49	10	24
Technical	309	0	1	0	25	0	0
Literacy program	16,464	n.a.	n.a.	n.a.	n.a.	n.a.	n.a.

Note: — = not available; n.a. = not applicable.

Student Annual Growth Rate 2005–09
percent

Education level	State	Northern Sudan
Preschool	34	15
Basic	7	5
Secondary	19	7

Share of Enrollment in Basic Education
percent

Schools	State	Northern Sudan
Nomadic	2	3
IDP	0	4

KEY POINTS

General
- School life expectancy higher than northern Sudan average (1 more year)
- Low level of spending per school-age population
- More efficient use of resources

Preschool
- High GER
- Sharp increase in enrollment for the latest year

Basic education
- Higher GER than the average
- Large increase in enrollment over the past 5 years

Secondary education
- GER a bit higher than the average
- Large increase in enrollment over the past 5 years

Educational Pyramid for South Kordofan (Basic and Secondary Only)

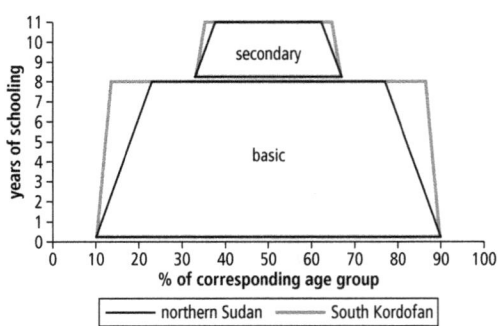

Internal Efficiency
percent

	Gross intake rate		Completion rate		Retention rate		Share of repeaters	
Education level	State	Northern Sudan	State	Northern Sudan	State	Northern Sudan	State	Northern Sudan
Basic	80	80	73	54	92	68	4	4
Secondary	34	34	30	25	88	72	—	14

Note: — = not available.

KEY POINTS

General
- Student flow very well managed

Basic education
- High intake rate but not universal
- High retention
- Relatively high completion rate
- Limited transition between basic education and secondary cycle

Secondary education
- High retention

Government School: Teachers

	Student-teacher ratio		Voluntary and national service (percent)		Teacher-nonteacher ratio	
Education level	State	Northern Sudan	State	Northern Sudan	State	Northern Sudan
Preschool	153	48	0	33	97	18
Basic	39	33	0	3	3	5
Secondary	22	16	0	8	2	1

Government School: Facilities

	Students per school		Students per form	
Education level	State	Northern Sudan	State	Northern Sudan
Preschool	—	—	—	—
Basic	246	332	39	48
Secondary	303	238	53	45

Note: — = not available.

Education Expenditures
percent

Indicator	State	Northern Sudan
Education as a percentage of all expenditures	14	27
Salaries as a percentage of education expenditures	86	85

Per-Student Spending at the State Level
Sudanese pounds

Indicator	State			Relative to northern Sudan		
	Preschool	Basic	Secondary	Preschool	Basic	Secondary
Total	41.1	201.7	416.3	0.3	0.8	0.6
Teachers	39.6	158.5	341.7	0.4	0.8	0.7
Nonteachers	0.3	37.6	62.9	0.0	1.3	0.5
Goods and services	1.2	5.7	11.7	0.2	0.6	0.3

KEY POINTS

General
- No use of volunteer teachers
- Education spending much smaller than the country average

Preschool
- Very high student-teacher ratio (more than three times the average)
- Even fewer nonteacher staff members than teachers
- Very low per-student spending

Basic education
- Smaller school size than the country average
- STR larger than the average but close to benchmark
- Fewer teachers than nonteachers
- Low per-student spending

Secondary education
- Bigger school size than the country average
- Per-student spending smaller than the country average
- Very small spending per-student on goods and services

Degree of Randomness in Teacher Allocations, Primary School

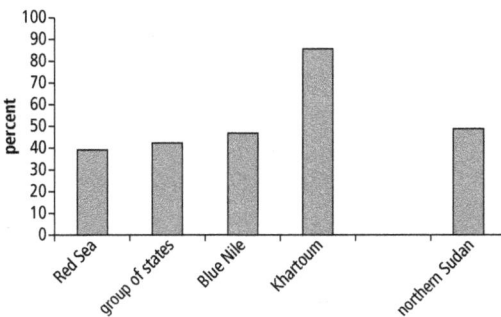

Note: *Group of states* is the average for all states in northern Sudan except for Red Sea, Blue Nile, and Khartoum. Disaggregated data were unavailable for the other states, so just the average is included.

Literacy Rates for Adults 20–30 Years Old, by Number of Years of School

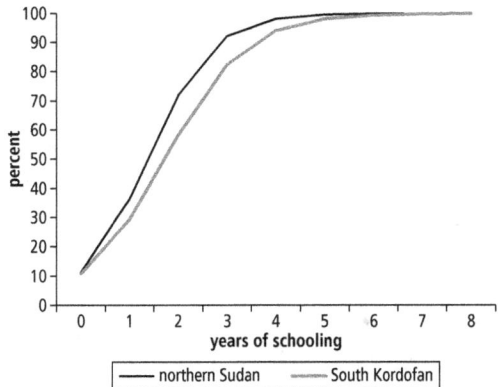

Appendix: State-Level Data Sheets—Northern Darfur • 221

State: Northern Darfur   Year: 2008–09

Indicator	State	Northern Sudan	State–northern Sudan ratio
Demographic pressure (population ages 5–16 as a percentage of total population)	32	32	1.00
School life expectancy, excluding higher education	5.6	6.3	0.89
Effort: spending per school-age population (SDG)	115	165	0.69
Efficiency of education spending: spending per child (in population) per year of SLE produced (SDG)	20	26	0.78

Student Flow and Socioeconomic Disparities

Education level	Enrollments	Gross enrollment rate (percent)		Share of girls in total enrollments (percent)		Share of private school enrollments (percent)	
		State	Northern Sudan	State	Northern Sudan	State	Northern Sudan
Preschool	46,094	32	37	52	47	—	—
Basic	346,779	67	72	46	46	3	5
Secondary	31,927	21	29	42	48	5	23
Academic	30,231	20	28	42	49	5	24
Technical	1,696	1	1	39	25	0	0
Literacy program	0	n.a.	n.a.	n.a.	n.a.	n.a.	n.a.

Note: — = not available; n.a. = not applicable.

Student Annual Growth Rate 2005–09
percent

Education level	State	Northern Sudan
Preschool	17	15
Basic	10	5
Secondary	–5	7

Share of Enrollment in Basic Education
percent

Schools	State	Northern Sudan
Nomadic	5	3
IDP	18	4

KEY POINTS

General
- School life expectancy lower than northern Sudan average
- Low level of spending per school-age population
- More efficient use of resources

Preschool
- Lower GER than the average
- Sharp increase in enrollment for the latest year

Basic education
- Lower GER than the average
- Higher increase in enrollment than the country over the past 5 years

Secondary education
- GER lower than the average
- Decrease or stagnation in GER over the past 5 years

Educational Pyramid for Northern Darfur (Basic and Secondary Only)

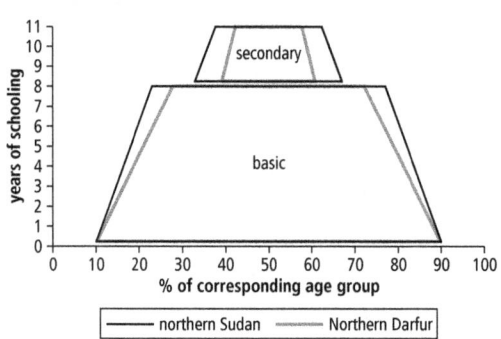

Internal Efficiency
percent

Education level	Gross intake rate		Completion rate		Retention rate		Share of repeaters	
	State	Northern Sudan	State	Northern Sudan	State	Northern Sudan	State	Northern Sudan
Basic	80	80	44	54	56	68	5	4
Secondary	22	34	15	25	71	72	—	14

Note: — = not available.

KEY POINTS

Basic education
- Intake similar to the country average
- Low retention and completion
- High dropout (occurring mainly within the cycle)
- Limited transition between basic education and secondary cycle

Secondary education
- High retention

Government School: Teachers

Education level	Student-teacher ratio		Voluntary and national service (percent)		Teacher-nonteacher ratio	
	State	Northern Sudan	State	Northern Sudan	State	Northern Sudan
Preschool	60	48	0	33	57	18
Basic	47	33	0	3	5	5
Secondary	18	16	0	8	2	1

Government School: Facilities

Education level	Students per school		Students per form	
	State	Northern Sudan	State	Northern Sudan
Preschool	—	—	—	—
Basic	315	332	49	48
Secondary	299	238	49	45

Note: — = not available.

Per-Student Spending at the State Level
Sudanese pounds

Indicator	State			Relative to northern Sudan		
	Preschool	Basic	Secondary	Preschool	Basic	Secondary
Total	99.4	171.3	606.7	0.8	0.7	0.9
Teachers	88.2	144.2	453.3	0.8	0.7	0.9
Nonteachers	5.3	20.8	114.7	0.8	0.7	0.9
Goods and services	5.9	6.3	38.7	0.8	0.7	0.9

KEY POINTS

General
- No use of volunteer teachers (or no data)

Preschool
- High student-teacher ratio
- Large number of teachers per nonteacher staff
- Low per-student spending

Basic education
- High student-teacher ratio
- Low per-student spending

Secondary education
- Bigger school size than the country average
- Per-student spending close to the country average

Degree of Randomness in Teacher Allocations, Primary School

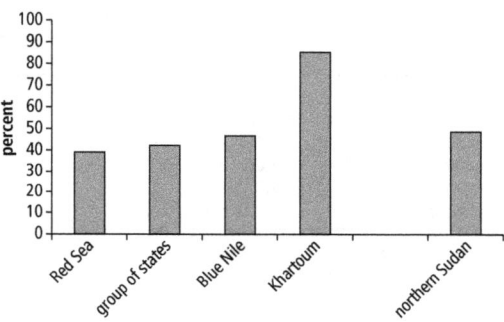

Note: Group of states is the average for all states in northern Sudan except for Red Sea, Blue Nile, and Khartoum. Disaggregated data were unavailable for the other states, so just the average is included.

Literacy Rates for Adults 20–30 Years Old, by Number of Years of School

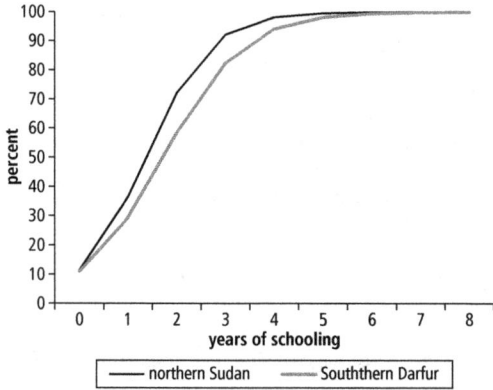

State: Southern Darfur   Year: 2008–09

Indicator	State	Northern Sudan	State–northern Sudan ratio
Demographic pressure (population ages 5–16 as a percentage of total population)	33	32	1.04
School life expectancy, excluding higher education	3.5	6.3	0.56
Effort: spending per school-age population (SDG)	64	165	0.39
Efficiency of education spending: spending per child (in population) per year of SLE produced (SDG)	18	26	0.70

Student Flow and Socioeconomic Disparities

Education level	Enrollments	Gross enrollment rate (percent)		Share of girls in total enrollments (percent)		Share of private school enrollments (percent)	
		State	Northern Sudan	State	Northern Sudan	State	Northern Sudan
Preschool	114,280	38	37	36	47	—	—
Basic	424,904	41	72	43	46	10	5
Secondary	52,263	17	29	40	48	33	23
Academic	51,030	17	28	41	49	34	24
Technical	1,233	0	1	7	25	0	0
Literacy program	0	n.a.	n.a.	n.a.	n.a.	n.a.	n.a.

Note: — = not available; n.a. = not applicable.

Student Annual Growth Rate 2005–09
percent

Education level	State	Northern Sudan
Preschool	47	15
Basic	7	5
Secondary	–1	7

Share of Enrollment in Basic Education
percent

Schools	State	Northern Sudan
Nomadic	5	3
IDP	18	4

KEY POINTS

General
- Very low school life expectancy
- Very low level of spending per school-age population
- More efficient use of resources

Preschool
- Share of girls very low

Basic education
- Very lower GER
- Small increase in GER, no clear sign of catch-up
- Lower percentage of girls than the country average

Secondary education
- Very lower GER
- Lower percentage of girls than the country average

Educational Pyramid for Southern Darfur (Basic and Secondary Only)

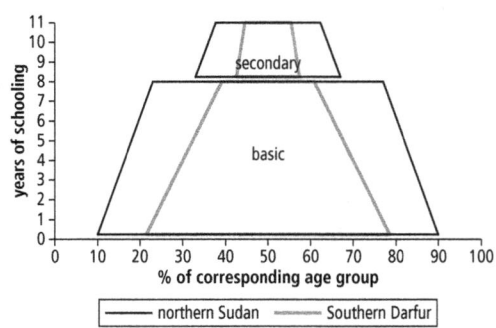

Internal Efficiency
percent

	Gross intake rate		Completion rate		Retention rate		Share of repeaters	
Education level	State	Northern Sudan	State	Northern Sudan	State	Northern Sudan	State	Northern Sudan
Basic	57	80	22	54	38	68	1	4
Secondary	15	34	11	25	74	72	—	14

Note: — = not available.

KEY POINTS

Basic education
- Low intake
- Very low retention and low completion
- High dropout (occurring mainly within the cycle)
- High transition between basic education and secondary cycle

Secondary education
- High retention

Government School: Teachers

	Student-teacher ratio		Voluntary and national service (percent)		Teacher-nonteacher ratio	
Education level	State	Northern Sudan	State	Northern Sudan	State	Northern Sudan
Preschool	64	48	0	33	8	18
Basic	44	33	0	3	5	5
Secondary	20	16	0	8	2	1

Government School: Facilities

	Students per school		Students per form	
Education level	State	Northern Sudan	State	Northern Sudan
Preschool	—	—	—	—
Basic	275	332	56	48
Secondary	360	238	55	45

Note: — = not available.

Appendix: State-Level Data Sheets—Southern Darfur

Per-Student Spending at the State Level
Sudanese pounds

Indicator	State			Relative to northern Sudan		
	Preschool	Basic	Secondary	Preschool	Basic	Secondary
Total	92.6	182.0	544.9	0.7	0.8	0.8
Teachers	82.2	153.2	407.4	0.7	0.8	0.8
Nonteachers	4.9	22.1	103.0	0.7	0.8	0.8
Goods and services	5.5	6.7	34.5	0.7	0.8	0.8

KEY POINTS

General
- No use of volunteer teachers (or no data)

Preschool
- High student-teacher ratio
- Fewer teachers per nonteacher staff members than the country average
- Low per-student spending

Basic education
- High student-teacher ratio
- Smaller school size than the country average
- Low per-student spending

Secondary education
- Bigger school size than the country average
- Per-student spending close to the country average

Degree of Randomness in Teacher Allocations, Primary School

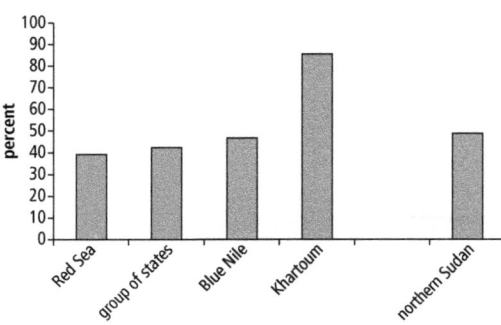

Note: Group of states is the average for all states in northern Sudan except for Red Sea, Blue Nile, and Khartoum. Disaggregated data were unavailable for the other states, so just the average is included.

Literacy Rates for Adults 20–30 Years Old, by Number of Years of School

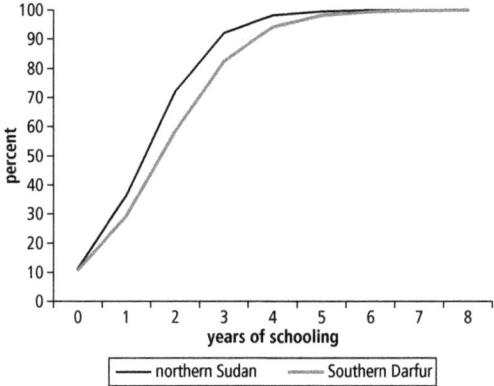

State: Western Darfur   Year: 2008–09

Indicator	State	Northern Sudan	State–northern Sudan ratio
Demographic pressure (population ages 5–16 as a percentage of total population)	34	32	1.07
School life expectancy, excluding higher education	7.2	6.3	1.13
Effort: spending per school-age population (SDG)	96	165	0.58
Efficiency of education spending: spending per child (in population) per year of SLE produced (SDG)	13	26	0.51

Student Flow and Socioeconomic Disparities

Education level	Enrollments	Gross enrollment rate (percent)		Share of girls in total enrollments (percent)		Share of private school enrollments (percent)	
		State	Northern Sudan	State	Northern Sudan	State	Northern Sudan
Preschool	25,134	26	37	50	47	—	—
Basic	283,355	88	72	44	46	2	5
Secondary	23,348	25	29	35	48	39	23
Academic	22,728	24	28	36	49	40	24
Technical	620	1	1	27	25	0	0
Literacy program	0	n.a.	n.a.	n.a.	n.a.	n.a.	n.a.

Note: — = not available; n.a. = not applicable.

Student Annual Growth Rate 2005–09
percent

Education level	State	Northern Sudan
Preschool	33	15
Basic	6	5
Secondary	21	7

Share of Enrollment in Basic Education
percent

Schools	State	Northern Sudan
Nomadic	8	3
IDP	24	4

KEY POINTS

General
- School life expectancy higher than northern Sudan average (1 more year)
- Low level of spending per school-age population
- More efficient use of resources

Preschool
- Low GER
- As many girls as boys enrolled

Basic education
- GER larger than the country average
- Percentage of girls lower than the country average

Secondary education
- GER smaller than the country average
- Percentage of girls lower than the country average

Educational Pyramid for Western Darfur (Basic and Secondary Only)

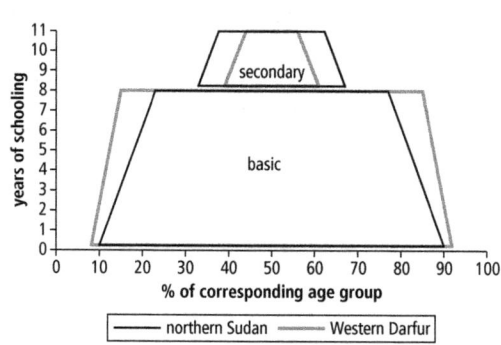

Internal Efficiency

percent

Education level	Gross intake rate		Completion rate		Retention rate		Share of repeaters	
	State	Northern Sudan	State	Northern Sudan	State	Northern Sudan	State	Northern Sudan
Basic	84	80	70	54	84	68	5	4
Secondary	22	34	12	25	55	72	—	14

Note: — = not available.

KEY POINTS

Basic education
- Intake rate a bit higher than the average
- Better retention and completion
- Very limited transition between basic education and secondary cycle

Secondary education
- Low retention
- High dropout
- Low completion

Government School: Teachers

Education level	Student-teacher ratio		Voluntary and national service (percent)		Teacher-nonteacher ratio	
	State	Northern Sudan	State	Northern Sudan	State	Northern Sudan
Preschool	195	48	0	33	8	18
Basic	64	33	0	3	5	5
Secondary	23	16	0	8	2	1

Government School: Facilities

Education level	Students per school		Students per form	
	State	Northern Sudan	State	Northern Sudan
Preschool	—	—	—	—
Basic	242	332	64	48
Secondary	391	238	48	45

Note: — = not available.

Per-Student Spending at the State Level
Sudanese pounds

Indicator	State			Relative to northern Sudan		
	Preschool	Basic	Secondary	Preschool	Basic	Secondary
Total	30.5	124.1	466.6	0.2	0.5	0.7
Teachers	27.1	104.5	348.9	0.2	0.5	0.7
Nonteachers	1.6	15.1	88.2	0.2	0.5	0.7
Goods and services	1.8	4.5	29.6	0.2	0.5	0.7

KEY POINTS

General
- No use of volunteer teachers (or no data)

Preschool
- Very high student-teacher ratio
- Fewer teachers per nonteacher staff members than the country average
- Extremely low per-student spending

Basic education
- High student-teacher ratio
- Smaller school size than the country average
- Very low per-student spending (half the average)

Secondary education
- Bigger school size than the country average
- Very low per-student spending (half the average)

Degree of Randomness in Teacher Allocations, Primary School

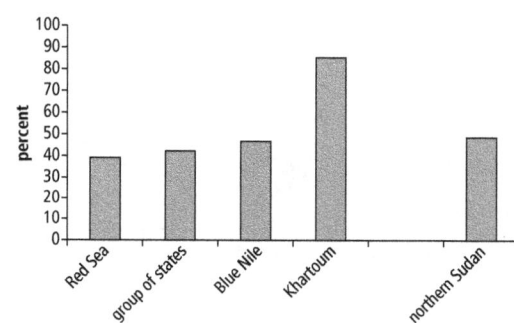

Note: Group of states is the average for all states in northern Sudan except for Red Sea, Blue Nile, and Khartoum. Disaggregated data were unavailable for the other states, so just the average is included.

Literacy Rates for Adults 20–30 Years Old, by Number of Years of School

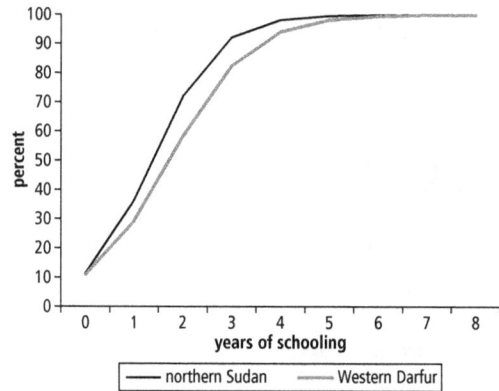

State: Kassala   Year: 2008–09

Indicator	State	Northern Sudan	State–northern Sudan ratio
Demographic pressure (population ages 5–16 as a percentage of total population)	35	32	1.11
School life expectancy, excluding higher education	3.9	6.3	0.61
Effort: spending per school-age population (SDG)	114	165	0.69
Efficiency of education spending: spending per child (in population) per year of SLE produced (SDG)	30	26	1.13

Student Flow and Socioeconomic Disparities

Education level	Enrollments	Gross enrollment rate (percent)		Share of girls in total enrollments (percent)		Share of private school enrollments (percent)	
		State	Northern Sudan	State	Northern Sudan	State	Northern Sudan
Preschool	17,616	17	37	51	47	—	—
Basic	182,372	46	72	42	46	8	5
Secondary	20,173	15	29	48	48	15	23
Academic	18,759	14	28	49	49	16	24
Technical	1,414	1	1	30	25	0	0
Literacy program	0	n.a.	n.a.	n.a.	n.a.	n.a.	n.a.

Note: — = not available; n.a. = not applicable.

Student Annual Growth Rate 2005–09
percent

Education level	State	Northern Sudan
Preschool	0	15
Basic	−2	5
Secondary	3	7

Share of Enrollment in Basic Education
percent

Schools	State	Northern Sudan
Nomadic	17	3
IDP	0	4

KEY POINTS

General
- Very low school life expectancy
- Low level of spending per school-age population
- Less efficient use of resources

Preschool
- Very low GER
- As many girls as boys enrolled
- No increase in enrollment

Basic education
- Very low GER
- Percentage of girls lower than the country average
- Stagnation in enrollment

Secondary education
- Very low GER
- Small increase in enrollment

Educational Pyramid for Kassala (Basic and Secondary Only)

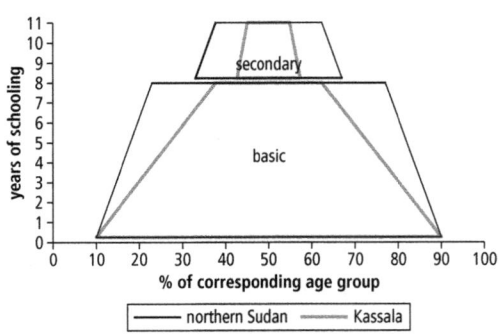

Internal Efficiency
percent

	Gross intake rate		Completion rate		Retention rate		Share of repeaters	
Education level	State	Northern Sudan	State	Northern Sudan	State	Northern Sudan	State	Northern Sudan
Basic	80	80	25	54	31	68	4	4
Secondary	15	34	10	25	67	72	—	14

Note: — = not available.

KEY POINTS

Basic education
- Intake at the average level
- Extremely low retention and low completion
- High dropout (occurring mainly within the cycle)
- Relatively limited transition between basic education and secondary cycle

Secondary education
- Low intake rate
- High retention

Government School: Teachers

	Student-teacher ratio		Voluntary and national service (percent)		Teacher-nonteacher ratio	
Education level	State	Northern Sudan	State	Northern Sudan	State	Northern Sudan
Preschool	76	48	25	33	3	18
Basic	31	33	9	3	5	5
Secondary	14	16	0	8	1	1

Government School: Facilities

	Students per school		Students per form	
Education level	State	Northern Sudan	State	Northern Sudan
Preschool	—	—	—	—
Basic	267	332	49	48
Secondary	293	238	44	45

Note: — = not available.

Education Expenditures
percent

Indicator	State	Northern Sudan
Education as a percentage of all expenditures	28	27
Salaries as a percentage of education expenditures	71	85

Per-Student Spending at the State Level
Sudanese pounds

Indicator	State			Relative to northern Sudan		
	Preschool	Basic	Secondary	Preschool	Basic	Secondary
Total	135.6	297.5	749.0	1.1	1.2	1.1
Teachers	59.6	226.0	515.9	0.5	1.1	1.0
Nonteachers	22.6	33.6	167.6	3.4	1.2	1.3
Goods and services	53.3	37.9	65.5	7.2	4.3	1.5

KEY POINTS

Preschool
- High student-teacher ratio
- Very small number of teachers per nonteacher staff members
- Per-student spending higher than the country average

Basic education
- Student-teacher ratio lower than the country average
- Smaller school size than the country average
- Per-student spending higher than the country average

Secondary education
- Bigger school size than the country average
- Per-student spending higher than the country average

Degree of Randomness in Teacher Allocations, Primary School

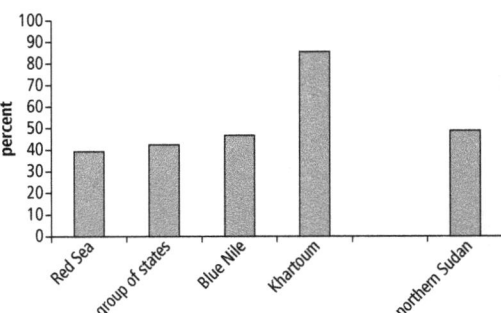

Note: Group of states is the average for all states in northern Sudan except for Red Sea, Blue Nile, and Khartoum. Disaggregated data were unavailable for the other states, so just the average is included.

State: Al Qadarif   Year: 2008–09

Indicator	State	Northern Sudan	State–northern Sudan ratio
Demographic pressure (population ages 5–16 as a percentage of total population)	37	32	1.15
School life expectancy, excluding higher education	5.5	6.3	0.87
Effort: spending per school-age population (SDG)	155	165	0.94
Efficiency of education spending: spending per child (in population) per year of SLE produced (SDG)	28	26	1.08

Student Flow and Socioeconomic Disparities

Education level	Enrollments	Gross enrollment rate (percent)		Share of girls in total enrollments (percent)		Share of private school enrollments (percent)	
		State	Northern Sudan	State	Northern Sudan	State	Northern Sudan
Preschool	34,730	36	37	46	47	—	—
Basic	222,083	70	72	45	46	2	5
Secondary	28,706	31	29	46	48	18	23
Academic	26,297	28	28	47	49	20	24
Technical	2,409	3	1	33	25	0	0
Literacy program	14,105	n.a.	n.a.	n.a.	n.a.	n.a.	n.a.

Note: — = not available; n.a. = not applicable.

Student Annual Growth Rate 2005–09
percent

Education level	State	Northern Sudan
Preschool	26	15
Basic	7	5
Secondary	8	7

Share of Enrollment in Basic Education
percent

Schools	State	Northern Sudan
Nomadic	2	3
IDP	3	4

KEY POINTS

General
- High demographic pressure
- Very low school life expectancy
- Slightly low level of spending per school-age population
- Less efficient use of resources

Preschool
- GER at the country average
- Sharp increase in enrollment

Basic education
- GER at the country average
- Steady increase in enrollment

Secondary education
- GER at the country average

Educational Pyramid for Al Qadarif (Basic and Secondary Only)

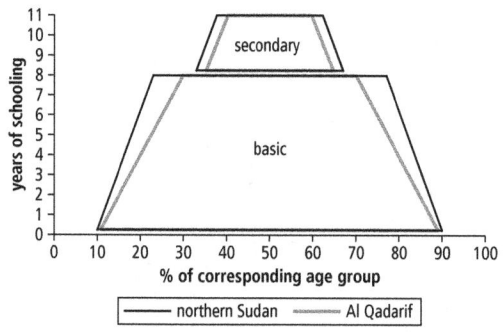

Internal Efficiency

percent

Education level	Gross intake rate		Completion rate		Retention rate		Share of repeaters	
	State	Northern Sudan	State	Northern Sudan	State	Northern Sudan	State	Northern Sudan
Basic	78	80	40	54	51	68	13	4
Secondary	30	34	19	25	66	72	—	14

Note: — = not available.

KEY POINTS

Basic education
- Intake at the average level
- Low retention
- Relatively high transition between basic education and secondary cycle

Secondary education
- Low retention

Government School: Teachers

Education level	Student-teacher ratio		Voluntary and national service (percent)		Teacher-nonteacher ratio	
	State	Northern Sudan	State	Northern Sudan	State	Northern Sudan
Preschool	47	48	0	33	38	18
Basic	38	33	4	3	6	5
Secondary	16	16	9	8	2	1

Government School: Facilities

Education level	Students per school		Students per form	
	State	Northern Sudan	State	Northern Sudan
Preschool	—	—	—	—
Basic	329	332	48	48
Secondary	245	238	48	45

Note: — = not available.

Education Expenditures

percent

Indicator	State	Northern Sudan
Education as a percentage of all expenditures	31	27
Salaries as a percentage of education expenditures	76	85

Per-Student Spending at the State Level
Sudanese pounds

Indicator	State			Relative to northern Sudan		
	Preschool	Basic	Secondary	Preschool	Basic	Secondary
Total	138.1	204.4	740.5	1.1	0.9	1.1
Teachers	125.5	171.2	537.6	1.1	0.8	1.0
Nonteachers	2.5	21.4	108.9	0.4	0.7	0.8
Goods and services	10.2	11.8	94.1	1.4	1.3	2.1

KEY POINTS

General
- Spending larger than the country average
- Share of salaries lower than the country average

Preschool
- Large number of teachers per nonteacher staff members
- Per-student spending higher than the country average

Basic education
- Student-teacher ratio lower than the country average
- Per-student spending on goods and services much higher than the country average

Secondary education
- Bigger school size than the country average
- Per-student spending higher than the country average

Degree of Randomness in Teacher Allocations, Primary School

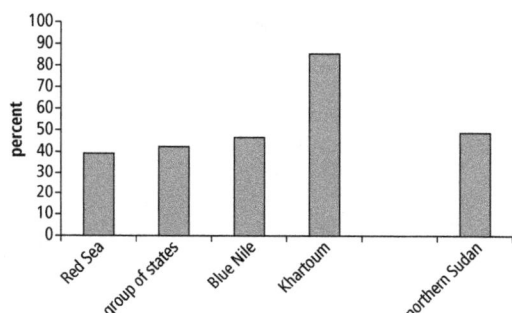

Note: Group of states is the average for all states in northern Sudan except for Red Sea, Blue Nile, and Khartoum. Disaggregated data were unavailable for the other states, so just the average is included.

Glossary

Child-friendly schools. A rights-based, child-friendly school has two basic characteristics:

- It is child seeking—actively identifying excluded children to get them enrolled in school and included in learning; treating children as subjects with rights that the states are duty-bound to fulfill; and demonstrating, promoting, and helping to monitor the rights and well-being of all children in the community.
- It is child centered—acting in the best interests of the individual child, leading to the realization of the child's full potential, and concerned both about the "whole" child (including her health, nutritional status, and well-being) and about what happens to that child (in her family and community) before she enters school and after she leaves it.

Dependency ratio. This ratio is defined as the school-age population as a share of the total population.

Development spending. This type of spending is for physical assets with benefits extending into the future.

Gender parity index (GPI). The GPI is calculated here as the gross enrollment rate for girls divided by the gross enrollment rate for boys.

Gini coefficient. This is a measure of the inequality of distribution. It is calculated as the ratio of the area between the diagonal and the Lorenz curve to the area of the triangle beneath the diagonal. A value of zero expresses total equality and a value of one, maximum inequality.

Gross enrollment rate (GER). The GER is calculated as total enrollment in the level of education divided by the population of relevant age for that level. The relevant age groups here are ages 4–5 for preschool, ages 6–13 for basic school, and ages 14–16 for secondary school.

Gross intake rate (GIR). This rate is calculated as the number of nonrepeaters in grade 1 divided by the number of students age 6.

Internally displaced persons (IDPs). "Persons or groups of persons who have been forced or obliged to flee or leave their homes or places of habitual residences, in particular as a result of or in order to avoid the effects of armed conflict, situations of generalized violence, violations of human rights or natural or human-made disasters, and who have not crossed an internationally recognized State border" (Guiding Principles of Internal Displacement 1998).

Khalwas. These institutions are traditional Islamic schools that teach the Quran. They enroll children of all ages.

Mahalya. The *mahalya,* or locality, is under the political leadership of an elected council of between 24 and 48 people, including a committee for education. Its administration is under the responsibility of an executive director appointed by the *wali* (state governor). He or she is assisted by a number of directors (including a director of education) in charge of various sectors of activity. The director for education in the *mahalyas* is often assisted by three officials, who are in charge of teachers, administration and finance, and students and statistics.

Net enrollment rate. This rate is calculated as the enrollment of 6–13-year-olds in basic school divided by the population of 6–13-year-olds.

Net intake rate. This rate is calculated as the nonrepeaters in grade 1 who are age 6 divided by the age 6 population.

Primary completion rate. This rate is calculated as the number of nonrepeaters in grade 8 divided by the number of students age 13.

R^2. This indicator measures the extent to which the number of teachers in a school is proportionate to the size of its enrollment. If the number of teachers deployed to a school is perfectly proportionate to the size of enrollment, then R^2 will be equal to one. Conversely, an R^2 of zero would indicate that there is no relationship between the number of teachers deployed to a school and the number of students enrolled in that school.

Recurrent spending. This type of spending is for assets or services to be consumed within one year.

Stunting. Moderate and severe: the percentage of children ages 0–59 months who are below minus two standard deviations from median height for age of the WHO (World Health Organization) Child Growth Standards. (WHO definition)

Underweight. Moderate and severe: the percentage of children ages 0–59 months who are below minus two standard deviations from median weight for age of the reference population from the National Center for Health Statistics (NCHS) of the U.S. Centers for Disease Control and Prevention and from the WHO. (NCHS/WHO definition)

Wasting. Moderate and severe: the percentage of children ages 0–59 months who are below minus two standard deviations from median weight for height of the WHO Child Growth Standards. (WHO definition)

ECO-AUDIT
Environmental Benefits Statement

The World Bank is committed to preserving endangered forests and natural resources. The Office of the Publisher has chosen to print **The Status of the Education Sector in Sudan** on recycled paper with 50 percent postconsumer fiber in accordance with the recommended standards for paper usage set by the Green Press Initiative, a non-profit program supporting publishers in using fiber that is not sourced from endangered forests. For more information, visit www.greenpressinitiative.org.

Saved:
- 6 trees
- 3 million British thermal units of total energy
- 591 pounds of net greenhouse gases
- 2,665 gallons of waste water
- 169 pounds of solid waste

www.ingramcontent.com/pod-product-compliance
Lightning Source LLC
Chambersburg PA
CBHW081219170426
43198CB00017B/2658